FOOD IN COLONIAL AND FEDERAL AMERICA

FOOD IN COLONIAL AND FEDERAL AMERICA

SANDRA L. OLIVER

Food in American History

Greenwood Press
Westport, Connecticut • London

Library of Congress Cataloging-in-Publication Data

Oliver, Sandra L. (Sandra Louise), 1947–
  Food in colonial and federal America / Sandra L. Oliver.
      p.   cm.—(Food in American history, ISSN 1552–8200)
  Includes bibliographical references and index.
  ISBN 0–313–32988–5 (alk. paper)
    1. Cookery, American—History—17th century.   2. Cookery, American—
History—18th century.   3. United States—History—Colonial period, ca.
1600–1775.   I. Title.   II. Series.
TX714.o466   2005
641.5973'09'032—dc22   2005018569

British Library Cataloguing in Publication Data is available.

Library of Congress Catalog Card Number: 2005018569
ISBN: 0–313–32988–5
ISSN: 1552–8200

First published in 2005

Greenwood Press, 88 Post Road West, Westport, CT 06881
An imprint of Greenwood Publishing Group, Inc.
www.greenwood.com

Printed in the United States of America

∞

The paper used in this book complies with the
Permanent Paper Standard issued by the National
Information Standards Organization (Z39.48–1984).

10 9 8 7 6 5 4 3 2 1

The publisher has done its best to make sure the instructions and/or recipes in this
book are correct. However, users should apply judgment and experience when
preparing recipes, especially parents and teachers working with young people. The
publisher accepts no responsibility for the outcome of any recipe included in this
volume.

To the community of Islesboro, Maine

CONTENTS

SERIES FOREWORD

This series focuses on food culture as a way to illuminate the societal mores and daily life of Americans throughout our history. These volumes are meant to complement history studies at the high school level on up. In addition, Food Studies is a burgeoning field, and food enthusiasts and food scholars will find much to mine here. The series is comprehensive, with the first volume covering American Indian food and the following volumes each covering an era or eras from Colonial times until today. Regional and group differences are discussed as appropriate.

Each volume is written by a food historian who is an expert on the period. Each volume contains the following:

- Chronology of food-related dates
- Narrative chapters, including
  Introduction (brief overview of period as it relates to food)
  Foodstuffs (staples, agricultural developments, etc.)
  Food Preparation
  Eating Habits (manners, customs, mealtimes, special occasions)
  Concepts of Diet and Nutrition (including religious strictures)
- Recipes
- Period illustrations
- Glossary, if needed
- Bibliography
- Index

ACKNOWLEDGMENTS

Many thanks are due the kind, helping hands who made this book possible. First, my colleagues in food history who patiently answered questions: Dr. Clarissa Dillon in Pennsylvania; Dr. Joanne Bowen and Martha Katz-Hyman at Colonial Williamsburg; Kathleen Curtain, Karen Goldstein, and Kathleen Wall at Plimoth Plantation in Massachusetts; and Karen Becker at the Museum of American Frontier Culture in Staunton, Virginia. Dr. Cheryl Foote made me a guest in her Albuquerque home for a week, and shared her years of knowledge and insights into the foodways of the Southwest, then patiently read what I thought I had learned and set me straight on the things I got wrong. Similarly, Peter Rose, of Salem, New York, an expert on Dutch Colonial cookery in the Hudson Valley, was exceptionally generous with her information. Leni Ashmore-Sorenson provided valuable insight on African American foodways, and is owed many thanks.

Also, many thanks are due Courtney Maclachlan, who served as my intern in the summer of 2003, using her librarian's skills to develop a bibliography for this book, and identified the libraries in the region where I would find the books I needed. She saved me many miles of travel and many hours of sleuthing, and proved a wonderful companion as well.

Alice Arndt and Susan Williams, authors of two other books in this series, have been helpful colleagues, sharing ideas, woes, and joys.

Closer to home, there was great support in my community. Linda Graf, the librarian at Islesboro's Alice Pendleton Library, tirelessly ordered for my use many volumes on interlibrary loan. Particular thanks to my dear friend Virginia Hall for a quiet place to work. Similar thanks are due to Roberta Heyne for quiet space in her home, and to my friends and good neighbors Roger and Marny Heinen for a month's use of a guest cottage within walking distance of my home, where I could work uninterrupted. Diane Winiecki reviewed portions of my manuscript and provided much cheerful encouragement—and dinner.

Credit is also due my husband, Jamie MacMillan, and my nephew Seth Johnson, who pitched in when needed. Many thanks, also, to Millie, who kept me company for many hours.

CHRONOLOGY

1567	First settlement in America is established at St. Augustine, Florida, by the Spanish.
1598	Don Juan de Oñate establishes a colony in New Mexico on the site of a commandeered Native American pueblo and names it San Gabriel. The Spanish abandon it in 1602.
1607	First permanent English colony is established at Jamestown, Virginia.
1609	Spanish establish Santa Fe as the new capital of New Mexico, and it becomes the permanent capital except for the twelve-year abandonment following the Pueblo Revolt of 1680.
1609–1610	Jamestown Colony, Virginia, suffers the Starving Time.
1620	Plymouth Colony is established in New England.
1625	Dutch establish New Amsterdam in New Netherlands, which later becomes New York City.
1627	Plymouth Colony divides the jointly held domestic animals among its households so that henceforth each raises its own animals for food.
1629	Baltimore, Maryland, and a colony in Georgia are established.
1654	Twenty-three Sephardic Jews arrive in New Amsterdam and begin the practice of kashruth (keeping kosher) in America.

1660 British monarchy is restored to the throne and more colonies are created in America after a hiatus of about eleven years.

1691 South Carolina's General Assembly votes to allow Carolinians to pay their taxes in rice, demonstrating that low-country rice production is well established.

1742 First cookbook printed in America, at Williamsburg, Virginia, by William Parks, is *The Complete Housewife; or, Accomplish'd Gentlewoman's Companion*, by Eliza Smith.

1767 England imposes the Townshend Acts, which tax tea and other imported goods. Many American colonists refuse to drink tea. Others drink only smuggled tea on which no tax has been paid.

1772 English cookbook by Susannah Carter, *The Frugal Housewife; or, Complete Woman Cook*, is published in Boston, and is regularly reissued. In 1829 Lydia Maria Child writes a cookbook titled *The Frugal Housewife*, but subsequently changes the name to *American Frugal Housewife*, noting that "there is an English work of the same name, not adapted to the wants of this country."

1773 England abolishes taxes imposed by the Townshend Acts except the one on tea. Boston colonists continue to resist by staging the Boston Tea Party, during which they plunder the tea cargo of three vessels, breaking open containers and heaving the tea into Boston Harbor.

1774 Greenwich, New Jersey, joins Boston in protesting the tax on tea by burning a cargo of British tea on Market Square. Charleston, South Carolina, Annapolis, Maryland, and Princeton, New Jersey, stage similar "tea parties."

1776 American colonies declare political independence from England and spend ensuing seven years fighting the War for Independence.

1782 Oliver Evans of Newport, Delaware, develops an automatic mill that cleans and, with a system of conveyor belts, moves grain and flour through a mill with less human labor required.

1783   American War for Independence ends.

1793   Connecticut native and American diplomat Joel Barlow writes "The Hasty-Pudding," a poem praising the many dishes made with cornmeal in the United States. Barlow's inspiration comes from encountering cornmeal in France, which prompted his memory.

1794   The Whiskey Rebellion occurs in western Pennsylvania. Farmers resent the tax on the whiskey they make as a major source of income, imposed by the new Federal government to pay in part for military protection of settlers against Indians. The Rebellion is also about economic inequities between western frontier settlers and established eastern businessmen and aristocracy.

1795   Oliver Evans publishes *The Young Mill-Wright and Miller's Guide*, which spreads advanced flour milling technology, thus increasing production of flour and especially of refined flour.

1796   The earliest known American cookbook, *American Cookery*, is published in Hartford, Connecticut, written by Amelia Simmons, who identifies herself as "an American Orphan."

1796   Massachusetts-born American Loyalist Benjamin Thompson, known as Count Rumford, publishes a work on a new fireplace design, the so-called Rumford fireplace, based on several years of working on improved cooking and heating methods. It quickly becomes the standard form of fireplace.

1803   United States buys the Louisiana Territory, which doubles the size of the country and opens land west of the Mississippi to settlement.

1805   Popular English cookbook *The Art of Cookery Made Plain and Easy*, written by Hannah Glasse, is reprinted in Alexandria, Virginia, with a section dedicated to recipes for Americans.

1825   Erie Canal reaches Lake Erie, opening eastern markets to western wheat, which greatly lowers the cost of wheat in the East.

CHAPTER 1

INTRODUCTION

In 1805, the popular English cookbook, *Art of Cookery Made Plain and Easy*, by Hannah Glasse, was reprinted in Alexandria, Virginia. To appeal to the American audience, the publishers (Mrs. Glasse had died in 1770) added a chapter titled "Several New Receipts Adapted to the American Mode of Cooking." Mrs. Glasse's cookbook, first published in 1747 and reprinted often throughout the eighteenth century, was very popular in England and among some English settlers in the Colonies. Many of her recipes were copied, sometimes slightly paraphrased, into handwritten recipe books brought to and used in the Colonies. A number of them survive in historical collections.

Twenty-six "American mode" recipes are given, although culinary historians identify only eighteen as truly having originated in the United States, and those were mostly dishes using American ingredients such as corn, maple sugar, or cranberries. Still, many of the recipes, even if they were really English-derived, must have typified American cookery, at least in the publisher's mind.[1]

Art of Cookery was not the only cookbook of the time that attempted to identify what was American about "American cookery." In 1796, a book titled *American Cookery* was published in Hartford, Connecticut, written by Amelia Simmons, who identified herself as "an American Orphan." Simmons depended heavily for recipes on previous English cookbooks, as did nearly all cookbook writers of the era, but she included instructions for cooking with American ingredients not mentioned in the 1805 *Art of Cookery*, such as blueberries and squash, and the first reference to a chemical leaven, pearlash.[2]

In the list of American dishes from these books, there are many familiar favorites: doughnuts, pumpkin pie, waffles, crullers, maple sugar and syrup, cookies, chowder, and cranberry sauce. Other, somewhat dated, favorites appear, too, such as Indian pudding; hoecake, johnnycake (a form of cornbread), and buckwheat pancakes; gingerbread; rye and Indian bread; election cake; and the use of corncobs for smoking hams. Many of these recipes, as one would expect from cookbooks written in the English language and published in the eastern states, had largely British and Dutch origins.

Some food historians compare America's foodways to a length of cloth, saying that it has a plain English warp into which are woven the threads of many nationalities. However, once one looks beyond the borders of the thirteen Colonies that declared independence of England to include both the Native nations and the colonists of other nations who established new homes in the American continent, it is clear that American food history is a good deal like a striped and checkered cloth. The foodways of Native Americans are all across the continent; the English predominate in the East; the French in the lower Mississippi Valley, Great Lakes region, and northern border; and the Spanish in the Southwest. Together, these form the background of American food, not always blending but often existing side by side. Into them were mixed during the Colonial era more English and French, German, Dutch, Scotch-Irish, and Africans.

American food history tells about people who traveled across an ocean, sometimes voluntarily and sometimes not; cleared land, built homes, raised families, created towns and cities; and eventually forged a society and culture that had not existed before. It was all made possible by an ample supply of food, prepared in as familiar a way as possible, to which were gradually added new ingredients and different combinations. Any modern American who breakfasts on a doughnut or corn flakes and coffee; lunches upon refried beans, tacos, and a chocolate shake; and dines on a steak and mashed potatoes, topped off with pumpkin or apple pie, owes something to the Native Americans who first lived here, and to the English, Dutch, Spanish, and many other peoples who came from great distances, bringing with them their favorite foods and their eating habits.

This book explores how this came about, from the earliest settlement to the development of regional food habits. It describes the foods the settlers found here, brought with them, and traded for. It considers their everyday meals, their holidays, and their special occasions. It describes their kitchens and their cooking utensils, and how they cooked on open hearths. It reveals how they kept themselves healthy and how their food choices reflected their spiritual beliefs. Through it all, readers will see that nearly any aspect of life is concerned with procuring, preparing, or consuming food.

FOOD AND INITIAL SETTLEMENT

Europeans crossed the Atlantic to establish new homes in North America for as many reasons as there were settlers, ranging from a desire for wealth to freedom of worship. For many more it was their best chance of doing better than their families had done in the Old World. In addition to owning land and creating commercial opportunities for themselves, "doing better" included having more and better food.

Few people today can grasp the difficulty of the first settlement experience, the first ten to twenty years of establishing a home in a new place. Subsequent immigrants, while having to make the adjustments any person would make in a new place, arrived in a land with familiar-looking homes, farms, domestic animals, gardens, orchards, and, later, cities, markets, and goods. Yet the first settlement experience of hardship was repeated all through the Colonial and Federal periods as settlers pressed westward into new American territory, just as it would be repeated after the Civil War when the farther western United States was settled.

Through it all, most colonists and subsequent settlers endeavored to provide themselves with sufficient and familiar food, cooked and consumed in their accustomed way. They gradually adopted or adapted new ingredients to their foodways, gave up others, and created dishes that modern Americans would recognize. But the first few years were always difficult, and many colonists did not survive.

Hardship, Disease, and Starvation

No matter where they came from and where in the new country they settled, colonists had similar experiences. Settlers carried with them to America the basic cooking equipment they would need, plus provisions intended to sustain them until they could grow or hunt food. However, almost all colonizing companies and proprietors, and the first settlers they sent, underestimated the cumulative effects of exhaustion from the sea voyage, the new climate, disease, and inexperience. Whether in New England, Virginia, or Louisiana, mortality from disease, starvation, or near-starvation was usually high among newly arrived colonists.

Survivors had the burden of clearing land, building homes, planting crops, and feeding themselves while doing so. Almost all of them depended heavily for food on the Native Americans on whose land they encroached, and with whom they ultimately battled. They also depended on arrivals of new settlers and provisions. All the while, they were obliged to the joint stock company or the proprietors who funded the colony and expected a return on their investment. The whole point of a colony, after all, was to provide the mother country with valuable resources, including foodstuffs, and a market for finished or imported goods, often including food.

The Spanish

The earliest colonies established in North America were settled by the Spanish in the mid-sixteenth century, first on the Caribbean islands and the Mexican mainland. From there they spread into territory that eventually became the United States, along the country's southern boundary in what are now states from Florida to California. Between 1550 and 1800 four efforts to settle resulted in Spanish colonies in Florida, Texas, New Mexico, and California. Each had its own origin, but all shared the characteristics of Spanish colonial government policies and showed the influence of the Catholic missions. Both government and church competed for the same Native American labor and Indian-occupied land.

Whether the colonists were missionaries or *adelantados* (the first comers into a region), the colonizing experience was usually beset with difficulty, and many more towns were established than survived the first decades. In Florida, Pedro Menéndez de Avilés built the town of San Agustín and several others along both the Gulf of Mexico and farther north on the Atlantic coast. St. Augustine, as it is now known, was both the first town and the only town to survive to the present. Jesuit and Franciscan missionaries penetrated Florida, searching for Native American settlements where they could establish missions. Spanish settlements were attacked frequently by the Native Americans or by the French, who were also interested in the territory. Even though many Native Americans died from diseases brought by the Spanish, many converted to Christianity and survived, only to be forced to construct churches and dwellings for missionaries, and to grow food or hunt and gather for themselves and the priests.

Similarly in the Southwest, where missionaries and colonists found more settled Indian villages called pueblos, the Spanish expectation of collecting tribute (called *encomienda*) in labor or material goods including corn, combined with competition between the religious and secular branches of settlement, alienated the Native Americans, who often turned on the colonists. Don Juan de Oñate led settlers to the northern Rio Grande in 1598, but most of them were driven back or fled to Mexico by 1602, and a subsequent settlement begun in 1609, near what has become Santa Fe, was disrupted by the Pueblo Revolt of 1680, reclaimed by Diego de Vargas in 1691, and experienced yet another, and last, revolt in 1696.

The Pueblo Indians were capable of growing enough food for themselves and even of storing food against the inevitable poor season, but the Spanish collection of corn tribute, some of which was intended for sale in Mexico, pushed the capacity of the Native Americans' agriculture beyond sustainability. Hunger and disease reduced the Indian population. Generally the Spanish colonies failed to prosper, and when their protection and care reverted to the Spanish crown, the colonies became burdens instead of sources of income.

The English

After a few false starts in colonies from Maine to Virginia, the English had established their first three permanent colonies by 1630. They hoped for new land for an ever-growing and often impoverished population moving into cities after being displaced by landowners who wanted land for sheep grazing. England also wanted new markets for wool and hoped to establish colonies where wine and olive oil, grapes for raisins, citrus fruits, and silk might be grown. Further, they hoped to harvest timber for shipbuilding, for which they were dependent on trade in the Baltic, and they wanted a source of tar and cordage as well. To begin the colonizing process they, like the Dutch and French, first established trading posts.

The Virginia Company sent its colonists, consisting of 120 men and boys, in three small ships to a spot on the James River. They landed in May 1607 and proceeded to build houses, a church, and a storehouse surrounded with fortifications. In June, when the ships returned to England, 101 settlers were alive, but in the next six months 51 died. Although new settlers arrived with provisions in January 1608, a combination of disease, organizational disarray, and a brief bout of gold fever resulted in two extremely difficult years. The Virginia Company owned the land, and the colonists were required to work to supply food and other products for the company, and to make a profit as well.

Captain John Smith wrote about this difficult time, "Though there be fish in the Sea foules in the Ayre, and Beasts in the woods, their bounds are so large, they so wilde, and we so weake, and ignorant, we cannot much trouble them."[3] However, recent excavation of the fort's site has revealed that in addition to consuming all the salt meat they had with them, the colonists caught and ate gulls and herons, oysters, raccoons, sturgeon, and land turtles. In the winter of 1609–1610, called the Starving Time, desperate settlers killed and ate all the domestic animals that they had brought with them, even those intended for breeding, and ate what they usually considered inedible, including poisonous snakes, horses, and musk turtles.

New settlers, some of who had been delayed by shipwreck in Bermuda, arrived in May 1610 and found the colony in very bad shape, with only a few dozen colonists left. A new governor, Sir Thomas Dale, set in place a rule forbidding the killing of any cattle, swine, poultry, even dogs. This rule, the breaking of which was punishable by whipping or the lopping of an ear, demonstrated the necessity of preserving animals for increase as insurance against future hunger.

In the next ten years, the Virginia Company continued to bring new settlers to Virginia, but disease still claimed lives, and a period of drought complicated agriculture. The Company finally made changes in its governing policy that put land ownership into the hands of colonists through a head-right system that allotted fifty acres to each person who could pay for his own or others' passage, including any family members or indentured servants. This relieved the Virginia Company of the burden of paying for its colonists' transportation at a time when it was growing ever deeper in debt. The policy repopulated the colony but also resulted in more dispersed settlement; that, in turn, crowded in on Native American land. Settlers' domestic animals destroyed Indians' crops and English insistence on land ownership led to bitter and often bloody conflict with the Native Americans.

Settlers on their own land were more motivated to grow food for themselves and their families, but the colony as a whole still needed to provide the Virginia Company with products. This they did with clapboards, pitch, potash, glass, and metals, but most of those products were of relatively low value and did not begin to meet the Company's expectations. Not until tobacco growing was established did the colony find a profitable product. The Virginia Company ended in bankruptcy, and the charge of the colony went to the crown. While England may have hoped to replace Spanish and French wines and luxury food products with ones grown in Virginia, and later in the Carolinas, the reality of the colonial experience was that once settlers survived the initial hardships, their first thoughts were to provide sufficient food for themselves and their dependents. Tobacco growing eventually became the way to make money.

The Plymouth Colony consisted of 102 emigrants, largely Puritan Separatists who, after time in Holland, crossed the Atlantic in the ship *Mayflower*. During the voyage, several died, and a delay in departure from England put the colonists on the Cape Cod shore in November 1621, just at the start of the winter. As in other colonies, the group lost nearly half its number to illness and hunger, even though they had some corn stolen from a Native American cache. Compared with the Virginia colonists, the Puritan settlers fared well. They occupied cleared land, and the surrounding Native population had been reduced by European disease before the colonists' arrival. But the Plymouth settlers, too, labored under a financial obligation to their English backers, tried to operate as a trading post, and attempted to hold land in common. Like the Virginians, the Plymouth people gathered wild food at first, mostly waterfowl, shellfish, and fish, but also grew reasonably good crops in the first few years and preserved domestic animals for increase. The colony abandoned communal land ownership within two years of arrival, much more quickly than in Virginia.

The third settlement, the Massachusetts Bay Colony, established itself at Boston in 1630. In this instance, the people who held the charter of the colony, and whose wealth backed it, came to New England themselves to live in the colony they founded. Like other colonies, they endured a hard winter (1630–1631) and lost many of their number, but were reinforced with even more immigrants, who came with cash to buy the food raised by the established colonists.

As the Plymouth and Massachusetts Bay Colonies grew and new towns were established deeper in the wilderness, they, like the Virginians, encroached on Native American lands, and bloody confrontations followed. Meanwhile, the New England colonists looked for products to pay back the stock companies that had lent them money for settling. Within ten to twenty years the New Englanders engaged in fishing and raised sufficient cattle and other food to feed themselves and to supply Caribbean sugar plantations.

The Dutch

The Dutch had explored the Hudson River, and from 1609 were trading with Indians who came to the upper reaches of the river from the interior of what is now New York state, and from lower Canada as far west as the Great Lakes. Near present-day Albany they created their first outpost, Fort Nassau (later renamed Fort Orange), and a village that they named Beverwyck, which seldom had more than fifty inhabitants though the 1620s. In 1625, to protect the mouth of the Hudson and to support the fledging colony of New Netherland, the Dutch West India Company established New Amsterdam, the town that eventually became New York City.

New Netherland seems not to have suffered a starving time or the loss of many inhabitants to disease and hardship in the first year. The Dutch settlers, however, held the Native Americans in very poor regard, and their focus on opening farmland, especially in New Amsterdam and environs, put them on a collision course with the Indians that ultimately resulted in the Dutch massacring Indians and Indians retaliating against outlying Dutch farmsteads and settlements.

Native American Help and Native American Conflict

Just how much any European settler was willing to learn from any Native American about food or agriculture depended a good deal on how desperate the settler was and how closely the food matched European concepts of edibility. Europeans were likely to regard the native populations at best as potential Christians, and at worst as absolute savages. The Spanish brought a feudal mind-set to their American colonies, relegating the Indians to the lowest levels of society while attempting to replace Indian culture with Spanish ways. The English and Dutch were more interested in establishing trade, acquiring land, and gradually eliminating Indian presence than in incorporating the Natives into their society. Most Europeans thought that they had little to learn from any Native American, and that, if anything, the colonizers had an obligation, often neglected, to make converts to Christianity. Interpreting Native American behavior in European terms, they usually failed to understand the Native cultures.

This resulted, at best, in Europeans discounting the Native wisdom and, at worst, led to the conflict that ultimately meant the virtual extermination of the Native Americans.

Land ownership is the best example of how this failure to comprehend played out. Along most of the eastern seaboard, the Native Americans of all nations engaged in seasonal hunting, gathering, and agriculture. They kept land clear by burning; planted corn, beans, and squash, using a hoe; and moved from one locality to another to give agricultural soil a rest. They grew only what they needed from one agricultural year to the next. In Virginia, for example, the colonists arrived in Jamestown in May, just when the Native Americans' food supply was at its lowest. The Indians had little enough to eat and little interest in sharing what was left, no matter what the English had to offer in trade.

For the Native Americans, land ownership was more about hunting privileges, and the English habit of enclosing land deprived them of part of their food supply. And in many places, the settlers allowed their domestic animals to run loose, and pigs and cattle ate the Indians' crops. Often the Indians killed the marauding animals, and that in turn caused conflict with the colonists.

Another example of colonists' misinterpretation centered on the Native American men hunting and fishing and the women doing the gardening. In Europe, hunting and fishing were recreational activities for the leisured classes, and agriculture was the work of mostly male farmers. To Europeans, it appeared that the Indian men were lazy, wanting only to hunt and fish while the women toiled at raising corn, beans, and squash in addition to minding children, gathering food, and cooking. Europeans did not comprehend that the Natives' hunting and fishing was as important a subsistence activity as growing food.

Nonetheless, under certain circumstances Europeans adopted or adapted foods, cooking styles, or agricultural practices. For example, they observed that Indians planted corn in hills among tree stumps, cultivating only around the hills. It made sense to the Europeans to plant newly cleared land, riddled with tree stumps, in this fashion until they could pull the stumps and begin plowing the ground. Similarly, the Natives planted squashes and pumpkins among the corn hills; they grew to cover the ground, shading out weeds, and beans planted at the base of the corn climbed the stalks. Further, in Plymouth Colony, the English-speaking Squanto taught the colonists the Native practice of burying a fish in each hill of corn. The Europeans adopted these practices until they could use their more accustomed plow, whereupon they reverted to many of their old agricultural habits.

Some Europeans had seen or heard of corn (maize) because explorers had brought it to Europe from the New World. Settlers quickly discovered that corn was a more reliable crop to grow, especially at first, than the English grains wheat, barley, and oats. This was also true of the other two of the so-called Three Sisters, squash and beans. Europeans found that the Native American beans could be used in ways similar to the European fava bean or even peas, and that eased their adoption. The English settlers similarly took to pumpkins and squash because they could be used in European-style dishes. Succotash, corn and beans stewed together, was similar to European pottages (thick soups), and cornmeal mush, sometimes called by the Native American name *suppawn*, was like a European porridge of wheat or oats. Without some degree of familiarity, Europeans generally looked askance at other Native dishes and sometimes were repulsed.

The Europeans brought seeds of familiar foods and planted them, often in preference to learning which indigenous wild foods could be gathered in the Indian fashion. Adriaen Van der Donck, in his *Description of New Netherland*, reported that among the many wild foods, especially berries, that the Dutch did gather there were "several other kinds of roots and fruits, known to the Indians, who use the same which are disregarded by the Netherlanders, because they have introduced every kind of garden vegetables, which thrive and yield well."[4]

Where settlers included women, either wives or servants, who would cook, the likelihood of European cookery habits persisting was stronger than where male traders or soldiers, or even captives of war, lived from time to time with Native Americans, or took Native American wives. For many of them the stews of wild meats thickened with corn or ground nutmeats resembled European pottages, but the Europeans were likely to report that they missed bread, salt (which the Natives used hardly at all), and sugar.

One difference between the English and the Spanish colonial experiences, especially in the Southwest, was that the Hispanic colonists who followed Don Juan de Oñate into what became New Mexico, and those who moved into California in the mid-1700s, were largely descendants of Spanish colonists in Mexico. Many had already adapted to New World foods, and some had married Mexican Indians and developed a distinctive cuisine blending the ancient foods of Mexico with Spanish imports and transplants. Spanish colonists were more open to Indian foodways than their English counterparts, partly because they were more open to intermarriage with Indian women. Among Spanish missionaries, as long as wheat and grapes could be grown to provide what was necessary for Communion wafers and wine, they seemed to accept what food could be obtained locally, with the occasional import of the more familiar fare when it could reach them. Yet they, too, brought with them domesticated animals and seeds of familiar vegetables and grains.

Over time, Native Americans adopted many European agricultural practices and foodstuffs. Squeezed off their lands, or outright displaced, they had to give up their traditional hunting, gathering, and seasonal agriculture. Having suffered the European pigs and cattle destroying their crops, they turned to keeping domestic animals.

The Columbian Exchange

The exchange of plants, animals, humans, and microbes between Europeans and Native American nations is known as the Columbian Exchange, named for Christopher Columbus. It began long before colonists came to America. On his 1492 and subsequent voyages of exploration in the Caribbean, Columbus introduced pigs and cattle and collected specimens of plants. He accidentally introduced diseases against which the Native populations had no immunity. He took back to Europe many American foodstuffs, including tomatoes, potatoes, and corn. Many other foods were taken from the New World to the Old World and sometimes, later, back to the New World again. Vanilla, chocolate, potatoes, and turkeys are New World foods that were taken to Europe and that returned with colonists.

Interdependence and Independence

Many new colonies experimented with communal food production and supplies for the first few years. Food was rationed so that all would be provided for. But that did little to motivate colonists to work hard to grow food. The Jamestown settlement struggled for nearly ten years before it turned to private land ownership. Plymouth Colony abandoned the communal approach after two years, allowing each settler an acre of ground to plant. The domestic animals held by the colony were divided among the households in 1627. With their self-interest engaged, settlers worked harder to provide for their families.

Hunting, Fishing, and Gathering

Many Europeans regarded hunting and fishing as sport. Settlers from wealthy classes, those regarded as gentlemen, were often skilled hunters, accustomed to shooting game. Many other settlers, however, whether or not they owned or knew how to use firearms, were not skilled in tracking large animals or, especially in "starving times," were not well or strong enough to hunt. Or they were so vulnerable to attack from Native Americans that they did not wish to venture out to find food.

Nonetheless, wild food provided an essential part of the diet in the first years of settlement until the colonists or settlers were established enough to feed domestic animals and raise them for eating. (In some areas, that meant having cleared land for pasturing and growing hay; in other areas, land on which animals could forage for themselves, and systems for branding and rounding up animals that had run wild.) Thereafter, a market for wild food existed in most places, and professional hunters brought in game for sale or trade.

Often throughout the Colonial period, the people most likely to turn to wild food were economically marginal and enslaved people who augmented their diet with food they could hunt, fish for, trap, or pilfer. Similarly, gathering edible plants and fruits was acceptable when the more essential work of gardening was finished. Gathering nuts and berries may have been essential in some instances for survival, and always provided variety, but most colonists preferred the activity as recreation and favored the reliability of garden, field, and orchard.

Climate determined how much wild food gathering was worthwhile. There was a great deal of difference in wild food available in the Northeast, with a growing season from June through October, compared with the longer season of the Southeast. It was one thing to dig for clams along the icy shore of New England in winter and quite another to fish along southern streams in the same season. Some regions were naturally abundant in certain foodstuffs while others were not. Hunters and gatherers, whether they were Native Americans or colonists, had to maintain a profitable balance between expending calories to find food and replacing those calories by eating it. Starvation and disease followed when more calories were spent getting food than were replaced by consuming it.

For much of the earliest settlement era, as in certain later periods, the best many settlers could hope for was enough food to provide the basic calories for living, clearing land, and beginning farms and gardens. In extremity, any food was good. Daniel Boone wrote in his memoirs that, as when he was an Indian captive in April 1778, the Natives' food was plain but sufficient: "My food and lodging was, in common, with them, not so good indeed as I could desire, but necessity made everything acceptable."[5] Necessity made a lot acceptable to many in the earliest years.

Self-Sufficiency and Markets

Hardly any colony, or subsequent settlement, was completely self-sufficient in the literal sense of the word. Without reprovisioning by colony proprietors or stock company, most of the earliest colonies would have failed; in fact, those which did, often failed because new or adequate food supplies did not reach them. Similarly, without a market for goods produced, new colonies had difficulty thriving. From the earliest settlement, colonists and settlers on the ever-expanding frontiers combined aspects of self-sufficiency with market activity. All needed some quantity of manufactured goods and imported foods, to buy which they sold produce or products.

Breaks or long delays in the supply may have had an adverse effect on the quality of imported foods such as spices, coffee, or tea, which could lose flavor. Olive oil, often called sweet oil, could become rancid. Dried fruits such as raisins and currants could become wormy, and nuts could become rancid. Although information is not clear enough to be able to assign this as a cause, nonetheless we may suspect that large quantities of spice may have been used in some dishes to obtain sufficient flavor, or that the high price and/or poor quality of these goods may account for their subsequent omission from the diet, especially in more remote parts of the country and among poorer folks.

As new settlers moved west through the 1700s and early 1800s, establishing trails and roads along which goods traveled, the time between new settlement and the appearance of merchants and stores shortened, so that periods of scarcity were also shortened, though cost and quality continued to be concerns for consumers. Some goods always had to be purchased, such as tea, coffee, rum, wine, brandy, cane sugar, and molasses. Whether other commodities, such as wheat, rice, cheese, and even meat and fish, were bought by consumers or sold for cash or credit depended on the region. New Englanders in the eighteenth century bought wheat and sold butter and cheese. Ohio consumers in 1820 sold wheat and purchased tea and tobacco, while Virginians purchased cheese and sold tobacco.

Markets and market effect appeared early. Within ten to twenty years of establishing a colony in Plymouth, farmers there raised and sold cattle to new colonists entering the Massachusetts Bay Colony in Boston. The Boston colony in turn enjoyed prosperity during the 1630s, providing goods to their newcomers until a pause in immigrants created a recession from which the colony tried to recover by selling wheat and other goods to Spain, the Canary Islands, and eventually the West Indies. Sometimes the value of food as a salable commodity would skew its use by the farmers who produced it, making it more valuable to sell than to eat.

The ideal of pure self-sufficiency among settlers who built homes and barns from timber they cut themselves, cleared land and grew their own food, spun their own flax and wool, wove their cloth and sewed clothing, churned their own butter, made their own cheese, and baked bread from the grain they raised, was hardly ever realized. Nearly everyone who came to America needed cash to purchase land and the animals required to work it and to provide food; they needed to buy or barter for metal farming and cooking implements; they had to pay taxes or tithes. Barter required time and labor or excess goods of recognizable value. Where there was a high level of self-sufficiency, very often hardship followed as settlers managed merely to survive and did without many of the goods and services that would have eased their existence.

A good example of this was described by a French general, the Marquis de Chastellux, who came to the Colonies in 1782 to fight with American troops against the British. While here, Chastellux visited western Virginia, where he had a conversation with a settler from North Carolina who described his way of life. Chastellux wrote in his journal that those settlements were "remote from trade" and depended entirely on the sort of agriculture that "consists in producing only what is sufficient for the owner's consumption." "It is easy," Chastellux wrote, "to conceive that there is . . . no deficiency of food," and that the settlers must make all their own clothing and shoes. "As for drink, they are obliged to content themselves with milk and water, until their apple trees are large enough to bear fruit, or until they have been able to procure themselves stills"—which would require money or barter goods—"to distill their grain." As idyllic as subsistence farming sounds, there was still plenty of motivation to find cash. One item that the settlers required was nails, which could be made only at the cost of labor and time. Chastellux asked the settler what had brought him 400 miles from home, and learned that he had been engaged in trading horses, which, he reported, multiplied quickly on the abundant pasturage, and could be driven to sale with the expenditure of the trader's energy but no cash outlay.[6]

For a colony or settlement to thrive or grow into a town, sufficient goods had to be produced to support a group of artisans such as blacksmiths, wheelwrights, millers, shoemakers, and potters, who produced the goods needed for daily life, and eventually to attract merchants, who brought desirable consumer goods, and the professionals such as ministers, lawyers, and doctors, who provided desirable services. While the artisans, businessmen, or professionals usually farmed in addition to conducting their craft or business, they were involved in an economy that depended on cash or goods whose value was calculated in cash.

Account books and diaries show the care with which people recorded their transactions and exchanges, many of which involved food, and they reflect a high awareness of the cash value of goods and services. One household might run out of butter but find another household willing to sell some butter. The seller might accept payment partially in cash and partially in an amount of grain or meat or cheese of value equal to the balance owed. Sometimes the buyer would continue to owe a balance calculated in cash until a later time, when the buyer would deliver a quantity of meat or of wool, or even pay an amount the seller owed a store in order to clear the debt. The transactions were often complicated and went unsettled for a long time, and sometimes involved third parties. They were effective in an economy that often lacked currency, and when, after 1820, most transactions were conducted with cash, hardship was created among people who had difficulty obtaining cash.

Other transactions were more direct. One person might, for example, record the "loan" of a quarter of a lamb, with the clear expectation that an equal quantity of lamb would be returned in the future. Other food was traded or given as gifts to cement bonds of friendship or family connection, even among wealthy individuals. A sudden surplus of perishable food could be distributed to prevent spoilage and show neighborliness.

Hardly any people in Colonial and Federal America, from earliest settlements through westward expansion after the Revolutionary War, provided all their own and their family's subsistence without being part of a network of community exchanges or participating in or being affected by market forces.

ISSUES IN EARLY AMERICAN FOOD HABITS

What people choose to eat and how they cook and serve it is subject to several influences. People desire what they consider to be edible and familiar. They like a food supply to be reliable. In the past, seasonality and climate often determined what food was available in a given place. In America, colonists and their descendants cooked many dishes from experience and memory, creating ones similar to those found in many parts of the world. These dishes eventually acquired an American character, either in their composition or in the manner they were prepared and eaten.

Preference for the Familiar and Reliable

Everyone has experienced new and different foods. Sometimes the encounter leads to addition of a new food to the diet, or proves to be one of many interesting but not repeated experiences of a new place or culture. Sometimes it proves to be unpleasant or unsettling, and the person eating it wishes to return to the familiar. Everyone likes knowing where the next meal will come from, and will describe hardship in terms of food scarcity or monotony. Over and over in the food history of America, and of the world, there are instances of encounters with new kinds of foods—the rejection of some, the adaptation of others—and the drive toward a steady, reliable supply.

There are, of course, many plants and animals in the world that are, strictly speaking, edible but are never incorporated into anyone's diet. Still other foods are eaten by some cultures and rejected as inedible by others, even to the point of being considered revolting. For example, insects are eaten around the world, but most modern Americans would avoid grubs or grasshoppers except in the most extreme survival situations. Similarly, Americans are repulsed by the idea of eating dogs or horses, though other cultures eat them. A later chapter will discuss the strictures of religion or health that affect people's choices in food and lead them to eliminate or add certain foodstuffs to their diets. What people choose to eat is determined mostly by what their culture designates as acceptable food.

Colonists and settlers certainly encountered new foods when they came to North America. In some cases, they learned from Native Americans what was edible. In other cases, they recognized a similarity between the North American plant, animal, fish, or bird and those they knew in Europe; settlers determined what might make good food based on experience and knowledge. As newcomers traveled through the Colonies and the regions that later became the United States, they observed and recorded descriptions of food resources. These descriptions, printed in England and Europe, sometimes painted an exaggerated picture of a land of plenty that was meant to encourage emigration, but at least cataloged some of what was found and showed which European foods thrived in North America.

For example, John Lawson, traveling in the Carolinas around 1700, described wild turkeys and deer, wrote what possum tasted like ("between young Pork and Veal"), saw many kinds of waterfowl, and listed the salad vegetables, wild and cultivated, that he saw: "The sallads are the Lettice, Curl'd. Red, Cabbage, and Savoy. Spinage, Fennel, Samphire in the Marshes is excellent, Dock, Pocket, Sorrel, French and English Cresses, purslain wild, Parsley—two sorts, Asparagus, White Cabbage."[7] Similarly, there is Rev. Francis Higginson's description of the fish along the New England coast in 1630: "There is a Fish called a Basse . . . altogether as good as our fresh Sammon [salmon], and the season of their coming was begun when wee came first to New-England in June, and continued about three month apace. . . . Also here is abundance of Herring, Turbot, Sturgion, Cuskes, Muskles and Oysters."[8] In *New Englands Rarities Discovered*, John Josselyn described all the plants, animals, insects, birds, and fish he saw on his trips to the region in 1638 and 1663, and commented on how such foods as cranberries, blueberries, squashes, and pumpkins grew and were prepared by the Indians and the English settlers.[9] Later the Pennsylvania-born naturalist John Bartram explored from Florida to Lake Ontario, identifying plants both edible and ornamental. He introduced many into cultivation, bringing such plants as sweet potatoes and West Indian peppers to the Middle Atlantic states to see how they could be grown there.

Wherever the colonists and settlers went, they took with them seeds of familiar vegetables and grains to plant. In 1609 the Virginia Company provided seeds for parsnips, carrots, cabbages, turnips, lettuce, onions, mustard, and garlic.[10] Colonists brought cattle, sheep, goats, pigs, and poultry. And while John Lawson, marveling at the democratic accessibility of deer and other game, hunting for which in England was the privilege of the gentry, exclaimed, "A poor Labourer, that is Master of his gun &c., hath as good a Claim to have Continu'd Coarses (courses) of Delicacies crouded upon his Table, as he that is Master of a greater Purse,"[11] most people preferred to have familiar, domesticated meat to accompany a reliable supply of vegetables and fruits.

Further, most settlers wanted bread with most meals, and bread required grain, which in turn required agriculture. The Europeans brought wheat, rye, oats, and barley, and took readily to corn. The first few decades of settlement in any region was a time of locating the best sections for growing various crops. Corn, being a native plant, proved to be a reliable and plentiful crop in most places and soon predominated as the staple grain, with wheat a second almost everywhere except New England. Similarly, while the English brought their familiar peas, they soon discovered that native beans fared better. Lawson, for instance, commented that English beans ended up dwarfed in the Carolinas, while the kidney bean, which was there before the English, and the climbing white and spotted beans, thrived.[12] Naturally enough, the colonists' effort gravitated toward the crops and husbandry practices that had greater yields and provided marketable surpluses.

Seasonality

For centuries humankind has sought ways to preserve plenty against scarcity, and to overcome the restrictions of the seasons. Today, one cannot walk into a store and determine the season of the year by the display of fresh foods. There are production, storage, and transportation systems that effectively eliminate most seasonal scarcities not only by drying, canning, and freezing, but also by supplying fresh, unpreserved foods. The chapter on food preparation will discuss specific strategies and technologies for food preservation in use in the Colonial and Federal eras. Part of the experience of life in the earlier days of the country meant accepting times of the year when there was no milk, or no eggs, or no green leafy food to eat, and only storable fresh foods such as apples.

It meant that the diet during some seasons was characterized by the monotonous repetition of certain foodstuffs, varied only by what could be eaten from the preserved supply or gathered fresh. Over the course of a year, there might be considerable variation in the diet, but that variety was not usually available within the course of one week. The harsher the climate and the more remote the settlement, the more true this would be. So in the colder northern regions or in the arid Southwest, for example, there might be considerably less variety in food than in the moderate climate of the Chesapeake or Middle Atlantic states.

The agricultural year did not necessarily match the change of seasons. Growing seasons varied from region to region, depending on temperature and rainfall. Settlers adjusted animal husbandry and grain and vegetable growing to take advantage of climatic conditions. For example, butchering in the fall made sense to northern farmers, who would select which animals they wished to feed through the winter and slaughter the rest. Cold weather allowed them to keep some of the meat fresh and cold, even frozen. Settlers in southern reaches of the country learned that some vegetables could not thrive through the hot and dry summer months, so they planted some vegetables early in the spring and again in the fall.

Universal Dishes

Over time, humankind worldwide has developed certain food preparation strategies that are remarkably similar from culture to culture. For example, nearly all cultures boil their staple grain or starch. Asians have boiled rice for centuries, and Africans have cooked such starches such as taro, plantains, sweet potatoes, cassava, and yams into a dish called *foo-foo*. Hawaiians have made poi from taro. In Scotland, oats have been sometimes ground, sometimes only broken, then boiled. In America, the Native Americans pounded corn and boiled it as a mush. When potatoes were introduced into Europe, they, too, were boiled. Similarly, staple legumes are often cooked into a soup or stewlike dish; the English boil peas into pease porridge, Asian Indians make dal from lentils, and Mexicans make refried beans.

Almost every culture makes some kind of bread from its staple grain, often a flat bread, simply mixed and quickly baked. Scots make an oat bannock; in the Middle East leavened wheat flour has been baked into flat bread for centuries; and in pre-Columbian Mexico the Indians made a flat bread of ground corn that the Spaniards named tortillas. Similarly, all cultures have soup; ferment beverages, even if they ultimately disallow their consumption; and value fat or oil. Most cultures have some kind of dumplings or pasta, and make pickles. Many have cheese made from the milk of their most important animal. Where there is sufficient fat or oil, there are deep-fried dishes. Most cultures have a way of cooking food in the ground, take advantage of natural cold to preserve food, and have adjusted their cooking methods to the amount of fuel available. Each culture develops a customary way of seasoning staple foods.

Each culture confers a certain status and symbolic importance on certain foods, and while any given food's status and meaning may change over time, some foods are nonetheless considered more important or special than others, and are served to special individuals or on special occasions. Other foods are considered suitable for everyday fare, and still others are repugnant and in some cultures are eaten only by the poor, the desperate, or the lowest castes or classes. Religious strictures often apply to certain foods, and believers may always avoid eating those foods or eat them only on specific occasions.

In American food history, all colonists, settlers, and subsequent immigrants have brought with them their home culture's habits and preferences, including dishes similar to dishes around the globe. Upon arriving in America, colonists adapted new ingredients to the dishes they were accustomed to making. For example, if settlers saw a root vegetable that looked like a potato and had the density and thin skin of a potato, they probably were inclined to peel, boil, and mash it. If it seemed bland, they might put salt, pepper, and gravy on it. If, on the other hand, it was sweet, they might add sugar and spices and eat it like applesauce, or even beat in eggs and cream and bake it in a piecrust for a dessert. They might give it a new name or name it after the dish it was based it on. But they would not have invented a dish as much as they would have developed one from what they already knew.

In the cluster of dishes that might be identified as early American there are many derived from European practice but made with native American ingredients. There are also European dishes that continued to evolve in North America, taking on new names as they changed and, sometimes, new significance. Then there are dishes that resulted from settlers adopting and adapting both Native American dishes and those of immigrants from other cultures. These will be identified and described shortly, but the role of everyday, plain cookery is considered first.

Vernacular Cookery

Most people have the experience of making something for themselves or their families to eat without consulting a cookbook. Most Americans can make a peanut butter and jelly sandwich, assemble a green salad, or fry a hamburger without instructions. They do not need a set of published menus to tell them that they like cereal and milk for breakfast, and prefer to carry a sandwich in a lunch bag rather than a plate of spaghetti and sauce. These habits are common, everyday practices that are followed almost unconsciously, just as when people speak a sentence, they organize the subject and verb in the right order without thinking about it very much. The term "vernacular cookery" will be used to describe this process in the past. (The word "vernacular" is usually applied to language, and means using the common or local dialect rather than cultured or literary language.) When people wish to adopt a certain style or create a special dish, they may choose to step out of everyday practice to cook and present a meal more self-consciously. A modern person, for instance, might cook a Chinese-style dinner even if he or she were not Chinese. Such a person might turn to friends, cookbooks, magazines or newspapers, the Internet, or television cooking shows for recipes and to learn how to prepare those dishes.

For 200 and more years, early Americans cooked many dishes and meals without formal instructions on how to assemble them, just as many of them constructed their houses without the help of an architect. Most cooks—and most cooks were women—learned from their mothers how to make the everyday foods that the majority of people ate. They cooked in the vernacular. In some instances, when a household attained a certain level of prosperity or wished to make something better than usual to serve to an important guest, or on a special occasion, the cook might turn consciously to a recipe that allowed her to demonstrate sophistication or wealth. Recipes might be found in one of the printed cookbooks that came from Europe, either brought by immigrants or imported for sale in the colonies.

Some women, particularly mistresses of gentry households, kept notebooks of handwritten recipes, some copied from printed cookbooks, others acquired from their mother, friends, or relatives. By

modern standards these recipe notebooks contain an amazing number of recipes for desserts or fancy dishes, but this merely points to
the recipes' uses for special occasions. For an everyday, ordinary meal,
people of high, middle, or lower class were very likely to cook from
memory and eat simple, vernacular dishes.

Some Early American Vernacular Dishes

Colonists brought wheat to America because it was their favorite
grain and had been for centuries. Wheat, however, did not grow uni-
formly well everywhere in the Colonies, whereas the native corn
(maize) usually did. The early settlers called all grains "corn" and distinguished the Native American from the English corn by naming it
Indian corn, or sometimes just "Indian." When pounded or ground
into meal, corn reminded settlers of oatmeal, and they cooked with
it to make dishes similar to ones they made with oats (and sometimes
wheat). This included simply boiling it and eating it with milk and
molasses or sugar. This was called mush, hasty pudding, or *suppawn*,
a name derived from the Native American word for a similar dish. In
the Spanish Colonial Southwest, settlers ate a very thin, souplike mixture of cornmeal and water (which the English would call a gruel)
named *atole*, which had been made by Indians since ancient times.

Colonial cooks made a stiff dough of cornmeal, water, and salt that
they patted out on a board or griddle and baked over or in front of
the fire to make a kind of bread that they called bannock, hoecake,
or sometimes johnnycake, a name that came from the word "joniken"
or "jannockin," a term used in the north of England for a simple oat-
meal hearth cake. When cooks lacked something to bake the dough
on, they would form the cornmeal mixture into a small cake and bury
it in hot ashes to bake; it was then called ashcake. All these simple
cornmeal mixtures made a plain flat bread such as could be found
around the world.

Sometimes cooks added other ingredients to the cornmeal mixture,
including shortening, eggs, milk, and a leaven, to make cornbread
(sometimes called Indian cake). During the later eighteenth century,
regional variations on cornbread appeared in the South and the
North. Made with a more liquid batter and fried on a griddle, this
became the pancakelike "Indian slapjack" recorded by Amelia Simmons in *American Cookery*, the first American cookbook, published
in 1796.[13]

Indian pudding was the American version of the English sweetened-milk puddings thickened with flour, rice, or bread. To make it, cornmeal and molasses, a sweetening commonly used in the Colonial era, were stirred into hot milk, and the mixture was baked in a dish or boiled in a cloth. Regional variations of this dish appeared, as will be seen in discussions of each region.

Pumpkin was another native American ingredient that colonists prepared as they had prepared similar foods at home, particularly apples. They boiled pumpkin and ate it as a sauce to accompany meat. Cooked pumpkin was added to cornmeal to enrich Indian cake. It was made into puddings and pies, ultimately the favorite way to use it. In some regions, pumpkin was baked and eaten with butter and sugar. Colonists came with no recipes for how to use pumpkin; nonetheless, they contrived familiar enough dishes that pumpkin became an important food.

The sap of maple trees offered another opportunity for colonists to adapt procedures used in Germany, Scotland, Scandinavia, and other European countries to a new setting. The goal of tapping maple trees and boiling the sap was to produce sugar, or at least a molasses substitute. Europeans were also familiar with other sugar-producing juices, most notably that of sugarcane, which during the Colonial era became an ever more important commodity, both to consumers and to the producers who made and sold it.[14]

Other American foods were more easily adapted to familiar dishes: fish, fowl, berries, and nuts fit easily into cooking procedures well known to European cooks, once a period of trial was past. Colonists found cranberries could be used in sauce, tarts, and eventually pies and puddings. The blueberry was used as currants had been.

Refinement and Gentility

Another influence with long-lasting effects on Colonial and Federal American eating habits was an ever-increasing awareness of refined and genteel dining. Increasing prosperity in early America put in the hands of the population more consumer goods, including imported china and silver. With them came more self-consciously genteel dining habits and manners, and a desire for more refined and elegant food preparation as well. These changes were well under way in Europe before America was colonized. During the Renaissance, the nobility adopted the use of forks and established elaborate food

Early seventeenth-century tableware. Clockwise from top: napkins, small mugs and jug, linens, redware baking plates, pewter and wooden spoons, decorated redware bowl, pewter platters, pewter bowls, tumblers, leather mug, and wooden trenchers. Wooden platters are in the center. Most English colonists used these sorts of utensils to set their tables and to eat with. (Courtesy of Plimoth Plantation, Plymouth, Massachusetts.)

presentation and higher cleanliness standards. The new refined habits of the nobility were imitated by the wealthy and gradually trickled down to the more prosperous merchant classes.

Most Colonial Americans, particularly the lower classes, were accustomed to eating with spoons and fingers, using their knives to cut pieces of meat and to convey them to their mouths. They used bread to sop up gravy or soup and sometimes served themselves from a common bowl. Even the gentry ate in this way in the fifteenth and sixteenth centuries, although they were more accustomed to individual place settings.

The greatest changes that appeared between first settlement and the post-Revolutionary War era were the adoption of forks, the appearance of equipment for making and drinking tea in many homes, and more individual place settings. The more prosperous often had a dining room dedicated to eating and entertaining.

The change to forks from knives and fingers was slower to occur in America than in Europe, where the wealthy began to adopt forks in the seventeenth century. When Plymouth Colony's Governor Winthrop died in 1676, the inventory of his estate included a fork. Few forks appear on estate inventories until the early 1700s. These forks most often had two tines, and as they came into popularity, table knives began to have a more rounded tip, and people ate from them. By the end of the Federal era, most people in the emerging middle class owned forks, even though many continued to eat from their knives.

When tea drinking was introduced around 1700, it was at first the province of the wealthy, who acquired teapots for brewing the tea, urns in which to keep water hot, caddies to hold the tea leaves, sugar bowls, milk pitchers, teacups and saucers, teaspoons, and special bowls for refuse. Making and drinking tea was an event performed with some care if not ceremony. Like many other things, tea drinking came gradually into the reach of the prosperous, and eventually more ordinary people. The appearance in the mid-1700s of teacups and teapots in middle-class estate inventories shows that the refined activity of tea drinking had diffused outward into society. The gentry continued the practice but used more expensive materials, such as silver for urns, pots, and other tea equipage, and purchased porcelain teacups. By the end of the Federal era, tea was a common beverage for nearly everyone and, accompanied by food, had become the name of a late afternoon or early evening meal.

Another aspect of refinement was the appearance of individual place settings for most people. As the Colonial era progressed, fewer and fewer people ate from a common serving bowl or platter. Only the poorest people would continue do so. The biggest change was from wooden plates, or trenchers, to pewter and redware pottery or Delft plates and platters, and eventually to china, either English or Chinese export. The wealthier classes acquired imported china, but as the standard of living improved in the Colonies, and as greater quantities of china were manufactured in England (and eventually in America), more and more people owned it. Table settings became more elaborate, with more specialized serving pieces and more expensive materials such as silver and porcelain.

In the earliest settlements, people were obliged to conduct nearly all their living in one room or, at most, two; cooking, sitting, entertaining, sleeping, and sometimes nursing the ill. Missions and governor's mansions might have a room dedicated to dining and entertaining, but most people ate their meals at a table in a common room. During the eighteenth century, as dining rooms became more fashionable in Europe, wealthy Americans interested in a genteel way of life dedicated a room for dining and furnished it with a table, matching chairs, and pieces for displaying silver and ceramics and for

food service. By the end of the Federal era, except in the most remote parts of the new country, gentry homes contained a dining
room, and having such a room became the goal of many middle-class
people in the 1800s.

Refinement went beyond dining habits to include cleaner streets,
well-thought-out city plans, confined animals, and flower gardens.
Genteel individuals learned neater handwriting, polite manners, and
easy conversation. They kept themselves and their clothing clean, and
dressed their servants in uniforms. Eventually refinement would even
change the way food was cooked and presented at the table, but for
most of the later Colonial era and the Federal era, the wealthy im-
pressed their guests with a generous variety of things to eat served in
beautiful platters and bowls and with a silver fork, knife, and spoon for
each guest. There were meats including fowl and game; soup in a
tureen; fish; side dishes of organ meats, vegetables, and fruits; sweetmeats (candied or crystallized fruit), jellies, custards, and cakes; and imported wines and liquors to drink. The middle class observed and, as
soon as they could, followed suit to whatever extent they could afford.

Speed and Efficiency

Despite the move toward gentility, one national characteristic
emerged during this era that mitigated somewhat the ease, comfort, and
elegance of refined dining. That was the American desire for conven-
ience and speed in food preparation, and an inclination to eat hastily.

Many cooks abandoned the practice of weighing ingredients and
instead measured them in cups, glasses or tumblers, and spoons that
surely varied in capacity. To some extent, this practice was a contin-
uation of one already under way. For example, in Gulielma Penn's
"receipt" book, many recipes call for ingredients weighed out in
pounds and ounces, to which liquids measured by the pint or quart
are added. But there is one recipe for a simple "buttered Lofe" that
calls for "a goode Dele of wheat flouer" and as many "yeolke of egs
as you thinke fitt," plus unspecified quantities of butter, sugar, cloves,
mace, and salt.[15] Even in Hannah Glasse's cookbook there are recipes
calling for "handfuls" of one thing, "some" of this, and a "little" of
that. Many people continued using pints and quarts, for the measures
appear in estate inventories, and weighed some ingredients by the
pound or ounce, but the frequency of measurement by weight was
shifting toward more informal and imprecise quantities. Quite possibly this, too, was a matter of economics: most people had a cup or

tumblers, but a set of scales and weights required cash. This tendency was more common in the North and on the frontier. More precise practices appeared to endure in wealthier homes in cities and on southern plantations.

This era also saw the beginnings of the use of chemical leaven. Previously, cakes were raised with yeast or beaten egg whites, but by the end of the 1700s, pearlash, the alkaline substance potassium carbonate, was added to an acid ingredient, such as molasses, sour milk, or lemon. The resulting gas bubbles raised the cake or biscuit; this eliminated the need to set yeast to rise in dough, then wait until it had risen sufficiently before baking. Chemical leavens such as saleratus, baking soda, and baking powder, which followed pearlash in the nineteenth century, made it possible to make biscuits in minutes. More important, it set America on the path to packaged mixes. Chemical leavens were embraced, in the North and along the frontier, wherever time was a valuable commodity, whereas more traditional baking practices endured longer among the gentry.

Among the colonial gentry, long dinners with two or more courses, followed by cracking nuts, eating fruit, and drinking toasts, were common, but among the middling and lower classes, there was little time for that. When the Englishman Henry Wansey traveled in America in 1794, he observed that there appeared to be no shyness in conversation at the table of a Boston tavern where he stayed, but that as soon as they finished eating, the Americans left to attend to business, "for," he said, "the Americans know the value of time too well to waste it at the table."[16] Few later travelers failed to note that average Americans ate quickly and did not linger sociably at the table. It seemed to be an American trait.

FOOD, LAND, AND PEOPLE

To understand American food habits, one must examine the larger context of colonial population and land. Who came? Where did they settle and move? What food did they grow, and how did they grow it? How did they obtain the food they could not grow?

The Starting Points

Once permanent colonies were established along the eastern seaboard at Spanish St. Augustine in 1565, Virginia in 1607, and

New England in 1621, and in the Spanish Southwest in 1598, others colonies were soon founded in the places that came to be called "the original thirteen" Colonies and in other parts of modern-day America. The Dutch established New Netherland in 1624; Salem and Massachusetts Bay Colonies were settled in 1626 and 1628, respectively. Baltimore dates to 1629, and New Hampshire's first settlement was in 1631. Seven years later, in 1638, Connecticut's first colony was established at New Haven, and Newport, Rhode Island, was settled in 1639.

After a hiatus that included the era of the British Commonwealth (1649–1660), the monarchy was restored in England and a new group of colonies was founded in America. Charleston, South Carolina, was established in 1670. Philadelphia became the first settlement in Pennsylvania in 1682. New Bern, North Carolina, was established in 1710, and Georgia was colonized in 1733. In 1699 French settlers began colonizing French-owned Louisiana.

Trading outposts and forts belonging to France, England, and Spain were scattered up and down the Mississippi, around the Great Lakes, and into what would be the Canadian Maritime Provinces and down into modern-day Maine. Spanish missions and outposts dotted the Gulf of Mexico and were scattered across the Spanish Southeast. The English Hudson's Bay Company had a post in the Pacific Northwest. While most of these forts and outposts were provisioned by the company or country that owned and maintained them, and they produced some of their own food by growing it or acquiring it from Native American or settler neighbors, they were usually so self-contained that they had very little culinary impact beyond their walls, and that tended to be in the nature of market effect.

Sweden had established a small colony in Delaware from 1638 to 1655, but it never quite thrived despite the support of the Swedish crown, and the Dutch took over the dwindling colony. The Swedes had only a small culinary impact on American foodways. Russians established a colony in 1784 on Kodiak Island, the first Alaskan settlement, and one in 1812 in northern California. Russian fare can be found today in Alaska, but there is little culinary evidence of Russian colonial cookery in California.

From these starting points, adjacent areas were settled, many of them reaching statehood by the close of the Federal era. Settlement was often uneven and depended upon political, economic, and national events, not the least of which were the French and Indian Wars and the American Revolution. England took over New Netherland,

and the Spanish relinquished their holdings in the Southeast. France was defeated in Canada by the English, and sold Louisiana to the young United States.

Food habits, though, did not carefully observe colony or state boundaries. They were carried by people who, whenever they could, moved into new areas, adjusted to new climates and soils, and met neighbors with sometimes different ways of eating. Even within one colony or state, if it was large enough and the terrain was variable enough, there were noticeable differences in food habits. Food habits take on and reinforce regional characteristics, and each region's food-ways are examined in chapter 4. For now, the Colonies will be considered, individually and collectively, to see how their populations were distributed and how they used the land.

Population

Population growth is important to the study of food because it is an indicator of the colonists' general health. Population increase, either by birth or by immigration, brought economic progress. Labor was always valuable and often hard to come by, so more people meant both more agricultural labor and more consumers. A decline in, or a leveling off of, population meant new land was cleared more slowly, markets for agricultural and manufactured goods flattened, and sometimes recession was triggered. This helps one understand why many people were encouraged to come to America: books describing the new country often mention natural abundance, fertile soils, and many opportunities.

For the first half of the 1600s, the population of the American colonies grew primarily through immigration, with most new settlers, estimated at around 40,000, coming from England to New England and Virginia, and from Holland to New York. Mortality in this period was higher in the Chesapeake than in New England, and because there were more than twice as many men as women, Virginia families were typically smaller than New England families.

By 1700, white people in America numbered about 235,000, and in the next seventy years, with even more immigrants from England, Ireland, Scotland, and Germany added to the large families that many northern colonists had, the number had risen to 108 million white people. This number implies, however, a concomitant decline in the Native American population. Death from communicable diseases brought by the Europeans had already claimed a large number of Indians in the East. Disease continued to destroy Indians everywhere the white settlers spread. Many Indians were forcibly driven off their lands, and many more lost their lives in settlers' attacks.[17]

The population of black people increased dramatically once slavery was established in the 1690s. Rising from about 13,000 in the seventeenth century to just under half a million in 1770, most of the blacks were brought involuntarily to the Colonies, though many were born here of enslaved parents.[18]

After the mid-1700s, immigration slowed somewhat, and most population growth was attributable to natural increase among both white and black populations. There is evidence that many early Americans married at a slightly younger age than their European counterparts and had larger families, averaging around seven children, in contrast to the four more common in England and Europe. This was partly attributable to the greater possibility that a young man would have land sufficient to support a family sooner, and that gave him and his wife more childbearing years in their marriage.[19]

Just before the Revolution, Virginia had the largest population of all the Colonies, with Massachusetts and Pennsylvania vying for the second spot. Pennsylvania had the largest city, Philadelphia.[20]

Northern colonists generally seemed to have longer, healthier lives than their southern counterparts. Once first settlement was past in most northern areas, mortality rates fell off, but it took longer, generally into the early eighteenth century, for Southerners to catch up. By the Revolution, southern mortality rates were more similar to northern ones. Scholars have not agreed on why many eighteenth-century Americans could look forward to living even into their late sixties and early seventies, but generally ample food; low population density, which slowed disease transmission; and sufficient wood for fuel meant people could better endure the winters even though settlement of America occurred during an unusually cold period called a little ice age.[21]

Distributing Land

Some English colonies were established by chartered joint stock companies, such as the Virginia Company and the Massachusetts Bay Company, which received the rights to land from the crown and paid the cost of establishing the colony in expectation of earning back the investment by the sale of the goods produced by the colonists. Other colonies were established by lords proprietor, individuals such as Lord

Baltimore in Maryland and William Penn in Pennsylvania, to whom the crown granted ownership and governance of large tracts of land. Proprietors in turn sold or gave land to settlers, but they, like the stock companies, expected a profit on their investment. Similarly, the Dutch West Indies Company gave large tracts of land along the Hudson River and westward-lying land to patroons, who promised to settle families. The Spanish crown sent agents and governors empowered to grant land to colonists. Throughout the Spanish Colonial Southwest, *adelantados*, such as Don Juan de Oñate, who came into what would be New Mexico, distributed large landholdings to the wealthier and better-connected colonists who traveled with them. Some of those individuals were entitled to the *encomienda*, which allowed them to collect tribute from the Indians. Because of their wealth they probably owned several farms or homesteads, many of which were established in the seventeenth century. Other farms or homesteads were owned by missions, but most belonged to ordinary colonists who had no other means of support. Many of these settlements in New Mexico were destroyed in the Pueblo Revolt of 1680, and not all were rebuilt when the Spanish returned to resettle in 1692.

In New England, the colonizing companies were ultimately acquired by the colonists, who then took charge of distributing the land and established towns by allotting tracts of land to organized groups of men who appealed to the General Court for permission to create a town. The town then recruited settlers, usually including a minister and often a miller. Parcels of ten to fifty acres were allotted in fairly compact settlements in the seventeenth century, though later 100-acre farmsteads were more common.[22]

Seventeenth-century proprietors were more likely to distribute large and dispersed tracts of land to their wealthy and prominent associates, who established plantations. In Maryland, Virginia, and some other southern Colonies, the head-right system allowed planters who could afford to bring family members and servants to the colony, in exchange for blocks of 50 to 100 acres per person, to build their plantations. The head-right system was used when colonists were sorely needed, so that a colony could get itself on sound financial footing. In the late seventeenth-century Carolinas, the head-right system was made available to farmers of modest means, at 150 acres per person. This encouraged settlers who created smaller plantations, but since the proprietors allowed the same head-right to wealthy slave owners, they also attracted large landowners who established rice and indigo plantations.

After initial land grants were made and settlements were built, native-born people hoping to own land had to inherit or buy it. In New England and other parts of the North, families left land to their children and divided it evenly among them. Within a couple generations, however, the land allotments were too small to support the young families who owned them. Young men wishing to farm were often obliged to look farther afield than their hometowns for land on which to settle, pressing westward or coastwise to new settlements. Portions of New Jersey and the Carolinas were settled not only by new immigrants but also by people from other colonies.

Another source of new settlers was people who had completed their indentured servitude. Many young people immigrated to America, most of them going to labor-starved Virginia and Maryland in the seventeenth and early eighteenth centuries, having agreed to a period of voluntary servitude, called an indenture, in exchange for the cost of their transportation to the colonies, living expenses, and other immigration costs. At the end of the indenture, usually lasting between four and seven years—during which they usually lived with their master's family, sharing bed and board—they received a sum of money, or occasionally land, and new clothing. They were free to marry, have a family, and establish their own farm or trade. In the Carolinas, about a third of the settlers began as indentured servants who gained 100 acres from the proprietors upon freedom; many acquired additional land afterward.[23]

Where there was a predominance of large landholdings, there was a higher percentage of tenant farmers in the late Colonial period, particularly in the formerly Dutch areas of New York and in the Chesapeake. Tenant farmers risked being stuck in largely subsistence farming, and had few prospects of owning their own land unless they were willing to move to the often dangerous frontier. Similarly, if a person chose to give up farming and become a craftsman, he risked being unable to feed himself and his family in the event of an economic downturn. Farmers at least could grow some food.

Colonial Standard of Living

Most free white eastern colonial families, whether they were farmers or lived in towns as artisans or business owners, generally had a better standard of living than their counterparts in Europe. In preindustrial societies, however, land ownership was a marker of well-being, even wealth, because land produced materials necessary for food, clothing, and shelter. Owning land also entitled a man to vote. Many colonists and their descendants made it a goal to own their own farm and to provide land for their children. Colonial farm families grew a great deal of their own food and owned a varied mix of livestock including cattle, sheep, swine, and various kinds of poultry. Most produced a marketable surplus, and could afford such imports as molasses, sugar, rum and other spirits, tea, coffee, and spices, as well as consumer goods such as ceramics, glassware, and tea utensils.

Two foods in particular, meat and wheat flour, signaled prosperity. Both of these were prized, and had been for centuries before America was settled; the elite was always able to have wheat bread daily and a variety of meat or, during church-designated fasts, fish. The less well-off seldom ate meat, and their bread was made of such coarser flours: as rye, barley, oats, buckwheat, and even ground legumes.

In America, however, even ordinary families ate meat daily, and by the close of the Federal era, it was not unusual to find meat on their tables three times a day, a phenomenon remarked on by foreign travelers in the new nation. Farm families raised and butchered animals for their own use, and strong markets developed for supplying cities and towns; thus herds of cattle were driven to market to supply butchers with fresh meat. Some town families with connections in the country owned animals or shares in animals raised by friends or relatives, and so provided their own meat. Only the poorest people had no meat at all. Fresh meat, particularly beef, was most highly valued, and salted meat was the fare of the less well-off, including most enslaved people.

Wheat flour was widely available except in New England, where, by the mid-1600s, colonists discovered wheat was subject to a rust, whereupon they purchased wheat from other colonies; Pennsylvania became a wheat-exporting state. In cities, where many people bought their bread at bakeries, wheat bread was more expensive than bread made from rye or corn, but people often purchased it in preference to other breads.

Food was usually plentiful in the American Colonies. While there were occasional economic declines making some foods more expensive for a while, and an occasional year of adverse weather that curtailed production, early America never experienced the kind of famines that periodically devastated Europe. The plenty contributed to the general health, which made for long lives, high birthrates, and high infant survival. It also contributed to a taller population. A study of the recorded heights of soldiers enlisted in the French and Indian and American Revolutionary wars showed that among American-born men, the average height was close to five feet, nine inches, roughly two inches taller than comparable British soldiers of the era.[24]

Slave treatment varied tremendously from owner to owner, but there is evidence that slaves were *usually* given sufficient food, although not consistently nor of consistently good quality nor in health-preserving balance. According to one study of antebellum slave populations,[25] slave children were very poorly fed, but once they joined the plantation labor pool, they were better fed and their growth rates increased. Adult slaves generally had the same mortality rate as the white population.

TRADE AND MARKETS

The market was an active force in Colonial and Federal economic life. Not only were there debts incurred by costs of colonizing, but there were products and materials that colonists wanted and that only trade could provide, including foodstuffs and tools and utensils for food production or preparation. Trade was always subject to regulation, because the mother countries wanted revenue from trade or an exclusive supply of or market for certain goods. America's distance from England and Europe helped lead to a breakdown of control over trade, as Americans figured out ways of avoiding regulations and gradually rebelled against them, especially taxation.

Colonists' first trading partners were Native Americans who supplied valuable furs, as well as corn and game, in exchange for metal goods, including iron cooking pots. Within relatively little time, however, the Colonies set up trade with each other and some foreign countries, mostly using coastwise and transatlantic water routes.

Common Trade Routes

In the first half of the seventeenth century, England enacted the Navigation Acts, which were intended to make sure the economic benefits of having colonies would remain with England. Only certain foods were subject to direct control by the Acts, particularly rice. In some respects, the Acts protected American shipping from competition with France, Holland, and Spain, but it also meant that certain European goods had to be imported through England, and not directly. These goods included sugar, rum, molasses, and rice. Of all the Colonies, Virginia and Maryland were most restricted because of tobacco, indigo, and rice, which were considered so valuable that they could be exported only to England, and not to European countries, where they probably would have brought a better price. The northern Colonies, because they produced goods very similar to those produced in England, had little to offer the mother country, so they turned to trade primarily with other Colonies and with the West Indies. Many food exports were not restricted, so the Middle Colonies established trade in flour, bread, and salted meat to southern Europe and the West Indies. In any event, control over trade could be maintained only where there was sufficient enforcement, and a great deal of molasses, rum, and sugar slipped by officials.

New Mexico's Hispanic settlers and missionaries relied on an overland supply route from Mexico, which took eighteen months one way to accomplish, so new supplies arrived once every three years. To Mexico they exported corn, wheat, piñon nuts, cattle, and sheep, and in return imported almonds, spices, and chocolate as well as church furnishings.

Important Trade Items

All through the Colonial era, among food products, molasses and sugar figured largely in foreign trade. Sugar was becoming an ever more important and popular commodity in England and Europe as it, and its cheaper form, molasses, increasingly became part of the diet of middling and even poorer people. As West Indian sugar production increased and new plantations were established, American colonies north and south engaged in provisioning them so that plantation owners did not have to divert slave labor to food production. Live cattle and horses, as well as barreled beef and pork, were regularly supplied by vessels setting out from New England and Virginia in the seventeenth and eighteenth centuries.

From the West Indies, New England imported a great quantity of rum, molasses, and sugar. More rum was distilled in northern Colonies and sold to other Colonies, where in the later seventeenth and the entire eighteenth century, it was the spirit of choice for most people. Besides rum, wine and fortified wines such as sherry and Madeira were imported from the Azores. Raisins, currants, wine, and salt came from Spain. While they were in the West Indies, American ships picked up lemons, nutmeg, and allspice.

Cod fishing had long been pursued off the New England coast, famous for its natural supply of fish. Europeans sailed from the coasts of France, England, Portugal, and Spain to catch, salt, and dry the fish in camps along the coast from Newfoundland to Maine. When New England colonists considered their natural resources beyond timber and furs, codfish was the most likely one to be exploited. Their markets were chiefly European Catholic countries and West Indies plantations—and, later, the southern Colonies. New Englanders pursued cod fishing for long-distance trade only for a couple of hundred years, preferring, in the early 1800s, to put their capital into textiles and shoe manufacturing.

For a period of time, New England joined with the Middle Atlantic Colonies and Virginia in exporting wheat, but by the mid-1700s, New England imported grain. After the Revolution, as more land was settled in western New York, Ohio, and Indiana, more grain was grown there and shipped east. At the close of the Federal Era, the Erie Canal at last connected the Great Lakes and the Atlantic via the Hudson River and the port of New York, creating much commercial opportunity for settlers growing wheat and corn in the Northwest Territories.

Developing Markets

Provisioning cities with enough food to supply a population engaged in nonfarm activities gave colonial farmers a market for their products. They did not, however, merely grow a surplus of what they themselves would use for food, but identified marketable goods and grew more or less of a commodity, depending on prices and demand.

Rural people obtained their nonfarm goods by traveling to a city or relying on merchants in nearby towns, who in turn relied on merchants abroad and in cities. Generally more wealthy colonists engaged in merchant trade, traveling to select goods or relying on agents. Colonial newspapers were full of advertisements describing the goods recently arrived in a warehouse or store.

Within about twenty-five years after the starving times of first settlement, American colonists managed to grow enough food to supply themselves and their families, and even to export to other colonies and parts of Europe. Gradually they adjusted to new ingredients and began the process of adjusting old habits of cooking and eating to new ones, adding the recipes and dishes of succeeding groups of settlers to those which were already here.

NOTES

1. Hannah Glasse, *Art of Cookery Made Plain and Easy, Which Far Exceeds Any Thing of the Kind Ever Yet Published* (Alexandria, VA: Cottom and Stewart, 1805), facs. repr. with historical notes by Karen Hess (Bedford, MA: Applewood Books, 1998), 137–144.

2. Amelia Simmons, *American Cookery; Or, the Art of Dressing Viands, Fish, Poultry and Vegetables* (Hartford, CT: Hudson & Godwin, 1796), facs. repr. with introduction by Mary Tolford Wilson (New York: Dover, 1984).

3. Wesley Frank Craven, *The Southern Colonies in the Seventeenth Century, 1607–1689*, vol. 1 of *A History of the South*, edited by Wendell Holmes Stephenson and E. Merton Coulter (Baton Rouge: Louisiana State University Press, 1949), 96.

4. Adriaen Van der Donck, *A Description of the New Netherlands*, edited with introduction by Thomas F. O'Donnell (Syracuse, NY: Syracuse University Press, 1968), 23.

5. John Filson, *The Discovery, Settlement, and Present State of Kentucke and an Essay Towards the Topography and Natural History of That Important Country* (Wilmington, DE: James Adams, 1784), facs. repr. as Garland Library of Narratives of North American Indian Captivities, vol. 14 (New York: Garland, 1978), 64.

6. François-Jean, Marquis de Chastellux, *Travels in North America in the Years 1780, 1781, and 1782 by the Marquis de Chastellux*, rev. trans. with introduction and notes by Howard C. Rice, Jr., 2 vols. (Chapel Hill: University of North Carolina Press, 1963), vol. 2, 390.

7. John Lawson, *A New Voyage to Carolina*, edited with an introduction by Hugh Talmage Lefler (Chapel Hill: University of North Carolina Press, 1967), 33, 83.

8. Francis Higginson, *New England's Plantation, with the Sea Journal and Other Writings* (Salem, MA: Essex Print and Book Club, 1908), 97.

9. John Josselyn, *New-Englands Rarities Discovered* (London: G. Widdoes, 1672), repr. with a (Boston: Massachusetts Historical Society, 1972).

10. Craven, 94, 95.

11. Lawson, 19.

12. Ibid., 82.

13. Simmons, 34.

14. There is very little agreement among scholars about whether the Native Americans either made sweetenings from sap before contact with Europeans or taught settlers to do so, but there is much evidence that once they acquired iron pots for boiling and found a market among settlers, they produced maple sugar.

15. Gulielma Penn, *Penn Family Recipes*, edited by Evelyn Abraham Benson (York, PA: G. Shumway, 1966), 65.

16. Henry Wansey, *The Journal of an Excursion to the United States in North America in the Summer of 1794* (Salisbury, UK: J. Easton, 1796), 46.

17. Edwin Perkins, *The Economy of Colonial America* (New York: Columbia University Press, 1988), 1.

18. Ibid., 2.

19. Ibid., 3.

20. Ibid., 2.

21. Ibid., 6.

22. Benjamin W. Labaree, *Colonial Massachusetts: A History* (Millwood, NY: KTO Press, 1979), 51.

23. Alan Taylor, *American Colonies: The Settling of North America* (New York: Viking, 2001), 224–225.

24. Perkins, 216.

25. Richard Steckle in Perkins, 216–217.

CHAPTER 2
FOODSTUFFS

The food supply in Colonial and Federal America was a mixture of plants, animals, and fish native to America that the colonists and subsequent settlers discovered when they arrived here, plus domesticated plants and animals that they brought with them. In nearly every instance Colonial Americans preferred a reliable supply of familiar food. That led them to pursue agriculture instead of relying for a long time on wild food and, in some cases, domesticating wild food. In turn, this preference led them to create marketable surpluses of food for trade for nonfood items, or for foods they either could not grow or could not grow in sufficient quantities for their needs.

Out of these foodstuffs, cooks made daily and festive meals. Most of the dishes thought of as typically American evolved from combinations of newly encountered ingredients and traditional ones, by cooks using both old, familiar ways of cooking and new ones that emerged in the new land.

GRAINS

Wheat

It is hard to overestimate the importance of wheat to most American colonists. It was the preferred bread grain for Europeans, and had been for centuries by the time they arrived in the Colonies. The flour was also used in a variety of pastries for crusts and for cakes.

Wheat was usually the first European grain colonists planted, and most of their agricultural practices—land clearing, plowing, sowing, harvesting, and threshing—were based on growing it. Although the native corn (maize) had higher yields, farmers grew wheat wherever climate and geography permitted, and found a market for it in other Colonies and abroad. The Middle Atlantic states, Virginia, and some of the backcountry regions grew wheat abundantly and sold it to the West Indies and the Northeast, where wheat showed a susceptibility to rust after 1660. In the Southwest, where corn truly was the premier crop, and in Florida, Christian Hispanic settlers planted wheat in order to bake sacramental wafers for the Eucharist and to supply gentry needs. Besides being ground into flour for bread and pastry, wheat was used whole in dishes such as frumenty, wheat kernels boiled until they were soft and had burst open.

Corn

Maize, usually called "Indian corn" by the colonists, was a New World grain, used by Native Americans for centuries before European settlers arrived. In England, "corn" was synonymous with "grain." Therefore, "English corn" usually signified wheat, and maize, which was obtained from the Indians, was called "Indian corn." After a while, Americans ceased making the distinction and merely said "corn" or used its nickname, "Indian."

Plymouth Colony Governor William Bradford and Edward Winslow, one of the first Plymouth colonists, described corn in *Mourt's Relation*: "thirty-six goodly ears of corn, some yellow, and some red, and others mixed with blue, which was a very goodly sight."[1] When John Winthrop, Jr., governor of the Connecticut Colony, reported on corn to the Royal Society in 1662, he wrote, "The Composure of the Eare is very beautifull, being sett in Even Rowes, every Graine in each Rowe over against the other, at equall distance, there being commonly Eight Rowes upon the Eare and sometimes more, according to the Goodness of the Ground."[2]

Over time, by picking and choosing seed corn, American farmers developed both white and yellow varieties, and flint and dent corns, flint being a hard, smooth-kerneled corn and dent, a softer corn that formed a dimple in the top of the kernel when it dried. Regional preferences for flint and dent and white and yellow types emerged in the North and South. Although most corn was ground for human consumption, it also proved to be good feed for animals.

Corn's nutritive value was improved by being processed with an alkali, often lye derived from wood ashes. Soaking or boiling corn kernels in lye water loosened the outer hulls, and the corn's niacin was freed for digestion. This process is called nixtamalization (from the Native Mexican word *nixtamal*, which is the flour ground from alkalisoaked corn), a process carried from Mexico into the Southwest for making tortillas. Colonial Americans on the eastern seaboard were less likely to grind soaked corn than to allow it to swell for use as a starch, as rice might be.

"Hominy," "samp," and "posole" were terms applied to corn prepared this way. "Hominy" and "samp" changed meanings from region to region and over time. "Hominy" could also refer to nonalkaliprocessed corn, ground or broken into grits to be boiled.

Colonists learned from Native Americans to eat corn in its fresh or "green" state as a vegetable roasted in its husk or boiled on the cob, or mixed with beans in succotash. They also learned to cook it when fresh, then dry it for use later; in the East this was called dried sweet corn, in the Southwest this was called *chicos*.

Rye

Rye, a bread grain introduced into America by European settlers, was generally not prized as highly as wheat except by German settlers. Still, it was usually one of the most commonly grown (with wheat and corn) for flour. It was also purchased by distillers to make into whiskey. Rye became very important in New England in the Colonial period when wheat could not be grown everywhere in the region because it suffered from a rust. Rye flour was mixed then with cornmeal and sometimes with wheat. Rye flour was at times used to make pastry for savory pies, and could also be used in porridges.

In the Middle Atlantic Colonies, German settlers grew wheat for market and rye for their own use. Rye was among grains grown in the South, but it was never as important as corn and wheat.

Meslin

A mixture of grains, usually rye and wheat, grown together on one field was called meslin or maslin. The two were harvested, threshed, and ground together, and sometimes the bread baked from the mixture was called meslin. Meslin was common in the North in the later seventeenth and early eighteenth centuries as a strategy for using soil where wheat began to fail.

Oats

Long a staple in the north of England and Scotland, oats were brought to America for human and animal consumption. They fared only indifferently in New England, but grew better in the South. Scottish and Scotch-Irish colonists and settlers continued using oats in soups, porridges, and, occasionally, bannocks. Since corn always yielded better crops, it largely replaced oats, and because cornmeal cooked up like oatmeal, cooks tended to substitute corn in dishes where previously they had used oats.

Buckwheat

Buckwheat was common in northern Europe, used in gruels and in porridges, or ground into flour for bread, and was often associated with poverty. It was grown in the American Colonies, although not as widely as other crops. It was particularly suited to new ground, where it provided flowers for bees and feed for cattle and poultry. The Swedish naturalist Peter Kalm observed in 1750 that the Swedes in Delaware used buckwheat flour in pancakes and puddings baked, on a stone or in a frying pan, and eaten with butter while warm. So did Acadians in northern New England. In America, too, buckwheat was sometimes food for the poor.

The Pennsylvania Germans preferred buckwheat for thickening *panhaas* (later more commonly called scrapple), the butchering-day pudding that used up the pig's head, feet, and small bits and pieces of pork left from making sausage. In the absence of buckwheat, cornmeal was used instead, or sometimes combined with buckwheat. Elizabeth E. Lea gave the following recipe for scrapple in her 1853 *Domestic Cookery, Useful Receipts, and Hints to Young Housekeepers.*

Scrapple

Take eight pounds of pork that will not do for sausage; boil it in four gallons of water; when tender, chop fine, strain the liquor and pour it back in the pot; put in the meat; season it with sage, summer savory, salt and pepper to taste; stir in a quart of corn meal; after simmering a few minutes, thicken it with buckwheat flour very thick; it requires very little cooking after it is thickened, but must be stirred constantly.[3]

Barley

Barley was grown in the Colonies mostly to be malted (sprouted, roasted, ground, and made into a mash for beer). Some households reserved barley for use in soups or puddings. Like wheat, barley proved to be less productive in parts of the Northeast, which may have helped nudge colonists toward making cider.

Rice

Rice was the premier crop of lowland South Carolina and Georgia by 1700, and subsequently was grown on some of the Colonies' largest plantations by slaves specifically imported from rice-growing regions of Africa. Rice was a huge and valuable export crop, much of it shipped to England. It was widely used in the South in bread, main dishes, and sweet dishes; much less was consumed in the northern Colonies, largely in sweet dishes. Carolina rice was so famous and of such good quality that it was mentioned by the name Carolina in some European cookbooks.

DOMESTIC MEAT AND FOWL

Beef

Beef was the most highly prized domestic meat among European settlers, and within a decade or two of colonization raising cattle became an economically important activity. In archaeological sites, bones of food animals usually reveal beef's importance in the diet almost everywhere in the Colonies. Zooarchaeologists use formulas to calculate the probable amount of meat represented by the bones recovered from a historical site. These calculations very often show that once the era of first settlement was past, wild food decreased in importance and beef usually predominated over other meats.

Because cattle could fend for themselves, during the early years of settlement, beef animals were branded and allowed to forage wherever they could find food. They were herded or lured back to farms for finishing before slaughter, or in some cases were herded together to be driven to market in towns or cities. In the South and on the frontier, this practice continued longer than in the North.

Dairy animals were kept closer to home and given better pasture, and in a few places, particularly in the North, a dairy-based agriculture arose. Tended animals provided manure for fields. Larger yields of milk in turn increased the cheese and butter business. But as settlers pressed into frontier areas, west or south, they allowed cattle to range freely to take good advantage of largely untamed land. This practice enabled settlers to meet the consistent demand for beef in more settled areas.

Today "cattle" most often means bovine (beef or dairy) animals, but in past times, the word could include oxen, pigs, and sheep. "Neat" and "kine" designated bovine cattle. Oxen are castrated bovine males that were usually raised and trained in teams for heavy work, such as hauling and plowing. At the end of their working lives, they were used as food.

Most people preferred to eat beef fresh, but the fattier portions were corned or salted, and some subsequently were smoked. "Dried beef" was a salted and smoked product, often sliced very thin for serving. In arid regions, beef and other meat was "jerked," simply dried. Making sausage was another way to preserve beef. The hard fat surrounding the kidneys, called suet, was used in making pastry and pudding; rendered beef fat, called tallow, was used for making candles. As with nearly all domestic animals used for meat, as many parts of the animal as possible were utilized; in the case of beef, hearts, livers, sweetbreads, tripe, and kidneys were all commonly used fresh, and tongues were often salted and smoked.

Pork

Hogs came with the earliest Spanish colonists to Florida, with the Dutch to New Netherland, and with English settlers in the North and Virginia. Like cattle, they foraged on their own in woods, eating acorns, nuts, and roots, and were kept just tame enough to be lured back to shelter for slaughter or wintering over. Sows had litters of up to a dozen piglets. As relatively the most prolific domestic animals, pigs could be harvested sooner after first settlement than cattle, which took longer to increase their numbers. Among bones found in archaeological digs, pigs usually place second after cattle in quantity; although they might outnumber cattle, they were smaller. Like cattle, hogs were driven to markets in towns and cities.

The words "pig," "hog," "shoat," "boar," and "sow" all have specific meanings, nowadays mostly to hog farmers, but in past times they were in common use among cooks. "Swine" referred to these animals generally, and "hog" was most often applied to mature ones. A boar is a mature male hog; a sow, a female. When sows were past usefulness for breeding, they were used for food. A shoat is a young hog, less than a year old, and the word "pig" was applied both to young hogs and to hogs generally. Suckling pigs, usually small, un-weaned animals, were roasted whole.

Domestic slaughtering was done in the fall and winter, with the onset of cooler weather, so that natural cold made it possible to store meat fresh for later consumption. Pork, high in saturated fats, took salt well, and hams, bacon, and sausage remained relatively unctuous even after smoking, a process that kept the meat good to use even into warm weather. The hard, white fat surrounding the kidneys, called lard, was tried out and saved for baking and frying.

Hogs are famous for their usefulness, and the saying "You can use everything except the squeal" is very nearly true. Besides the meat and fat, the organs—liver, kidneys, heart, tongue, brains, and lungs—were eaten. The small and large intestines were cleaned and stuffed for sausage. Stomachs were cleaned, filled, and boiled as a pudding. The English had a tradition of making head cheese, and the Germans a tradition of making scrapple from the head and feet. Some colonists saved the blood to make black pudding.

Mutton

Mutton is the meat of mature sheep, deemed best if the animal is four to five years old; the meat of wethers (castrated males) is considered finest. Both British and Spanish colonists appreciated mutton, and though they favored beef and pork, it was one of the domestic meats eaten in early America. More mutton was consumed by the end of the Federal era in New England than elsewhere; it was rare in early Chesapeake settlements and gradually increased in Virginia as the eighteenth century progressed. The Southwest has the longest continuous tradition of eating mutton, and it was an export from New Mexico to old Mexico. Mutton can still be found among the Pueblo Indians.

Unlike other cattle that were better able to forage on their own, sheep required protection and good pasture. In Colonial times, when labor for tending them was scarce, sheep were often grazed on small islands. Local conditions, mainly suitable and safe pasturage, determined whether or not farmers engaged in raising sheep. Mutton production also depended a great deal on the market value of wool. When wool brought a good price, farmers tended to prefer live animals for shearing over using them for meat. During the Revolutionary War, the trade in wool with Britain was interrupted, and Virginia, for example, passed a resolution that no sheep was to be killed for mutton, except in case of necessity, and then only the most unprofitable animals were to be culled.

Mutton was most often eaten fresh. The sheep, a relatively small animal, was often divided among family and neighbors and used quickly, but it was also salted like pork, and some early cookbooks refer to mutton hams. As with other animals, the organs of sheep were eaten.

Veal

Calves' meat, called veal, was the natural product of dairying, which depended on cows giving birth annually and having milk. Usually born in the spring, calves were weaned quickly and allowed to mature from one to three months, whereupon they were slaughtered and eaten as fresh meat during the summer months, especially if they were males. The females (heifers) were often kept to mature into milk cows. Like lambs, calves were small enough to be eaten in a short time by farm families and their neighbors. Wherever dairying was conducted, veal was a fairly important meat.

The lining of a calf's stomach yielded the curdling agent rennet, needed for making hard cheese. Housewives saved the stomach lining of newly weaned calves that had not yet begun grazing, and salted, stretched, and tied it to dry on a hoop of wood. To obtain the enzymes in the rennet for curdling, pieces of the stomach lining were clipped and soaked in water, and that water was added to the milk destined to be cheese.

Like the other animals that have been discussed, as many parts of the calves were used for food as possible. Calf's head soup was fashionable for a while in early America. Young animals' joints were rich in cartilage that when cooked yielded gelatin, so calves' feet were essential to making dessert and wine jellies, the forerunners of modern gelatin desserts (not to be confused with preserved fruit jellies).

Lamb

Lamb is not well represented in most bone remains from archaeological sites, nor does it appear often in account book records of food sales and exchanges. For nearly all of the Colonial era, when sheep were kept at all, it was primarily to produce wool, so adult animals might be harvested and eaten but the young were kept for increase. Like veal, lamb, when it *was* killed, provided fresh meat in the warmer summer and early fall months, when a small animal could be consumed in a short time by one family or among neighbors.

Chevon

Chevon is the name given goats' meat. Goats were brought to the colonies early, usually for milk, because they were hardy and could forage for food. But cows were favored, and within a few decades goats were hardly seen. Massachusetts settler Edward Johnson, in *Wonder-Working Providence* (1650), reported that in New England goats had been "in great esteeme at their first coming, are now almost quite banished."[4] No doubt valuable to the few families who kept them, goats ultimately were a negligible part of the Colonial and Federal diet.

Poultry

Domestic chickens, turkeys, ducks, and geese were brought by some of the earliest settlers. Poultry care was considered part of the housewife's work. Chickens were kept primarily for eggs and were harvested when their useful laying life was over, except among the prosperous, who could afford to kill younger birds. Duck eggs were gathered for food, and duck meat was eaten. Roasted turkeys and geese appeared especially on festive occasions. All poultry is relatively underrepresented in bone remains, and poultry eating must be understood in the context of labor-intensive preparation. Most poultry was small and yielded little meat, but required quite a bit of effort in the plucking and cleaning for cooking, compared with large animals, which, once butchered, weighed hundreds of pounds and provided many meals' worth of meat.

WILD MEAT AND FOWL

Venison

Most English settlers in America regarded venison as a high-status food because in England it was the privilege of the gentry to hunt deer as a sport in game parks reserved for their use. A meal at which venison was served, accompanied by other game or fowl, marked a special occasion. In America, deer were, for all intents and purposes, free for the taking, and were hunted so widely that by the close of the seventeenth century, the taking of deer was restricted to a certain season in New England. On the frontier through the entire Colonial and Federal eras, however, settlers continued to hunt deer, and venison often constituted a large part of the diet until domestic animals could be established.

Venison is a very lean meat, so cooks larded it before roasting it, or braised it. The fashion for venison dishes led to the creation of mock-venison dishes, such as mutton cooked venison-style and venison pasty recipes that used beef, mutton, or rabbit meat.

Small Animals

Squirrels, raccoons, rabbits, beavers, woodchucks, and possum are all edible, and had a place in the American diet during and well past the Colonial and Federal eras. Travelers and explorers describe the flavor and cooking qualities of many of them. For example, the naturalist and surveyor John Lawson, writing in 1700 about North Carolina, remarked of possum that it "tasted between young Pork & Veal, their Fat being as white as any I ever saw."[5] Raccoon was also considered suitable for the table. Dutch settler Adriaen Van der Donck reported of raccoons: "When their meat is roasted, it is delicious food, but when stewed, it is too luscious, on account of its fatness."[6]

Moose

Large animals such as moose yielded a great deal of meat from one individual, and the animals were hunted as long as they were to be found in an area. Early Massachusetts settler Thomas Morton reported in 1622, "There flesh is very good foode, and much better then our redd Deare of England," high praise indeed, for red deer was greatly prized.[7]

Bear

Bears were seldom taken except on the frontier. Their meat is often described as being as fat as pork, good for roasting. The grease, saved, was a suitable substitute for butter in cooking—stirred, for example, into mush or pottages, and even used as an oil for dressing salad.

Buffalo

Found mostly on grassy plains beyond the Appalachians, buffalo provided much food for new settlers. Observers described the meat was excellent, and Van der Donck even said that it was "more desirable than the flesh of the deer."[8] The eighteenth-century naturalist John Brickell, describing North Carolina in 1737, said of buffaloes, "Their Flesh is very coarse, and nothing to be compared with our Beef, but their Calves are said to be excellent good Meat." He further observed that were buffalo and beef cattle to be bred together, it would "much improve the Species for largeness and Milk."[9] That is, in fact, done today, producing a meat called beefalo.

Elk

Settlers found elk on the same grassy western reaches of the Colonies where they found buffalo. A venison-like meat, it made up part of the wild food diet of early settlers all across the West, as it had for the Native Americans. Brickell described the meat as coarser and stronger-flavored than deer meat.[10]

Turkey

Plentiful during early settlement, wild turkey was considered excellent wildfowl. The birds' habit of roosting on tree branches in a row and their refusal to scatter under fire meant that many could be taken at one time. Accounts of this come from in New England, New Netherland, and westward into Kentucky. Van der Donck wrote that the birds slept in the same trees night after night, in large flocks, and gunners would simply go and kill a dozen or more at a time. Accounts of their size may have been exaggerated, but many writers reported turkeys weighing twenty to thirty pounds. In New England in 1622, Morton wrote, "Of these there hath bin killed that have weighed forty-eight pound a peece."[11] John Lawson's party ate a great deal of turkey during its trip through the Carolinas in 1700, and he reported that the Indian guide killed birds that weighed no less than forty pounds.[12]

Van der Donck said of turkeys, "When they are well cleaned and roasted on a spit, then they are excellent, and differ little in taste from the tame turkeys; but the epicures prefer the wild."[13] They could not prefer it for long; turkey abundance was short-lived in the wake of settlement, as was true of much wild food. In New England, for example, turkeys were already becoming rare by 1670, though as new territory was opened for the next hundred-plus years, settlers found new large flocks to exploit.[14]

Wildfowl

Most early descriptions of the American Colonies list in great detail the wildfowl available for hunting. The earliest colonists, following a centuries-old custom of the gentry favoring a variety of exotic fowl for the table, ate many kinds of birds now not considered suitable for food, including swans, cranes, herons, cormorants, eagles, and many smaller songbirds, such as larks and thrushes. Most of these fell out of fashion by the end of the eighteenth century. At times, some of these birds were taken as survival fare. *Mourt's Relation*, January 1620–1621, reported that Captain Miles Standish of Plymouth Colony and a small group of men "shot at an eagle and killed her, which was excellent meat; it was hardly to be discerned from mutton."[15]

Game birds such as quail, pheasants, partridges, pigeons, woodcocks, and many others were all considered worth taking. Wild waterfowl such as geese and ducks were favored in particular, and supplemented the domestic waterfowl raised by many colonists.

Most fowl in the seventeenth and eighteenth centuries were hung to ripen a couple days before they were cooked, which helps explain the instructions in some early cookbooks for cleaning the birds to remove taint should the meat be hung too long. Smaller birds were roasted on bird spits, devices with many small hooks, or strung on longer meat spits. They were also stewed or cooked in pies, sometimes with other fowl or meat. Many of the birds were fairly lean, and were wrapped in slices of fat before roasting.

Pigeons deserve special mention because they were so abundant. Nearly all observers in the early Colonial period comment on the huge flocks: Van der Donck is typical: "The pigeons . . . are astonishingly plenty. Those are most numerous in the spring and fall of the year, when they are seen in such numbers in flocks, that they resemble the clouds in the heavens, and obstruct the rays of the sun."[16] They were shot in great numbers, and large quantities were taken in nets. They were plucked and roasted.

FISH AND SHELLFISH

Fish and shellfish consumption showed regional patterns because of habitat differences, although colonists in the North and the South had in common preferences for certain seafoods. Upon arriving in

America, they recognized new species of familiar families of fish and shellfish, and cooked them as they always had.

In New England the most frequently mentioned saltwater fish were cod, alewives and herring, mackerel, shad, bass, haddock, eel, and salmon. Trout was the favorite freshwater fish, and lobsters and oysters were the favored shellfish. The Dutch ate mussels, but most English settlers shied away from them except when absolutely necessary, and clams were poorly regarded.

In the South, sturgeon, sheepshead, black drum, red drum, striped bass, perch, and catfish predominate in archaeological sites. The French army officer François-Jean de Beauvoir, the Marquis de Chastellux, who came to aid the Colonies in the Revolutionary War, was served sturgeon and shad in Virginia, about which he said that they were "two kinds of fish which are at least as good in Virginia as in Europe, but which make their appearance only in the spring."[17] Plantation owners set slaves to fishing for alewives and herring, which were netted, salted, and barreled for the slaves' food supply.

Along the shores of the Ohio River in Kentucky and Ohio, buffalo fish, catfish, trout, mullet, rockfish, perch, gar, and eel were caught. Around the Great Lakes, lake trout, whitefish, lake herring, lake chub, yellow perch, sturgeon, burbot, whitefish, and others were caught.

In the Middle Atlantic Colonies, colonials ate shad, herring, oysters, crabs, perch, trout, sturgeon, bass, and rockfish.

All fish were generally preferred freshly caught and cooked, but some—particularly cod, mackerel, shad, herring, and alewives—could be salted and saved for use in other seasons. Generally, fish with large or few bones were preferred over fish with many small bones. For this reason cod, salmon, and sturgeon were very popular. Nonetheless, alewives and shad, both spring-running anadromous fish, were caught in large quantities in the North and the South.

Large fish were roasted on spits or planked, or stuffed and baked; small fish were considered better fried or broiled.

Shellfish were used in ragouts, soups, or sauces. Lobsters were boiled shortly after being caught and, in cities, sold in the street by the fisherman himself. Oysters were ever popular: stewed for a supper, or fried and stuffed into rolls, or even pickled. In the Chesapeake, crabs were food for those who caught them and ate them soon after harvesting. They were more perishable than oysters, so they do not appear as a marketable shellfish, although many people ate them seasonally. The gentry used them in soups or sauces; other people probably ate crabs as subsistence fare.

In the late Colonial period, a fad for turtle soup resulted in recipes for it appearing in most cookbooks. They called for the sea turtle, which is now protected from harvest. Turtle soup was so fashionable that a mock turtle soup was developed, using a calf's head to replace the turtle.

Alewives

Alewives, like shad, are anadromous fish. That is, they live in salt water but lay their eggs in fresh water, so each spring they swim upstream from the sea to spawn. They were harvested wherever they gathered at rapids or fall lines. Large numbers were netted, salted, and barreled. Being small fish, they were ideal panfish. Colonials learned from the Indians how to use alewives as fertilizer in corn hills.

Cod

New England is famous for salt cod, which was primarily a commodity, but which most families served once a week. There were different grades of salt cod; and the best was called dunfish, for the buff color it acquired in the salting and drying. Settlers from New England moving to the West took with them the taste for salt cod, and the product could be found in markets there. Salt cod was also eaten in the South.

Oysters

Settlers arrived in the Colonies with a taste for oysters, and welcomed their abundance. Oysters were most abundant in New England and Chesapeake waters, and supported a commercial fishery in both places. New England fished out its oyster population before the end of the Federal era, and raided the Chesapeake for oysters—and later for seed oysters to carry back to Long Island Sound and Cape Cod Bay to establish oyster farms.

Salmon

Salmon were held in high esteem in England and Europe because of their large bones and meaty pink flesh, and colonials caught and ate the salt- and freshwater salmon they found here. Cookbook author Amelia Simmons described salmon in her 1796 *American Cookery* as "the noblest and richest fish taken in fresh water."[18] Like alewives and shad, salmon are anadromous, and, like the others, were easily caught during their annual upstream runs.

Shad

Although most people did not enjoy oily and bony fish as much as they did white-fleshed fish such as cod, shad were popular because of their abundance and because they were caught easily during the spring migration upstream to spawn. Farmers, fishermen, and trades-men held specific sites along streams (often at the fall lines) and caught, cleaned, and salted the fish for later consumption or for ex-change or sale among neighbors. George Washington's troops put an end to the hunger of the Valley Forge winter of 1777–1778 by shad fishing in the spring. There was also a commercial shad fishery, and the preserved fish were supplied to plantations as food for slaves, and to city markets.

Sturgeon

Sturgeon was popular because the fish were so large, sometimes weighing as much as 600 pounds, and because they had external car-tilaginous plates and fewer internal bones than many fish. They were found in saltwater and fresh water, and in most regions of the coun-try. One observer humorously commented in the nineteenth century, "When sturgeon fishing was of great importance on this [Hudson] river Albany was the chief mart, and hence the name "Albany beef." On the James River in Virginia, sturgeon was nicknamed "Charles City bacon."[19]

DAIRY PRODUCTS

Milk

Milk from cows or goats was a desirable product in Colonial and Federal America. Cows' milk was the favorite, and dairying was women's work. Used both as an ingredient in cooking and as a bev-erage, milk in large quantities was also required for making cheese. During early settlement, it was a seasonal product, because cows ceased giving milk in the winter months and did not produce milk again until after calving. Milk production relied on good pasture, and in the early years, cows were allowed to graze wherever they could, and thus gave less milk than they did later, when they grazed on land planted in English grasses.

Many colonists kept at least one cow expressly for milking, and milk formed an important part of one to two meals a day for many. Breakfast and supper often consisted of bread and milk, or milk in a hasty pudding or porridge.

Soured milk was a useful ingredient in cooking and was not considered spoiled food, particularly after the adoption of chemical leavens; sour milk and buttermilk provided the necessary acid to combine with the alkaline pearlash to form the leavening gases.

Cream

The quality of cream, the fat from milk, depended a great deal on the richness of the milk, which in turn depended both on the breed of cow and on the richness of the pasture. Cream floated to the top of milk left in a cool place in a large, shallow bowl, called a milk pan, whereupon it could be skimmed off and set aside for use as cream or to be churned into butter. As it is today, cream was a popular sauce, sometimes slightly sweetened with sugar or even molasses, for fruits, berries, and other desserts.

Butter

Butter, sometimes salted to promote its preservation, joined cheese as the usual accompaniment to bread for breakfast or supper. It was also an indispensable ingredient in better cookery, used in pastry, cakes, and puddings, and was sometimes melted as sauce for vegetables. It was also used for frying. Melted butter was sometimes used to seal the tops of potted meats to exclude air.

Cheese

Cheese made from cows' milk predominated in the eastern Colonies, whereas goats' milk predominated in the Southwest. While some Middle Eastern countries have a sheep's milk tradition, and some colonists kept sheep, they seem not to have milked them to make cheese. Most cheese consumed in the colonies was eaten with bread or biscuit, and less often incorporated into recipes.

Cheese was made both from milk curdled by use of rennet or a culture, and from milk soured either naturally or by addition of acid. Most colonial cheese came from English and Dutch cheesemaking traditions, and included both hard, aged cheese, and fresh semisoft and soft cheeses. After taking them from the press, housewives rubbed hard cheeses with salt and sometimes butter, then aged for months, turning them faithfully to give them a rind. Softer cheeses were eaten within a week or even days. Makers varied their cheeses by leaving more or less butterfat in the milk. The Dutch added cumin seeds to cheese; New Englanders added sage.

Colonists also imported Parmesan from Italy, and Cheshire and Gloucester cheeses from England.

Eggs

Another part of women's work was the care of chickens, ducks, and other egg-laying poultry. Eggs were a seasonal product, though they were oiled or stored in ashes to extend their usefulness. Besides using beaten egg whites as a leaven in baking, colonists found eggs were a handy food, eaten at breakfast or as an accompaniment to meat at another meal. They were roasted by being buried in hot ashes by the fire, or boiled or fried. Early recipes sometimes call for what seems to be startling numbers of eggs, but seventeenth- and eighteenth-century eggs were smaller; modern cooks should use three large eggs for every four eggs called for in historic recipes.

VEGETABLES

Vegetables were important to the Colonial American diet, but colonists did not consider them to be as essential as meat and bread. That they ate vegetables at all kept them in good health, and slaves who grew their own vegetables in plots allotted them preserved their health.

Vegetables' place in the diet is revealed by the description of them as garden sauce, or "sass," an accompaniment to meat. Still, some diarists, such as Maine midwife Martha Ballard, record eating them with what sounds like enjoyment. For example, Mrs. Ballard's July 27, 1795, entry reports that they dined on "roast Lamb, String beens & Green Peas and Cucumbers." Since she had primary responsibility for the vegetable garden, she may have been deservedly noting her accomplishments.[20]

Many travelers in early America painstakingly list every vegetable that grew in the Colonies, but those lists cannot be taken as descriptions of the typical garden. Credit is often given German and Dutch immigrants for more varied and careful vegetable cultivation than was typical of the English and Scotch-Irish, who were often described as being careless of their gardens.

Which vegetables a household grew and ate depended a good deal on the region, season, and economic status of the home owner. Some vegetables were very fashionable and required a fair amount of cultivation; others were casually planted and tended. Where growing seasons were relatively short, preference was given to root vegetables that could be stored over winter, or winter-keeping cabbages, squashes, and pumpkins. Also, early Americans showed a preference for more substantial, starchy vegetables such as peas, beans, and corn.

Asparagus

Asparagus was a fashionable vegetable in Europe and Colonial America. Sometimes called "sparrow grass" or "sparagus" in the early seventeenth century, it required intensive cultivation and was not widely planted except by the wealthy. It was usually boiled and served with olive oil or butter and salt and pepper.

Beans and Peas

Peas and beans were eaten both fresh and dried. When fresh, they were often called "green" or "new," terms that also applied to corn. Dried peas were sometimes termed "old," but "old" also referred to a starchy state, not yet dried. Dried beans, soaked and boiled, were a good source of cheap protein.

Some beans were good as "string" (or green) beans, edible before they had completely filled out their pods, and also as "shelling beans," which were allowed to mature into fleshy firmness and shelled out of their pods to cook. Beans also were allowed to mature on the stalk, were harvested dry, and were flailed to break the pods. The dried beans were then swept up, winnowed, and stored for winter use. Peas were similarly treated. Indigenous to America, beans grew slightly better in all the Colonies than did peas, which had been favored in England. During the Colonial period there were hundreds of beans varieties mentioned in diaries, newspaper seed advertisements, and gardening accounts.

Sometime between 1650 and 1750, the practice of baking a pot of beans in the oven became established, in the Northeast; it spread into newly opened areas of the West by the end of the Federal period. Most ethnic groups had a variation of beans stewed or baked with meat; the dish is directly descended from the bean and pea pottages of England and Europe, in which soaked beans were cooked slowly at a low temperature, usually with a piece of salt meat. Early bean dishes were not sweet; molasses in any amount was not introduced until the nineteenth century. The combination of beans or peas and salt pork also points to the association of dried legumes with poverty; salt meat being relegated to poorer people. The following recipe for baked beans comes from Lydia Maria Child's 1833 edition of *The American Frugal Housewife*.

Baked Beans

Baked beans are a very simple dish, yet few cook them well. They should be put in cold water, and hung over the fire, the night before they are baked. In the morning, they should be put in a colander, and rinsed two or three times; then again placed in a kettle, with the pork you intend to bake, covered with water, and kept scalding hot, an hour or more. A pound of pork is quite enough for a quart of beans, and that is a large dinner for a common family. The rind of the pork should be slashed. Pieces of pork alternately fat and lean, are the most suitable; the cheeks are best. A little pepper sprinkled among the beans, when they are placed in the bean pot, will render them less unhealthy. They should be just covered with water, when put into the oven; and the pork should be sunk a little below the surface of the beans. Bake three or four hours.[21]

Baked or stewed pork and beans is a good example of a vernacular or folk dish, and recipes for making it do not appear in printed cookbooks that in the eighteenth century were generally printed for upper-class cooks.

Peas were eaten and relished fresh as long as they were available. In the eighteenth century there were varieties with tender pods, called sugar peas, that could be eaten pod and all. Dried peas were used in soup and pea porridge, or often stewed, as the beans were, with salt pork.

Okra

A tropical plant native to and widely grown in Africa, okra spread to other tropical areas. It came to the Caribbean and American Colonies by way of the slave trade, and was planted by slaves in their gardens. Though it has had many names, the African word *gumbo* is the most familiar one today, and the dish gumbo takes its name from the ingredient. The pods are harvested when they are young and tender, and because the vegetable releases a sticky substance, it is useful for thickening soups and stews. Okra was, and is, also pickled, fried, and stewed alone or with tomatoes.

Cabbages, Coleworts, Collards, and Kale

Cabbages, coleworts, collards, and kale, hardy and ancient members of the brassica family, grew well all through the Colonies where settlers introduced them. Cabbage formed a tight head when mature, and could be kept in storage for extended periods. Coleworts, collards, and kale formed looser heads and were used fresh and new only, although some resprouted after cutting, providing harvestable greens again.

Most cabbages were considered coarse fare, appropriate for hardworking, common people, and thus had a reputation for being rustic food, sometimes associated with poverty. These, with root vegetables, were very common in gardens. The cabbage family includes cauliflower and broccoli, but these did not commonly appear; they were grown mostly by gentlemen gardeners. Headed cabbages and the looser-growing kales and collards were very common.

Cabbage heads stored well for the winter and provided a fresh vegetable. Cabbages, particularly the red, were pickled by the English; the Germans made green cabbage into sauerkraut. Stuffed cabbage was common. Everyone boiled cabbage, and the Dutch made a salad of it.

Collards, coleworts, and kales are probably the oldest forms of the cabbage family. Some scholars believe that the word "collard" was a corruption of the English term "colewort," used to describe both young cabbage greens eaten after they were pulled to thin a patch of cabbage, and the vegetable we call kale. Others believe that collards had diffused into Africa and were brought with slaves to America. Whatever their origins, they were and are widely grown in the South, and in Colonial times apparently were more common there as part of the garden produce grown by slaves and other poor farmers.

Cucumbers

Used fresh or pickled, cucumbers were extensively grown. Some early varieties were strikingly different from modern cucumbers, being shorter, yellow, and very prickly. In England and cooler parts of Europe, cucumbers proved difficult to grow, and the gentry grew them with the aid of hothouses, but in America, where summer was hot and dry, cucumbers did well and became a very common vegetable. Cucumbers fermented when salted, which soured and preserved them, and they could be pickled by immersion in spiced vinegar and salt; both methods were used in early America.

Hops

Hops vines were brought to many parts of the America Colonies so that their delicate blossoms could be harvested and dried for use in brewing ale and beer. Hops are known now to have an antibacteriostatic action that may have helped in beer fermentation by controlling which yeasts would thrive while adding a desirable bitter flavor. Hops shoots were among the earliest spring greens that some families harvested for use as a vegetable.

Lettuce and Spinach

Leafy vegetables such as lettuce and spinach often fell under the heading of "salad herbs," and were commonly eaten both raw and cooked.

Onions and Leeks

Widely grown and used, onions and leeks were very old vegetables by the time America was settled. Both were grown and used here, with onions receiving somewhat more frequent mention than leeks. In the late 1780s, Wethersfield, Connecticut, specialized in growing onions for export. They were found in home gardens and in market gardens near large colonial towns and cities. Onions were pickled as well as used in savory dishes.

Potatoes

Two kinds of potatoes appear in the colonial record—the white-fleshed kind called Irish, and a yellow-orange sort called sweet.

Irish potatoes were actually a New World plant native to the South American Andes. They were introduced to Europe, where they became a valuable source of starch, even replacing bread for poor people because potatoes could be grown in relatively small spaces. They were introduced to Ireland, where they became a staple, and came to North America with colonists by the late 1600s; they are mentioned by William Penn in 1685 as a vegetable that grew in his colony. Scotch-Irish settlers in New Hampshire brought potatoes with them, and by the mid-1700s they were very common on New England tables. By the end of the Federal era, potatoes were an indispensable daily vegetable nearly everywhere in America settled by Northerners or Scotch-Irish. They were propagated by planting sections of potatoes with eyes from which sprouts came.

Sweet potatoes are frequently confused with yams, which are a different vegetable. Sweet potatoes, too, are a New World plant taken to Spain by Columbus, whence they dispersed, reaching Tudor Britain by Henry VIII's time. Sweet potatoes were favored slightly over Irish potatoes in England, and in mid-eighteenth-century cookbooks such as Hannah Glasse's, E. Smith's, and others, it is possible to see their use mostly in sweet dishes. When a "potato" pie or pudding calls for sugar, it almost always indicates that sweet potato was used, unless it specifies otherwise. Sweet potatoes were propagated by being allowed to sprout, and the small plants or "slips" were planted out.

Squashes and Pumpkins

The word "squash" comes from the Algonquian word *askut asquash*, which means something that is eaten green, or unripe. Today a distinction is made between squash and pumpkins, but they are both actually squashes. Obtained from the Native Americans, they were usually cooked in European fashion. Part of the "Three Sisters," which included corn and beans, they were planted so that their vines ran among cornstalks. They thrived and provided a reliable source of food, especially in the early years. Pumpkins were also grown as a field crop for animal fodder.

As their Alquonquian name origin suggests, these vegetables could be eaten before they formed the hard exterior shells that make them good for keeping into winter. Both could be dried for use later, although they also stored well into the winter when kept cool and dry. For summer eating, there was in the Colonial era and later, primarily in the South, a squash called cymling (pattypan), often mentioned in southern culinary sources. Yellow crooknecks, another old variety, were found in New Jersey and spread through the early 1800s. Another squash of the South was the potato or sweet potato pumpkin, which reputedly was introduced in the late eighteenth century from Jamaica via the slave trade.[22] Many of the varieties known today, such as Hubbard and turban squashes, were developed or introduced in the nineteenth century.

Squashes and pumpkins were cooked in several ways, including baked and boiled, eaten plain or made into puddings or pies. One of the earliest recorded recipes for cooking squash is found in *New England's Rarities*, by John Josselyn:

The Ancient New-England Standing Dish

But the Housewives manner is to slice them when ripe, and cut them into dice, and to fill a pot with them of two or three Gallons, and stew them upon a gentle fire a whole day, and as they sink, they fill again with fresh Pompions, not putting any liquor to them; and when it is stew'd enough it will look like bak't Apples; this they Dish, putting Butter to it, and a little Vinegar, (with some Spice, as Ginger, &c.), which makes it tart like an Apple, and so serve it up to be eaten with Fish or Flesh: It provokes Urin extreamly and is very windy.[23]

Root Vegetables

Beets, carrots, parsnips, turnips, and radishes were the most important root vegetables grown by colonists and settlers. Among the seeds that English settlers brought were those of parsnips, carrots, and turnips, all of which the Virginia Company provided for its colonists. Beets came with colonists from the Continent, particularly Germans. Sugar beets, were grown as food for cattle and saw some experimentation for sugar production, largely unprofitable until the nineteenth century.

Skirrets, salsify, and Jerusalem artichokes also appear among root vegetables in cookbooks, which dutifully offer directions for cooking them. It is very hard to tell how popular these vegetables were in common households. Like other vegetables, they are listed by colonial botanists, and heirloom varieties of them survive to the present. Skirrets and salsify both have long, slender roots and take quite a bit of care to prepare. Salsify was also called oyster plant. Both are a little sweet. Jerusalem artichokes have small, rounded roots, are mealy when cooked, and are bland.

Root vegetables were primarily boiled for eating, sometimes alone and sometimes mixed with other vegetables and with meat. Carrots and parsnips were made into puddings.

Tomatoes

Tomatoes, a New World plant back carried to Europe after Columbus's explorations, spread slowly there as Spanish and Italian cooks learned to use them. Most of the English, however, believed that the bad smell given off by tomato leaves and stalks indicated the plant was harmful, so they tended not to use tomatoes except medicinally. Consequently, they were scarcely mentioned until later in the eighteenth century, after more English people had experience with them, particularly English Jews who had connections to Spain and Portugal, where tomatoes were used.

In America, tomatoes were probably carried to Florida by Spaniards or by colonists to the low Country from the West Indies. They were subsequently grown and used in southern colonies in the middle 1700s, appearing in at least one manuscript source by 1770.[24] They spread into Pennsylvania and northward into New England, and westward into the Northwest Territory and the Mississippi valley, by the early 1800s.[25] In the Spanish Southwest, tomatoes were among the vegetables introduced by Hispanic settlers and missionaries.

In most of the northern Colonies, tomatoes were accepted more slowly than they had been in South. Some people were suspicious of them, believing them to be unhealthful, but most objections to them related to culinary unfamiliarity, the fruit's sourness, and the plant's bad smell.[26] Tomatoes were widely accepted after the Colonial and Federal eras.

Wild Greens

How many wild greens, and which sorts, were actually gathered by colonial housewives is very difficult to ascertain; it went largely unrecorded. Many edible greens are mentioned in botanical and travel descriptions, such as purslane or pigweed, dandelions, sorrel, sassafras, wild garlic (ramps), wild onions, and others used as seasonings or remedies. William Wood reported, "There is likewise growing all manner of herbs for meat and medicine, and that not only in planted gardens but in the woods, without either the art or the help of man, as sweet marjoram, purslane, sorrel, penerial [pennyroyal], yarrow, myrtle, sasparilla, bays, etc."[27] In the Southwest, the Native Americans gathered a large number of wild plants, and the settlers there, as did settlers in the East, learned from them which were useful.

Greens were gathered especially in the spring, when they were most welcome as a tonic after a long winter. But like all wild food, there was a balance to maintain between energy expended and nutrition gained; sickly or weak colonists or settlers would be hard pressed to gather even beneficial wild food. As always, the Native Americans used a wide range of wild food that the Europeans often ignored or rejected, preferring domesticated plants.

FRUITS

Apples

Apples were the primary domesticated fruit of the Colonial and Federal periods, more popular and more widely grown than any other, and even planted by Hispanic ranchers in New Mexico by 1815. By the start of the 1800s there were hundreds of apple varieties across America. Once land was cleared and the basic grain and food crops were assured, settlers and householders planted orchards, with apples predominating. Proof of a homesteading claim required an established orchard containing both apple and peach trees. John Chapman, known as Johnny Appleseed, assisted this process in portions of Ohio and Indiana by planting apple tree nurseries in advance of settlement, then selling trees to new settlers.

Apples were widely used in a great variety of dishes, from applesauce to pies, puddings, dumplings, and plain baked apples. Juice pressed from apples was fermented into hard cider, a beverage that rivaled beer in popularity. In some places cider was boiled down to make a molasses-like sweetener. Many apples were cut and dried, then used in sweet and savory dishes. Preserves were made from apples, including apple butter. When they were very plentiful, apples were fed to cattle and swine.

Apple dumplings were one way to prepare the fruit, and this description from the Swedish botanist Peter Kalm explains how to make them: "One apple dish the English prepare is as follows: take an apple and pare it, make a dough of water, flour and butter. Roll it thin and enclose an apple in it. This is then bound in a clean linen cloth, put in a pot and boiled. When done it is taken out . . . the crust is cut on one side. Thereupon they mix butter and sugar which is added to the apples."[28]

Pears

Pears consistently appear on the lists of travelers and botanists recording the produce of the American Colonies, but they seem not to have been planted in large numbers. Farmers throughout the

Northeast grew pears, but Peter Kalm observed that in the Middle Colonies "the orchards have seldom other fruit than apples and peaches. Pear trees are scarce in this province."[29] The fruit, besides being eaten fresh, was also made into a sauce similar to applesauce.

Quince

Similar to apples in shape, though usually yellow when ripe, quince were another popular domesticated fruit, but now are hard to find. They were favored for preserves, often made into a thick marmalade, and also were preserved whole in a sugar syrup as a wet sweetmeat.

Peaches

Peaches were among the most common stone fruits grown in early America. Introduced by Spanish colonists in Florida, peaches grew so prolifically in the South that early travelers thought they grew wild. Native Americans also favored and cultivated peaches once they were introduced. Along with apples trees, a peach orchard provided evidence of an established homestead for claim purposes. Peaches were eaten fresh were used in pies and other sweet dishes, and often were preserved as wet sweetmeats.

Plums

Wild plums grew throughout the colonies and were characterized by early botanists and visitors as good-tasting. For example, New England colonist William Wood, author of the first printed account of New England, *New England's Prospect*, wrote around 1634 about the wild plums: "They be black and yellow about the bigness of a damson, of a reasonable good taste."[30] But settlers seemed to prefer domesticated plums, which met with mixed success in the Colonies. Often termed Damsons in cookery books, they were used fresh and preserved in sweet dishes; dried, they were called prunes. John Brickell observed that Damsons thrived in 1737 Carolina: "Planters wives and Daughters make good Dishes of its Fruit."[31] German settlers, however, found they could not grow enough plums to make their favored plum butter, and rather than turn to wild plums, they made butter out of apples instead.

Cherries

A popular domesticated fruit for fresh eating as well as preserving, cherries were found all through the colonies, where, as with pears and plums, local conditions determined how well they would grow and yield. Kalm wrote that in Pennsylvania, "They sometimes have cherry trees, but commonly by the sides of roads leading to the house, or along the fences." As he proceeded farther from Philadelphia, he saw fewer cherry trees until he arrived at Staten Island, where he saw them in abundance again, although most were sour cherries rather than sweet black ones.[32]

Raspberries and Blackberries

Raspberries and blackberries grew wild in America, but colonial gardeners also brought domesticated raspberries to plant. Colonials were less interested in planting domesticated blackberries because the wild were so common. Both fruits were used in preserves, in pies, and in tarts. Blackberries were often made into wine.

Citrus Fruits

Lemons, oranges, and limes were familiar to colonial Americans even if they were not always available.

Limes originated in ancient Malaysia and were carried to Europe, where they grew only in the warmer regions. Shortly after Europeans discovered the New World, the Spanish introduced limes to the West Indies and Mexico, where they thrived and spread. Early limes were more like the small, very tart Key or Mexican limes of today, and their juice was used primarily by American colonials in beverages, mixed with rum and sugar for punches. Inventories of colonial tavern keepers, even in New England, show large quantities of lime juice in storage, which points to quantity production and shipments of limes and/or their juice.

Lemons seem to have originated in northern India but were used by the Romans, and subsequently by wealthy Europeans. Like limes, they were introduced into the New World. Columbus brought them to Haiti, where they thrived, when he established a settlement there on his second voyage. From the 1600s to the 1800s lemons became much more common in European cookery than they had been before. Spaniards carried lemons to mainland Florida in the sixteenth century, and Hispanics took them to California in the 1730s. They were used in cookery all through the Colonies wherever imported goods were available. Lemon peel and juice in particular were commonly recommended seasonings.

Oranges, like limes, originated in Asia, and were domesticated early. Columbus introduced them along with lemons and limes on his second voyage, and the Spanish settlers in Florida established orange orchards at St. Augustine in the sixteenth century. By the early 1700s, St. Augustine was trading the fruit with English colonists to the north. Oranges also grew in the Carolina low country, according to Brickell in 1737. He said they "thrive tolerably well."[33] More perishable than lemons or limes, oranges did not have as wide a circulation as the other citrus fruits until the steamship transportation of the nineteenth century. They were, however, used in sweet cookery, made into preserves, and eaten by the very prosperous.

Grapefruit, found in the mid-1700s in Barbados, were called shaddocks until 1814, when the name grapefruit was given to them. The fruit is mentioned only occasionally. The French Count Odette Philippe is credited with introducing grapefruit to Florida, near Safety Harbor on Tampa Bay, where he settled in 1823, but they were not sold commercially until later in the nineteenth century.

Pineapples

Originally from Brazil, the pineapple spread northward to the Caribbean islands, where Columbus discovered it. Pineapples were taken to Europe, where they were highly prized but grown only with mixed success. They were, however, carried in coastwise trade to the American colonies, where they were served fresh and made into a sweetmeat. As tremendously popular but also exotic fruits, they were expensive and usually were served only by the wealthy, who in the late Colonial and early Federal eras sometimes grew them in hothouses.

Citron

In Colonial and Federal America the term "citron" was applied to more than one food item. One kind of citron was the candied peel of a citrus fruit native to northeastern India that, like the lemon and lime, spread throughout the Middle East and Europe and became important in sweet cookery, particularly in fruited cakes, mincemeat, and rich puddings. Jewish cooks used it during the harvest festival

Sukkoth. Spanish settlers introduced it into the Caribbean and parts of Florida. As an import, it appears in the historic record as a sweet-meat.

The other citron is the citron melon, a member of the watermelon family, brought by European settlers. It was used as a cheaper substitute for imported citron because housewives grew it in their gardens and preserved it as candied peel.

Melons

Spanish colonists introduced cantaloupes and watermelons into their Florida colony. Native Americans so liked the fruit that they passed seeds along to other Native nations across the southern part of America. The fruits also traveled up from Mexico and took hold among Native Americans in the Southwest. Some travelers among American Indians assumed the fruit was native to the country.

Cranberries

Cranberries grew wild in many parts of America, particularly southern New England and coastal New Jersey. Native Americans regularly harvested them, and settlers adopted them for use as a condiment with turkey and venison. They were also preserved in sugar and used in pies and puddings. They kept very well into the winter if barreled and stored in a cool, dry place. Cranberries were popular enough that a market for them existed even in the seventeenth century; Native Americans picked and sold cranberries to New Jersey settlers.[34] The wild crop could not keep pace with the popular demand in the early 1800s, which led to cranberry cultivation in the mid-1800s.

Currants

Two different fruits were and are called currants. The dried fruit called currant is actually a small grape, the Black Corinth or Zante grape. The Black Corinth was grown in ancient times near Corinth, Greece, and since currants, also called *currans* in early cookery texts, have been used for centuries, the name may be a corruption of the word Corinth. Very commonly used in early American baking, puddings, mincemeat, and some savory dishes, currants were imported from the Mediterranean and were one of the products some English colonizers hoped could be grown in America. (Indeed, they now are grown in California.)

The other fruit called currant is a juicy, red, very tart, domesticated berry, most commonly used fresh in the past to make jelly and wine.

Elderberries

Elderberries grew wild and were often used medicinally. They were also made into preserves and wine.

Gooseberries

Gooseberries are grape-sized, translucent, and very juicy domesticated fruits. Some varieties were red when ripe; some, green. They did not thrive in America as well as in England, being subject to a powdery mildew, but gardeners continued to try growing them. They were commonly used in pies and tarts, and were sometimes made into preserves.

Strawberries

Wild strawberries are native to America, and some varieties were transplanted into settlers' gardens. But the colonials also brought with them domesticated berries that grew slightly larger fruits. A great favorite, strawberries were eaten fresh, made into preserves and wine, and used in pies.

Blueberries

Blueberries grew wild in many parts of America, and settlers distinguished among several kinds of them. Some grew very low to the ground and were a bright, light blue. Darker ones grew on taller bushes. Various sorts of blueberries go by the name of whortleberries, huckleberries, and bilberries. Naturally sweet and dry, they were used primarily in pies and puddings, or eaten fresh, as John Josselyn reported: "They usually eat of them put into a Bason with milk, and sweetened a little more with Sugar and Spice." They could also be dried; in fact, Native Americans sold dried blueberries to settlers, who, according to Josselyn, "make use of them instead of Currence [currants], putting of them into Puddens, both boyled and baked, and into Water Gruel."[35]

Grapes

Many kinds of grapes, growing abundantly and wild in the colonies, have been identified as native to America, including those known by the names mustang, muscadine, frost, and long. The Concord grape is often cited as a native grape, but it was developed from native grapes by Concord, Massachusetts, resident Ephraim Bull in the nineteenth century. The scuppernong, a muscadine type, is usually attributed to North Carolina, and from there was somewhat domesticated. Colonists and settlers, by transplanting the grapes from the wild into gardens or yards, taking cuttings, and sharing the fruit, did much to propagate various wilds sorts in places where they were not native.

Grapes were harvested and made into wine or preserves. In her 1796 *American Cookery*, Amelia Simmons reports that grapes "grow spontaneously in every state in the union." Of the domesticated grapes, she writes, "The *Madeira*, *Lisbon*, and *Malaga* Grapes, are cultivated in gardens in this country, and are a rich treat or desert." She claimed that "Trifling attention only is necessary for their ample growth."[36]

While there was great hope that the southern Colonies would produce grapes in sufficient abundance that America would become a wine-growing region for England, the grapes did not thrive well enough for that, but there was some domestic winemaking. Grapes for wine and table were carried by Hispanic settlers into the Southwest. In New Mexico, along the northern reaches of the Rio Grande where wine grapes could be irrigated, settlers grew wine grapes on farms and at missions. The Temperance movement of the 1800s put an end to much domestic winemaking and retarded the development of commercial wineries. Winemaking became a commercial venture later in American history.

Dried Fruits

Raisins and currants, the two most common dried fruits imported to the colonies, were used frequently in baked dishes and puddings, and were essential to mincemeat and plum puddings. (Currants are described above.)

Raisins were (and are) dried grapes. Until the late 1800s, when seedless grapes were developed, raisin grapes were dried with seeds in them. Many recipes instruct the cook to "stone" the raisins (to remove the seeds). These raisins were quite sizable, much larger than the modern seedless raisins, and when they were soaked, they became quite plump; thus, some recipes recommended chopping the raisins. Most early recipes with the word "plum" in the name call for raisins.

Raisins were also served with nuts and other fruit at the end of the meal, and very likely were still in a small bunch. A popular dish among the Dutch was raisins soaked in brandy, served in a small bowl and eaten with a spoon.

Among other imported dried fruits were figs and dates, though fresh figs were grown in the low country.

Pawpaws

The pawpaw is a native, largely southeastern, American fruit. It grew wild, quite possibly was spread by Indians, and is now cultivated. The fruit is described as being creamy, or custardlike, with a flavor like banana mixed with other tropical fruits.

Persimmons

Persimmons are a native American fruit found in the country's warmer climates. They were known to the Indians, and the Algonquian word for them, *putchamin* (also *pasiminan* and *pessemmin*), was corrupted into the English name. Very tart, the wild sorts, which grew to about the size of a grape, were edible after becoming fully ripe. The English botanist John Bradbury, who explored the interior of America, traveled along the Missouri River in 1811 and ate with the Petit Osage Indians, who offered him "square pieces of cake, in taste resembling gingerbread. On enquiry I found it was made of the pulp of persimon," which he identified by the Latin name *Diospyros virginiana*, "mixed with pounded corn. This bread they call stan-inca."[37]

Colonists used persimmons medicinally, preserved them as a sweetmeat, and brewed beer from them. The persimmons available in stores today are a domesticated relative from the Orient.

Nuts

Many sorts of nut trees, both native and introduced, abounded in the colonies. Nuts provided mast (for pigs) that foraged in woodlands. Settlers in the North and the South gathered nuts—including chestnuts, walnuts, hickory, butternuts, and pecans—wherever they grew, to add a bit of variety to the diet and sometimes for market as well.

Elegant colonial meals ended with fruit, nuts, and wine. The Marquis de Chastellux described a meal taken with George Washington during the Revolutionary War at which nuts were served: "After [the meal] the cloth was taken off, and apples and a great quantity of nuts were served, which General Washington usually continues eating for two hours, 'toasting' and conversing all the time. These nuts are small and dry, and have so hard a shell that they can only be cracked with a hammer; they are served half open, and the company are never done picking and eating them."[38]

Almonds were imported. They had been a very important ingredient in Europe, particularly for fast day cookery, when they were ground to make a milk substitute. Spanish settlers in the Southwest and Florida and the English desired almonds for cookery.

Pine Nuts

Hispanic settlers in the Southwest gathered pine nuts (piñons) from cones of the piñon pines. Similar to Italian pignoli, pine nuts were already familiar to the Spanish, who used them in their cookery. Pine nuts were plentiful and valuable enough to be exported to Mexico from New Mexico.

Peanuts

Originally a New World food from South America, peanuts, also known as groundnuts, were taken to Africa by the Portuguese in the sixteenth century, and subsequently they were reintroduced from Africa to America. (Another wild food is called the groundnut was dug and eaten by Native Americans and European colonists alike, but is not the same plant as the peanut.)

There is some debate about how and exactly when peanuts were introduced into the Colonies. Since they were widely grown in the Caribbean, low-country settlers from the islands may have brought peanuts with them to the mainland. But slave ships also had peanuts among their provisions with which to feed the slaves, who later grew peanuts in their garden plots. The slave and peanut connection is the strongest and most probable method of introduction.[39]

Clearly, however, during the Colonial and Federal eras, peanuts were food for slaves, and also sometimes for chickens and pigs. Peanuts were eaten as other nuts were, snack-fashion, in the early 1800s by other Americans, but they did not become important in the general diet until later in the nineteenth century.

HERBS, SPICES, AND OTHER SEASONINGS

Herbs

At the time of earliest settlement, the word "herb" encompassed some food plants that today are called vegetables. Salad herbs, for example, included lettuces and cresses, and potherbs included vegetables such as spinach and dandelion greens. In addition, certain herbs were used primarily medicinally, though there is some crossover in the categories.

The plants grown for seasoning that today are commonly considered herbs were found in all Colonies, with some ethnic variations. In seventeenth-century English cookbooks, herb citations abound, but Amelia Simmons summed up the English colonial favorites at the end of the eighteenth century when she listed sweet marjoram, summer savory, sage, parsley, and sweet thyme. It is very hard to determine just how commonly any of these herbs were used day-to-day. Martha Ballard in Maine, who recorded many of the vegetables she grew, mentioned only one culinary herb, parsley, saying she wanted it to use in her gravy.[40] Many recipe books and manuscripts merely call for "sweet herbs," leaving the specifics to the cook.

The Dutch used a group of savory and sweet herbs similar to those used by the English, to which they often added lovage, oregano, and horseradish.

In his 1709 travels in the Carolinas, John Lawson observed herbs being grown, and among "sallads" listed fennel and parsley. His list of "pot herbs" included borage, burnet, clary, marigolds, marjoram, and summer and winter savories. He also lists dill, caraway, coriander, cumin, and anise, apparently all used as seeds.[41]

Capsicums

In the Spanish Colonial Southwest, juniper berries, safflower, oregano, wild parsley, and garlic were used in addition to chile for seasoning. Chile (with an "e") peppers, one of many capsicums, were used green and roasted; and, red, ripe, and dried, were strung in *ristras* for storage. Both were made into sauces for meat dishes.

In the low country, particularly those parts settled by Barbadians, and the former Spanish Florida, where Creole settlers moved from Caribbean islands, other capsicum peppers lent their heat to foods. Hot pepper use spread from northward to the Chesapeake, and since hot peppers were grown and used by slaves, they were gradually introduced to the white population. The famous Philadelphia pepper pot soup was seasoned with one such pepper, and another became the base for Tabasco sauce in Louisiana.

Spices

Spice use was an established part of English, Dutch, and Spanish culinary practice before those nations colonized America. As expensive imports, their use was a mark of wealth and refinement, and some early recipes call for startling quantities of them, giving rise to the erroneous idea that heavy spicing was used to mask the bad smell and flavor of spoiled food. In fact, people in past times did not eat spoiled food, and the wealthy, who could most easily afford spices, were most likely to have access to good fresh meat at all times. Lavish spice use demonstrated wealth.

Colonial-era seasonings included loaf sugar (top center), stick cinnamon in the round box, with lobes of light-colored ginger in races, and small, nut-shaped nutmegs. Raisins are piled on the plate, and a bag of black pepper is open next to it. Vinegar and sweet (olive) oil are in the bottles. The wooden stand holds salt. All the spices had to be pounded and sifted or grated before use. (Courtesy of Plimoth Plantation, Plymouth, Massachusetts.)

By the time the colonies were settled, spice costs had declined somewhat. Many early Americans used spices with a heavier hand than most modern people are accustomed to, and put them in dishes no longer seasoned in that fashion. For example, most modern meat recipes do not call for nutmeg or mace, but both were used in past times with fish, chicken, and red meat. In Colonial port cities and towns, it was easier to obtain imported spices, and they were fresher than those which traveled miles to the interior, losing quality and strength along the way but still costly. Spices were usually imported whole, and it was the cook's job to pound and sift them for use in cookery.

Salt and pepper were the most available seasonings for most classes. Salt had an important role in food preservation and was essential wherever people settled, either as a locally produced or as in imported item. Pepper came from India and was the chief object of much pre-colonial spice trade over which the Dutch and British bitterly competed. It is now grown in tropical areas around the globe.

Nutmeg and mace were the next most common spices. They come from the same tree, the mace forming a net of petals around the outside of the nutmeg's husk. The mace petals were called blades, and early recipes sometimes call for a "blade of mace." The nutmeg husk is cracked, and the nut within is used for spice, usually grated on a grater specifically for nutmegs. Nutmegs came from continental Asia and Indonesia, as did cloves. Nutmeg trees were transplanted to the West Indian islands, where they grow today.

Cloves are the dried buds of an evergreen tree native to the tropics. Widely used in savory and sweet cookery, cloves often appear together with nutmeg and mace in early American pickle recipes.

Cinnamon and cassia are very similar in flavor although they come from different trees. Cassia has a stronger flavor and was slightly less expensive than true cinnamon in early America. Consequently, most cinnamon used here was really cassia. Both were imported from Asia. Dutch cooks often used cinnamon in preference to nutmeg in apple dishes.

Ginger appears frequently in colonial dishes, from pickles to gingerbread. It was imported from India and Jamaica in the form of small, flattened, dried lobes, called races, that were pounded and sifted to make ginger powder. In the early part of the Colonial era, ginger was popular in savory cooking, but by the eighteenth century was used mostly in sweet baking. It is not unusual to read early gingerbread recipes that make no mention of the spice among the ingredients, the assumption being that cooks knew to add it.

Allspice was imported from Jamaica, and in earlier times was sometimes called Jamaica pepper, or pimento (from the Spanish *pimiento,* pepper). Its flavor combines that of other spices, hence the name. Whole allspice is round and dark brown, larger than a peppercorn. Like nearly all other spices of the time, it had to be pounded and sifted for use.

Rosewater, made from distilled water in which rose petals had been steeped, was still popular in the eighteenth century and early nineteenth century, though by the end of the Federal period its popularity was waning. It harked back to the era of the Crusades, when Europeans encountered it in the Holy Land, adopted it, and used it in sweet cookery, particularly puddings and custards, but also in cakes and pastries. Orange flower water occasionally appears in seventeenth- and eighteenth-century recipes, but less frequently. Brandy was used to flavor baked goods and sweet dishes. Vanilla was not commonly used.

Seeds

Caraway, coriander, and sesame seeds were commonly used in English Colonial and Federal era baking, a practice that gradually faded toward the end of the era. They were often incorporated into small cakes, sometimes called seed cakes. Both caraway and coriander could be grown in a kitchen garden. Sesame seeds, also called benne seeds (from the West African word *benni*), grew in the South, particularly the low country, brought there by slave traders with the West African slaves who were imported to grow rice.

The Dutch used cumin in cheese, and it was an ingredient in curry powder. Anise was more popular among Spanish colonials.

Some seeds, nuts, and whole spices were given a sugar coating to be made into confits, a kind of candy, during this era. They were made mostly by professional confectioners.

CONDIMENTS

Cooks seasoned most dishes during preparation, but there were some items put on the table with which diners could adjust the seasoning to taste. Salt, for instance, appeared on the table hundreds of years before American settlement. In the Colonial era, the wealthy had caster stands that held bottles with oil, vinegar, salt, mustard, or other sauces. (In the nineteenth century, these were found in middle-class homes.) Lesser households placed at least salt dishes on the table, and sometimes pepper and bottles with oil and vinegar.

Horseradish and Mustard

Horseradish and mustard appear as ingredients in recipes of the era, but it is less clear how often they were offered as condiments on the seventeenth- or eighteenth-century table. Horseradish was widely grown, and mustard was both imported and raised in the Colonies. The early term "made mustard" meant mustard that had been mixed with water or vinegar to make a sauce.

Vinegar

Vinegar was widely used as a condiment, sprinkled on salads and on boiled dinners. The sharpness contrasted with the saltiness of some preserved food. It was included in rations to soldiers and sailors. Vinegar was sometimes seasoned with herbs or spices; in the South, vinegar or sherry was infused with capsicum peppers to make a kind of a hot sauce still seen in the Caribbean islands today.

Butter

Butter was placed on the table for the diner to put on bread or anything else he or she chose. In wealthy households, chips of ice underneath the special plates holding the butter kept it cool in hot weather.

Ketchup

Ketchup in colonial America more closely resembled Worcestershire or steak sauce than modern tomato ketchup. The word comes from a corruption of the Chinese word *kêtsiap*, originally a fermented fish sauce brought to Europe by the Dutch. Early ketchups were made from a variety of ingredients, including mushrooms, anchovies, and walnuts, in vinegar or ale, and highly seasoned. Early cookbooks include recipes for making them, but there is scant reference to their appearing on American Colonial tables. Eighteenth-century English cookbooks often call for ketchup as seasoning, and the practice continued into the early nineteenth century among American cookery writers. Most people today are familiar only with tomato ketchup; in 1833, New England cookbook author Lydia Maria Child wrote in *The American Frugal Housewife* that "the best sort of catsup is made from tomatoes," although other cookbooks continued to offer recipes for the older-style ketchups.[42]

Drippings and Rendered Fats

Any drippings from roasted meat not used in a sauce or gravy with the meat, and the pot skimmings from boiling meat, or rendered fat from frying meat, were reserved for cooking to replace more desirable lard, suet, or butter. Drippings were also spread, as butter was, on bread.

Anchovies

An imported food, anchovies are small, oily fish found in warm oceans around the world. They are usually heavily salted. Anchovies in Colonial America were largely from the Mediterranean, barreled and exported for use in sauces and to garnish poultry and fish dishes.

SUGARS, SWEETENINGS, AND SOURS

Colonial cooks used many grades and kinds of sweetenings, both solid and liquid. Virtually all were derived from sugarcane. A brief interest in developing a beet sugar industry at the end of the Federal period, particularly in Pennsylvania and the Ohio valley, attracted speculators but did not materialize as a profitable industry. Sorghum was introduced in the later nineteenth century. Maple sugar was made in the Northeast, western Pennsylvania, Ohio, and the Northwest Territory.

At earliest settlement in America, sugar was used both medicinally and to season dishes lightly. By the beginning of the nineteenth century, it was called for in a substantial number of recipes for baked goods, puddings, and pies. Many regarded it as essential for sweetening bitter beverages such as tea, coffee, and chocolate. To supply this increasing demand for sugar, the Caribbean islands and the American South became ever more involved in growing canesugar and refining its juice for export. A labor-intensive crop and process, the production of sugar consumed the lives of many African slaves without whose unpaid work it would not have been so profitable.

The primary forms in which sugar was sold during the Colonial period were white refined sugar in loaves; soft, brown sugar; and molasses. All sugar was boiled out of the juice extracted from the crushed sugarcane. The juice was cooked until granules of sugar began to appear in the thick molasses, whereupon it was packed in barrels. Molasses was allowed to drain out, and the barrels were sent to the refiners or sold as raw, or *muscavado*, sugar. Refining was another complicated process, and there were several refining methods used in the Colonial era.

Loaf Sugar

Loaf sugar was formed by packing damp, refined granulated sugar into inverted cone-shaped molds with a small hole in the tip. Any remaining molasses dripped through the holes, leaving harder sugar in the molds. Processors further refined that sugar by covering the base of the cone while the sugar was still in the mold with wet clay through which they poured water. The water washed out any remaining molasses, leaving the loaf mostly white. The loaves were baked to dry them, wrapped, and exported.

To use loaf sugar, cooks broke off pieces and pounded them into something similar to modern granulated sugar. There were usually some impurities in the loaf sugar, and nearly all period cookbooks caution the cook to clarify the sugar for use. Because it was expensive, cooks generally reserved loaf sugar for best baking, making preserves, and sweetening beverages.

Raw, *muscavado*, or brown sugar was damp dark sugar. Relatively inexpensive compared with loaf sugar, it was often used by people who could not afford loaf sugar for baking. Even cheaper was molasses, which was a very common sweetening for ordinary people all through the Colonies, used in baking cakes, sweetening puddings, and even added to cream to make a sweet sauce.

Maple Sugar

The high value of sugar and its increased use through the Colonial and Federal eras made maple sugar a valuable commodity, and some who promoted settlement hoped it could rival cane sugar. Although it never did, maple sugar was made wherever the sugar maple grew in the hardwood forests of the Northeast, western Pennsylvania, Ohio, and in the Northwest Territory. The process was known to Europeans before settlement. Though there is some controversy about whether Native Americans used or made maple sugar before contact with Europeans or taught colonists how to make it, it is true that once Native Americans had access to iron pots through trade, they made maple sugar and sold it to settlers.

Maple trees were typically tapped, and the sap collected, during the spring run. The sap was heated at a high temperature to drive off water and reduce the sap to a thick, dark syrup, called maple molasses, which was used as cane sugar molasses was. When makers wanted a granulated product, the molasses was boiled until the sugar crystallized, and at that point it was turned out of the kettle into a wooden trough for clashing, pounding with a wooden beater to break up clumps of crystals. The sugar was yellow and retained some maple flavor. People who produced maple sugar often saw it mostly as a cash crop while keeping some for their own use. The goal of maple sugaring was to make sugar. Maple syrup is now the main product, but historically it was not.

Honey

Colonists brought bees with them to America, where they thrived and spread into the interior ahead of white settlers. They were more commonly raised in the Middle Atlantic Colonies, and the honey and beeswax were valuable commodities in Philadelphia by the late seventeenth century.[43] Backcountry and frontier areas, where imported molasses was harder and more costly to obtain, used honey in addition to maple sugar and molasses. Households that clung to old ways of doing things, especially in early settlements, may have also used honey to brew the beverage mead, but most honey was used to sweeten dishes and beverages, and to spread on bread.

Verjuice

Verjuice, the tart juice of crabapples or green, sour grapes, and other unripe fruits, was used to add piquancy to a dish in the same way that lemon juice is used today. It appears often in sixteenth-, seventeenth-, and eighteenth-century European cookbooks, but gradually disappears in the nineteenth century. It was probably used more by the gentry in Colonial America than among the less well-off, who would have used the more readily available vinegar.

Vinegar

Besides its use as a condiment, vinegar was an ingredient in some remedies and was indispensable in pickling. It was made from wine, cider, maple sap, or other sweet juices, including plain sugar water, according to a recipe in Hannah Glasse's English *Art of Cookery* (1805), which called for yeast added to sugar and water to promote fermentation.[44] Vinegar replaced verjuice in many later seventeenth- and eighteenth-century recipes. Among the frugal, pickle juice, essentially the flavored vinegar from various sorts of pickled vegetables, was also used in recipes. Homemade vinegars varied in acidity, but once vinegar was sold commercially, its acidity was regulated.

BEVERAGES

Water

Water was an acceptable beverage for most early colonists in the absence of the preferred beer or cider. In the newly settled areas, a reliable source of good water was highly desirable, but water supplies did not always remain good as populations became more dense. Some settlers distrusted water, and drank other beverages whenever possible.

Beer and Ale

Brewing beer and ale, both popular beverages among most European colonists (particularly the English and northern Europeans), was one of the housewife's chores. They were made by malting grain (barley being favored), by lightly soaking it and allowing it to begin sprouting. It was then roasted slightly, ground, and made into a mash with water to which yeast and hops were added. Set aside to ferment in casks or tubs until it was done, it was then drawn off into bunged kegs or stoppered bottles. Much home-brewed beer in early times was "small" or "near" beer—that is, it had a low alcohol content— and was consumed with a meal by young and old.

Wine

Most wine consumed in the Colonies was imported from Spain and the Canary Islands, and Portugal and the Azores; some came from

France and the Rhine River valley. The supply of French wines was interrupted periodically in the Colonial era because they were imported through England, and France and England were frequently at war.

Colonists generally preferred sweet and fortified wines. Fortified wines had alcohol added, which acted in part as a preservative that kept the wine in good condition on its voyage across the Atlantic and during storage in the Colonies until it was consumed. When households could afford to, they bought large quantities of wine in pipes, hogsheads, or butts, and bottled it themselves to settle after the voyage. Few people, however, could afford to maintain a wine cellar where wine was stored at ideal temperatures, and since fortified wines did not need that kind of storage, they were popular especially in hot and humid regions of the Colonies from Spanish Florida north to the Chesapeake.

Madeira was among the wines most frequently mentioned in letters and journals, in cookbooks, and in store advertisements. It was followed by sherry, malaga, fayal, claret, sack, champagne, and others. The more prosperous colonials drank the most wine, often using expensive serving pieces including wine glasses, wine coolers, and glass decanters.

Wines and spirits were also used in recipes for sweet and savory dishes, for a range of remedies, and for home-made beverages such as cordials and fruit brandies. Housewives produced wines from dandelions, currants, persimmons, blackberries, and even wild and domesticated grapes.

Cider

Making cider was a part of the British foodways tradition in districts of England where apples grew abundantly. In the American Colonies where apples thrived, cider sometimes edged out beer, depending on how reliable a crop barley proved to be, but cider never completely replaced beer. Apple juice was pressed, barreled, and fermented, sometimes with the addition of yeast or raisins to promote fermentation. Making cider was also a way of preserving large quantities of apple juice for drinking year-round.

Mead

Mead and metheglin were very old-fashioned alcoholic beverages by the time America was colonized. Very often homemade, they were brewed from honey and water, sometimes with raisins and herbs added. Recipes for them appear in cookbooks used in Colonial America but scant mention is made of them elsewhere, and it is hard to determine how common they were.

Brandy

Brandy is a spirit distilled from wine imported from France. Housewives used brandy as a flavoring in sweet dishes, added it to homemade wines, and steeped fruits in it to preserve the fruit or to make a beverage.

Rum

Rum, a spirit made by fermenting cane sugar by-products, was produced in both the Colonial West Indies and mainland locations, particularly New England, which imported a great deal of molasses for the purpose. Rum formed the alcoholic base for many seventeenth- and eighteenth-century beverages, sweetened and mixed with fruit juices to make punches and shrubs. Rum was a common, relatively inexpensive spirit, given in rations to soldiers, sailors, and, on special occasions, slaves. The earliest appearance of the word "rum" in print is 1654, and is thought to be a contraction of "rumbullion" or "rombostion," both names for rum.

Whiskey

Whiskey making came to the Colonies with settlers from the British Isles. Based on fermenting a mash of grains and distilling the liquid, whiskey making in Great Britain, particularly in Scotland and Ireland, chiefly used barley but also rye and wheat. The word "whiskey" comes from a Gaelic word meaning "water of life." In America, colonists experimented with using corn in combination with the traditional grains to make an American whiskey. Whiskey production allowed the corn-growing settlers of the upland South to sell their corn transformed into a high-value product that paid back the cost of transportation to market.

The corn-based whiskey called bourbon was refined in the upland South. Erroneously credited as the invention of Rev. Elisha Craig in Kentucky, the name bourbon's became attached to any whiskey produced in the former Bourbon County of Kentucky, which has since been divided into several counties. These whiskeys, transported by flatboat to the port of New Orleans, were identified as being from "Old Bourbon" county, and the whiskey was eventually identified by the name.

Corn-mash whiskey is a unique American product. To qualify as genuine bourbon, it must consist of 51 percent corn mash, be aged for two years in new charred oak barrels, and be made in the United States. In actual practice, most bourbons were, and are, made of a higher percentage, often close to 75 to 80 percent, corn mash.

Other Spirits

Gin, a grain-based alcohol flavored with juniper berries, came from Holland and was imported by Americans, but was far more popular in England. In the Spanish Southwest, an alcoholic beverage called pulque was made by fermenting agave juice. (Tequila is a distillation of a similar fermented product.)

Milk and Buttermilk

Milk was a common Colonial beverage for young and old, used frequently at breakfast, sometimes heated. Buttermilk was a by-product of making butter. Cream skimmed from milk for butter was set aside to accumulate until there was enough to churn, during which time it sometimes soured slightly, a step that promoted its ability to churn well. When it was churned, the fat solids collected and the milky liquid left had a slightly tart flavor, which some thought made it an agreeable beverage.

Chocolate, Coffee, and Tea

Chocolate, coffee, and tea appeared roughly simultaneously in seventeenth-century England, tea coming from Asia, coffee from the Near East, and chocolate from America. In Europe, certain conventions and equipment became associated with each of the three beverages, and were brought to the Colonies along with the ingredients for making the drinks. Also, all three were bitter beverages and contributed to the increasing consumption of sugar in the seventeenth and eighteenth centuries as people became accustomed to adding a sweetening to them. All were consumed first by the wealthy classes, but gradually were adopted by the rising middle classes, and eventually even by poorer families. As early as the 1690s all three were sold in the Colonies.

Chocolate. A raw cocoa seed is not edible; it must be fermented, dried, roasted, and winnowed to remove the shells. The beans are then heated slightly and ground into a paste that hardens into cakes. When cocoa was needed, the cakes were scraped, and the chocolate was mixed and heated with milk and sugar to become a beverage. As with tea and coffee, the elite were the first to use chocolate, and the beverage had its own equipment.

Chocolate was imported by missions and settlers in the Spanish Colonies east and west in the seventeenth and eighteenth centuries, but it did not become popular in the other American Colonies until the eighteenth century. Spanish chocolate was thick enough to be eaten with a spoon, and was not made with milk or sugar.

Coffee. In England, coffee was frequently drunk in coffeehouses by men conducting business or discussing news and politics. It seemed to be a public beverage, whereas tea seemed to be a domestic and private, albeit sociable, one.[45] Coffee enjoyed a small upsurge in popularity when some colonists boycotted tea because of the tax imposed on it and other imported goods by the Townshend Acts in 1767.

Coffee beans were picked and exported green, and roasted often by the consumer, who also ground them to brew the beverage.

Tea. Tea was served in the Colonies first among the gentry, who could afford to adopt the English fashion and the specialized equipment for brewing and serving it. A scattering of references to tea in the first decades of the 1700s gradually gives way to frequent mentions of it by the mid-eighteenth century as a common breakfast beverage and as one for later afternoon.

One indicator of increasing prosperity among the eighteenth-century middle classes was the appearance in their homes of tea equipage, at least a teapot to brew it in and teacups to drink it from. A full set of tea equipment included, besides the teapot, a slop bowl into which one poured the dregs with leaves still in them or emptied the contents of the tea strainer; a sugar bowl; sugar tongs; a cream pitcher; a canister to store tea leaves in; spoons; and a tray for the spoons. In the wealthiest homes, the tea service might be of silver, with china teacups. There might also be a tea table; a stand on which the tea kettle holding the hot water rested; and, later in the eighteenth century, an urn in which to heat water or keep it hot. Pewter, porcelain, or ceramic sets were more common farther down the social ladder.

At this time, teacups had no handles, and in America, most English colonists liked to drink it very hot, holding the cup in one hand and the saucer in the other. Tea parties with food served were firmly established by the end of the eighteenth century, and in some homes, tea was the name of a meal as well as a beverage.

Tea, an imported item, was more costly the farther it had to travel. Newspapers of the era mention many kinds of tea by name—for example, souchong, hyson, bohea, pekoe, green, and others. It was sold to merchants loose in chests, having been sorted and priced according to leaf size.

Tea was subject to import duties, the tax that caused such a furor in the Colonies. Many people gave up drinking tea, and others looked for tea that had been smuggled and so had not been taxed. In 1774 John Adams, upon arriving in Falmouth in the District of Maine, inquired of his landlady, "Is it lawfull for a weary Traveller to refresh himself with a Dish of Tea provided it has been honestly smuggled, or paid no Duties?" She informed him that she had relinquished all tea, but that she would make him coffee. "Accordingly," Adams wrote, "I have drank Coffee every Afternoon since, and have borne it very well. Tea must be universally renounced. I must be weaned, and the sooner the better."[46]

NOTES

1. William Bradford, *A Journal of the Pilgrims at Plymouth: Mourt's Relation*, edited by Dwight Heath (New York: Corinth Books, 1963), 22.

2. John Winthrop, Jr., "Letter to the Royal Society (1662)," repr. *New England Quarterly* 10, no. 1 (1937): 121–133.

3. Elizabeth E. Lea, *Domestic Cookery, Useful Receipts, and Hints to Young Housekeepers* (Baltimore: Cushing and Bailey, 1853), 171–172.

4. Edward Johnson, *Wonder-Working Providence of Sions Saviour in New England*, edited by J. F. Jameson (New York: Charles Scribner and Sons, 1910), 78.

5. John Lawson, *A New Voyage to Carolina*, edited by Hugh Talmage Lefler (Chapel Hill: University of North Carolina Press, 1967), 31.

6. Adriaen Van der Donck, *A Description of the New Netherlands*, edited with introduction by Thomas F. O'Donnell (Syracuse, NY: Syracuse University Press, 1968), 47.

7. Thomas Morton, *The New English Canaan* (Boston: Prince Society, 1883), 203.

8. Van der Donck, 45.

9. John Brickell, *The Natural History of North-Carolina* (Dublin: James Carson, 1737), facs. repr. with introduction by Carol Urness (New York: Johnson Reprint, 1969), 107.

10. Ibid., 108.

11. Morton, 192.

12. Lawson, 33.

13. Van der Donck, 50.

14. William Cronon, *Changes in the Land* (New York: Hill and Wang, 1983), 99–101.

15. Bradford, 44.

16. Van der Donck, 51.

17. François-Jean, Marquis de Chastellux, *Travels in North America in the Years 1780, 1781, and 1782 by the Marquis de Chastellux,* rev. trans. with introduction and notes by Howard C. Rice, Jr., 2 vols. (Chapel Hill: University of North Carolina Press, 1963), vol. 2, 379.

18. Amelia Simmons, *American Cookery; or, the Art of Dressing Viands, Fish, Poultry, and Vegetables* (Hartford, CT: Hudson & Godwin, 1796), facs. repr. with introduction by Mary Tolford Wilson (New York: Dover, 1984), 6.

19. George Brown Goode, ed., *The Fisheries and Fishery Industries of the United States,* 8 vols. (Washington, DC: Government Printing Office, 1884–1887), vol. 2, 659.

20. Martha Ballard, *The Diary of Martha Ballard, 1785–1812,* edited by Robert McCausland and Cynthia MacAlman McCausland (Camden, ME: Picton Press, 1992), 340.

21. Lydia Maria Child, *The American Frugal Housewife. Dedicated to Those Who Are Not Ashamed of Economy,* 12th ed. (Boston: Carter and Hendee, 1833), 51.

22. William Woys Weaver, *Heirloom Vegetable Gardening: A Master Gardener's Guide to Planting, Growing, Seed Saving, and Cultural History* (New York: Henry Holt, 1997), 277–278.

23. John Josselyn, *New-Englands Rarities Discovered* (London: E. Widdoes, 1672), repr. with a foreword by Henry Lee Shattuck (Boston: Massachusetts Historical Society, 1972), 91.

24. Andrew F. Smith, *The Tomato in America: Early History, Culture, and Cookery* (Columbia: University of South Carolina Press, 1994), 19, 25; Harriot Pinckney Horry, *A Colonial Plantation Cookbook: The Receipt Book of Harriot Pinckney Horry, 1770,* edited with introduction by Richard Hooker (Columbia: University of South Carolina Press, 1984), 89.

25. Smith, 30–36.

26. Ibid., 40–43.

27. William Wood, *New England's Prospect,* edited by Alden T. Vaughan (Amherst: University of Massachusetts Press, 1977), 36.

28. Peter (Pehr) Kalm, *Peter Kalm's Travels in North America: The Amer-*

ica of 1750, Reprint of English version of 1770 translated from the original Swedish by John Forster, and edited by Adolph Benson, 2 vols. (New York: Dover, 1966), vol. 1, 173–174.

29. Ibid., 41.

30. Wood, 41.

31. Brickell, 103.

32. Kalm, vol. 1, 41, 324.

33. Brickell, 105.

34. Angus Kress Gillespie, "Cranberries," in *Rooted in America: Foodlore of Popular Fruits and Vegetables,* edited by David Scofield Wilson and Angus Kress Gillespie (Knoxville: University of Tennessee Press, 1999), 60–88.

35. Josselyn, 60.

36. Simmons, 17.

37. Bradford, 35.

38. Chastellux, vol. 1, 109.

39. Andrew F. Smith, *Peanuts: The Illustrious History of the Goober Pea* (Urbana: University of Illinois Press, 2002), 12–13.

40. Ballard, 535.

41. Lawson, 83–84.

42. Child, 35.

43. Percy Wells Bidwell and John Falconer, *History of Agriculture in the Northern United States 1620–1860* (New York: Peter Smith, 1941), 32.

44. Hannah Glasse, *Art of Cookery Made Plain and Easy* (Alexandria, VA: Cottom and Stewart, 1805); also facsimile with historical notes by Karen Hess (Bedford, MA: Applewood Books, 1998), 221.

45. Rodris Roth, "Tea Drinking in 18th-Century America: Its Etiquette and Equipage," *Contributions from the Museum of History and Technology,* paper 14, U.S. National Museum Bulletin 225 (Washington, DC: Smithsonian Institution, 1961), 66.

46. John Adams to Abigail Adams, July 6, 1774, in *The Book of Abigail and John: Selected Letters of the Adams Family, 1762–1784,* edited by L. H. Butterfield, Marc Friedlaender, and Mary-Jo Klein (Cambridge, MA: Harvard University Press, 1975), 61.

CHAPTER 3

FOOD PREPARATION: COOKING AND COOKS

American Colonial and Federal cooking was dominated by fireplace technology. The earliest settlers cooked on open hearths, but by the end of the Federal period many households had participated in a great shift that continued into the middle 1800s, from cooking on a hearth to using a stove. Increasing refinement in the manner of living, including food preparation and housekeeping, gradually embraced by most Americans in the nineteenth century, started in this period its diffusion from the gentry classes downward to middle-class Americans.

Women, free and enslaved, performed the food preparation and preservation work in the vast majority of American households. Cooking, dairying, baking, brewing, care of poultry, vegetable gardening, and preparing remedies for the sick were all women's work. To these chores were added the care of children, the ill, and the infirm, as well as the many chores of housekeeping, spinning, weaving, and making clothing, and helping seasonally with agricultural chores such as hoeing or harvesting. Food-related trades and professionals such as bakers, brewers, maltsters, butchers, confectioners, and millers also had a hand in the food supply.

KITCHENS AND OTHER FOOD-HANDLING SPACES

From earliest settlement to the end of the 1820s, kitchens changed somewhat, but not as dramatically as they would during the later

1800s. Since food preparation and storage were so important in Colonial life and people then were more flexible about how they used their houses than many modern people are, food-related activity occurred in rooms from cellar to attic and in buildings outside as well.

Earliest Kitchens

Kitchen arrangements varied less from northern to southern colonies than from one social class to another and, to a lesser extent, among ethnic groups. The kitchen was an integral part of any new colonial dwelling. Newest settlers usually erected one-room shelters where all domestic activity occurred, and where the family slept as well. As soon as a household could afford it, that shelter was im-

A kitchen hearth of 1627, re-created at Plimoth Plantation in Plymouth, Massachusetts, has a cast-iron pot and a brass kettle hanging over the fire. A fowl on a spit rests on hooks on the face of the andirons, and a dripping pan is beneath. Dry food is stored in cloth bags hung on the wall. Cooking hearths like this one were found in the first settlers' homes from New England to the Chesapeake in the 1600s, and even later in the backcountry. (Courtesy of Plimoth Plantation, Plymouth, Massachusetts.)

Improved eighteenth-century hearth. This house, the Major John Bradford House in Kingston, Massachusetts, was built in 1674; the kitchen and fireplace have been improved since then. On the left an oven has been built outside the fireplace opening in the fashion more typical of the late 1700s. A crane extends from the right fireplace jamb. A mechanical jack is installed above the hearth on the chimney wall at right, and indicates that the house owners were prosperous. (Courtesy of the Library of Congress, Historic American Buildings Survey, HABS, MASS, 12-KING, 1-7.)

proved with additions or was replaced it with a new house, at which time rooms were set aside for specialized activities such as cookery, food storage, dairying, socializing, and eventually dining. City dwellers, with homes on small pieces of land, often put kitchens in the basements of their homes.

The poor in all regions and the enslaved dwelled in the simplest sort of structure, a one-room home or, at best, a one-over-one-room house, where they may have designated spaces for cooking and keeping food, for sitting, and for sleeping, but did not differentiate space beyond that.

Northern Kitchens. In cold-weather colonies, having a kitchen in the main structure of the house was highly desirable. The constantly burning kitchen fire kept the entire chimney stack heated, radiating heat into other rooms. As homes were improved during the fifty or so years after first settlement, kitchens might be plastered or wainscoted, and walls freshened with whitewash. Beams overhead held hooks for hanging food stored in bags, safe from flies or vermin. A fireplace occupied one wall.

When home owners expanded their houses, the kitchen often represented the older part of the house, with the new added onto it around the existing chimney, to which new flues were added to accommodate fireplaces in other rooms. In New England particularly, the old kitchen might then have small rooms added to each end of it, to create on the northern end a cold room, and on the southern end a kitchen chamber, or bedroom.

In the North, so-called summer kitchens sometimes appeared in the later 1700s in prosperous homes. They were usually located in an ell at a distance from the main part of the house. Households most likely used these spaces for heavy, messy tasks such as making candles or soap, laundering, and some butchering activity, though certainly in the heat of August a family might have been glad to see the cooking fire moved away from the center of the house.

Southern Kitchens. In warm-weather regions, the constant heat, longer fly season, and increased use of enslaved cooks made moving the kitchen apart from the main house more attractive, though even Virginia's gentry kept kitchens in their homes until the later Federal era. The often-cited fear of fire as a reason for the removal of kitchens from the main dwelling cannot account alone for the practice that seems to have predominated among prosperous southerners.

The separate southern kitchen was usually part of a complex of outbuildings at the back of the main house, opening onto outdoor workspace. A door and sometimes a window or two ventilated the kitchen, which was dominated by the hearth and chimney. It often served as the dwelling for the cook and her family, which meant that the slave cook was often isolated from other slaves, whose quarters might be at a distance from the main house. At the beck and call of the owner around the clock, like all the domestic slaves, the cook often ended up more constantly at work than field hands.

In the late eighteenth- and early nineteenth-century South, when kitchens were generally separated from houses, some householders continued using the in-house kitchens. While hot and large-quantity cooking was conducted in the separate kitchen, the mistress of the

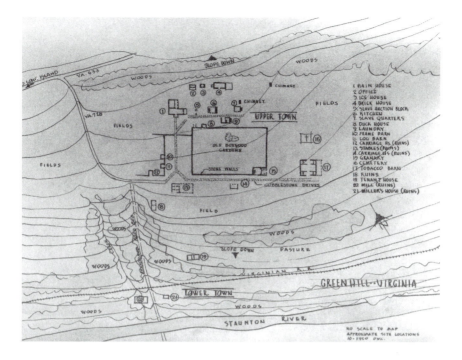

This drawing of the layout of Green Hill Plantation in Campbell County, Virginia, shows the relationship among the main house, the slave quarters, and the kitchen, as well as the existence of food storage spaces in a granary and ice house. The legend on the right side identifies each structure. (Courtesy of the Library of Congress, Historic American Buildings Survey HABS, VA, 16-LONI, V, 1-2.)

Green Hill Plantation. Building probably began in 1797 with the ell, and continued until the mid-1800s, but this photograph is a good example of how Federal era and later plantations were arranged. It shows the plantation in the early twentieth century. (Courtesy of the Library of Congress, Historic American Buildings Survey HABS, VA, 16-LONI, V, 1-1.)

house may have prepared fancy and/or cold dishes herself or directly supervised their preparation in the main house kitchen. These kitchens are often described as warming kitchens, and indeed, in cooler seasons or under certain circumstances, they may have been used to keep food warm prior to serving it. But it is as likely that these kitchens were used as "cool kitchens" in the French tradition of a "office" for preparing cold desserts such as custards or the ices so fashionable at the end of the eighteenth century.

Kitchens in the Spanish Colonial Southwest. In many parts of the Spanish Colonial Southwest, early dwellings constructed of adobe bricks plastered over with clayey mud have largely disappeared along with their kitchens. The first Spaniards to live among the Pueblo Indians in this region were priests who built missions with Spanish-influenced kitchens. For example, the interpretation of the archaeological remains at Mission San Gregorio at Abo, New Mexico, theorizes a wall against which cooks built their fires; smoke escaped through a hole in the ceiling. A stone bench along one end of the kitchen space may have provided a place to sit or work.

Other furnishings probably included pottery cooking and storage pots and a few cooking pots of brass or iron brought from Mexico. Manos and metates for grinding corn into masa harina for tortillas were ubiquitous even up to recent times, and surely were part of the kitchen equipment. Since they were used by Indian cooks who knelt on the floor before them, and cooking was done over floor-level fires, there were few tables or benches. The Spanish also introduced ovens, called *hornos*, freestanding adobe and clay structures that worked in the same way as beehive ovens elsewhere in the world and were, as they still are, outdoors.

Other Southwest colonists, as elsewhere, built very simple dwellings at first, and cooked outdoors or in fire pits under smoke holes in the roof, as the Native Americans did. As more homes and ranches were built, the very few that remain show a gradual progression from the later seventeenth-century *cocina con fogón de pastor* (kitchen with a shepherd's fireplace) to the eighteenth-century *cocina con fogón de campana* (kitchen with a bell-shaped fireplace). Spanish Colonial kitchens were furnished according to the householder's prosperity. Much work was done on the floor or, in more prosperous households, on simple tables. Households that could afford imported ceramics from Mexico or even China had decorative shelves hung on the wall

This *horno* was found in the Acoma Pueblo, in Valencia Country, New Mexico. (Courtesy of the Library of Congress, Historic American Buildings Survey, HABS, NM, 31-ACOMP, 1-80.)

for displaying dishes. Kitchens and an adjacent storeroom (*dispensa*) opened onto courtyards that served as work spaces in the same way as the yards adjacent to the separate Southern kitchens. If a household had a *horno*, it might be situated in the courtyard, too.

Other Food-Related Spaces

The less well-off any household was, the less likely it was to have more than one kitchen or to have a kitchen far from the main house. However, most households, even poorer ones, needed food-related work spaces. While city dwellers obtained their food supply daily from the market or from vendors selling door-to-door, country people had to store produce for their own use in other seasons or before they conveyed it to market. Cellars, storerooms, springhouses, dairies, pantries, smokehouses or smoke chambers, attics, and icehouses served as spaces for food and beverage preparation and storage. What region of the country the house was in, to what social class the household belonged, how large a household was served, and whether commercial food production was involved, determined where and how many of these spaces there were, and what their capacities were.

Cool Storage. Most homes needed a cool place to store root vegetables, fruits, pickles, dairy products, and barrels of salted meat, cider, beer, or wine, and, in cold seasons, fresh meat for short periods of time. House cellars or smaller underground spaces served these needs. Archaeological digs on sites of slave dwellings have uncovered pits in cabin floors that are interpreted as food storage places. Some households stored food for a short time in a spring or well, in containers set into the cold water or in the cooled air near it. Only the very wealthy built and maintained icehouses or dedicated large sections of cellars to wine storage.

Households engaged in dairying and making cheese and butter needed ample cool storage for milk and cream. If only enough for family use was required, a room on the north side of a house or in a cellar or a small springhouse might suffice, but larger operations might need a separate building equipped with many shelves to hold milk pans.

An icehouse like this one at Green Hill Plantation in Virginia took advantage of below-ground storage to make the ice last longer. (Courtesy of the Library of Congress, Historic American Buildings Survey HABS, VA, 16-LONI, V, 1H-1.)

Dry Storage. Large quantities of flour, meals, beans, peas, and similar dry foods were stored in barrels, casks, or chests. Smaller quantities were kept in sacks or bags hung from beams or pegs on walls. Only in larger, more prosperous homes was there a room dedicated to food storage; most people kept dry foods in the kitchen. For squashes, pumpkins, and onions, which rotted if kept in cool, damp cellars, householders needed winter storage in dry, cool spaces that never froze. Attics in warmer parts of the country might suffice, or lofts over warm kitchens in colder regions, even if those were also sleeping areas. Toward the end of the 1700s pantries appeared in prosperous homes, and gradually in more ordinary homes as well.

Smoking. Householders, especially in colder regions, sometimes built chimneys with smoke chambers in them. Others constructed freestanding smokehouses ranging in size from a fairly small space in

Plantation smokehouse. The Oaks Plantation in Leighton, Alabama, begun in the late Federal era, once had 300 slaves on its 10,000 acres. This smokehouse gives a sense of the scale of meat preservation on southern plantations. (Courtesy of the Library of Congress, Historic American Buildings Survey, HABS, ALA, 17-LEIT, V, 1-12.)

which four or five hams and a couple sides of bacon could be hung, to a small building. There are scattered examples of small plastered rooms through which a chimney ran with many hooks in the ceilings and a hole in the chimney that, when opened, let smoke into the space, where hams and slabs of bacon were hung for smoking. Larger setups usually implied commercial operations because much more meat could be processed than one family typically used in a year. Freestanding smokehouses, often large, were very common in the South because of the many hundreds of pounds of meat processed on plantations to feed both family and slaves.

THE OPEN HEARTH

During earliest settlement, a cooking fireplace dominated the main, or only, room of any home. Subsequently, once a space was designated as a kitchen, it had the largest fireplace in the house.

Fireplaces

Whether a fireplace and chimney were constructed of fieldstones, bricks, hardened clay applied to a wooden frame, or adobe brick, all cooking was done on its hearth over an open fire or on hot coals heaped next to the fire. Baking was done in wood-fired ovens or in kettles designed for baking.

During the 1600s and up to the late 1700s, fireplaces were deep and wide, with large openings leading upward into chimneys that gradually became smaller as they reached the roof peak. If there were other fireplaces in the home, the flues emptied into the main stack. These chimneys were inefficient by later standards, requiring great fires and drawing a great deal of warmth up and out of the house—certainly a blessing in southern summers but a distinct disadvantage in northern winters.

New Netherland Dutch colonial homes had jambless hearths with a hood projecting over the fireplace to catch the smoke and direct it up the chimney. The Dutch built in this fashion up to the mid-eighteenth century. In more prosperous homes in the later eighteenth century and early 1800s, descendants of Dutch settlers built kitchens that resembled English ones.

German settlers were accustomed to working on a hearth raised as high as thirty-six inches, on which they maintained small fires, using small pieces of wood. Many Germans came first to Pennsylvania, sometimes spending ten to twenty years there, before migrating into the South or West. They gradually adapted to American conditions and dropped the hearths to eighteen inches or even six inches. Plentiful firewood made a lowered hearth and wide fireplace opening more practical.

In the Southwest, fireplaces and hearths were considerably different from those in the East. The seventeenth-century hearth, in a *cocina*, whether it had a shepherd's fireplace (*fogón de pastor*) or not, was built along the wall or in the corner of a room, with a hole in the ceiling or a small chimney to draw smoke away. If it had a *fogón de pastor*, a platform of wood and adobe was built with one end over part of the hearth. These hearths, with openings not much wider than two feet, accommodated only small fires that probably sufficed to keep the corner of the room warm and dry.

This arrangement was succeeded by the eighteenth-century *cocina con fogón de campana* (kitchen with a bell-shaped fireplace), in which the fireplace also occupied a corner of the room and had a bell- or funnel-shaped chimney leading the smoke upward. As in the earlier southwestern fireplace, the opening was not large. Since New Mexico had a somewhat warmer climate, the huge hearths and blazes of the colder Northeast were unnecessary, and if a larger fire for roasting was wanted, it was built outdoors. Round, three-legged iron stands held pottery cooking pots and griddles for baking tortillas, Called *comales*, that were made of stone or, more rarely, iron. Iron, copper, and brass cooking utensils were costly in the Colonial Southwest because they had to be brought overland from Mexico by a wagon train that took a year and a half to reach New Mexico, making many stops along the way. Household use of metal competed with needs for military armament and farming equipment, and pieces of ironware, even simple tools, were bequeathed to the next generation. Much cookery was done in pottery vessels.

Modernizing Fireplaces

In 1796, Massachusetts-born Benjamin Thompson, a Loyalist who had fled to England during the Revolutionary War, published a work on fireplace design based on several years of working on improved cooking and heating methods. Thompson, upon being named a count, chose the name Rumford, after his wife's birthplace in New Hampshire. Thompson's design, the so-called Rumford fireplace,

Rumford fireplace and stove. The Randlett-May House kitchen in Portsmouth, New Hampshire, was equipped with a Rumford stove and oven. Besides a small fireplace with a crane, and an oven just to the right of the fireplace with a slightly curved door, there was another barrel-shaped oven with a firebox beneath. Inside the oven were shelves to bake on. On the window wall was a stew stove. The square iron doors beneath are for the fireboxes. A counter was installed later that covered the openings on the top of the stew stove where the cook placed pots and pans. (Courtesy of Historic New England/SPNEA.)

quickly became the standard form of fireplace. It was shallower and had a smaller chimney throat than earlier fireplaces. It burned less wood but radiated more heat. Older-style fireplaces were sometimes retrofitted as Rumford fireplaces. The old opening was filled in with brickwork and an oven was created on the side.

After the first decades of settlement, high-style gentry homes, particularly in Colonial cities, added stew stoves or *potagers*. These benchlike brick structures had small, usually square, surface openings fitted with iron grates. The fireboxes underneath the openings held a small fire, coals, or burning charcoal. Stew stoves were common in Europe, and had been for a couple centuries before Americans adopted them. They also appeared in more prosperous southwestern ranch homes in the later eighteenth century and into the nineteenth, but those were the result of Spanish influence.

Eastern gentry sometimes equipped their kitchens with charcoal burning grates on waist-high hearths, and jacks and spits for roasting. While even middle-class households might have spits, usually only the wealthy could afford jacks to drive them. Some jacks were built into the fireplace, powered by a vane in the chimney that turned as heat rose; some were driven, clockwork fashion, by weights and gears. In other instances, children were pressed into service to turn the jacks by hand or servants, often enslaved, did the work.

During the first decade of the 1800s, some gentry homes, particularly the most progressive and well-to-do, adopted Rumford designs for metal cooktops with fireboxes underneath, a kind of cross between the old *potagers* and the cookstove yet to come. There were also horizontal, barrel-shaped ovens with shelves in them, and cooking kettles set into brickwork heated by fireboxes beneath them and equipped with stove pipes that carried away the smoke. These were expensive installations and generally appeared only in wealthy homes, taverns, or institutional kitchens where quantity cooking was routinely performed.

Fireplace Equipment

Kitchen fireplaces needed a way for the cook to suspend a pot over the flames. During the 1600s and early 1700s, a lug pole of green wood or iron was installed inside the chimney, centered over where the fire was built. From this hung trammels (pothooks) from which cooks hung pots and kettles by their handles. To move a kettle on or off the fire, a cook stepped into the hearth opening, carefully avoiding the fire.

In the mid-1700s, lug poles were gradually replaced with cranes, iron arms hinged to one side of the fireplace opening that swung out, enabling the cook to take pots and kettles off the hooks without having to step into the fireplace. Rumford-style fireplaces required cranes because they closed off the chimney throat where the lug pole had been installed.

In many houses dating from this era, cranes were installed in fireplaces of parlors and bedrooms. This points to a more flexible use of rooms than might be imagined. In these fireplaces people heated water for hot tea or chocolate, warmed porridges or soups for tea or supper, or heated water for washing.

Many people used andirons to support burning logs, but perfectly usable cooking fires were built without them. Tongs, shovels or peels, and fire pans, on the other hand, were hard to do without. Cooks managed fires by using tongs to move burning wood. They used shovels and peels for moving hot coals, and fire pans for carrying live embers from one fireplace to another, the easiest way to start a new fire when one had gone out. Striking flint and steel into tinder to make a new fire was, in this era before matches, a common skill, but most households kept their fire alive by banking it at night under a deep bed of ash, then reviving it in the morning. If a fire went out, the householder carried coals from another fireplace or house, if there were nearby neighbors. Keeping fire was a valuable skill. Only the poorest households lacked at least this much fireplace equipment.

The Oven

Not all colonists had their own oven. Heating an oven required a great deal of fuel, which was scarce or costly in many parts of England and Europe. Some cooks were used to taking their bread and pastries to a baker's shop, where they rented oven space. In newly settled America, households sharing ovens was not unusual, but once settlers were past their first decades of clearing and building, having a fireplace oven or a freestanding oven outside became increasingly common even in middle-class homes.

The earliest northeastern ovens were frequently built into the chimney's back wall and used the chimney itself as the flue. Later in the 1700s, particularly after Rumford fireplaces were widely adopted, an oven at the side of the fireplace opening was more usual. This oven had its own flue leading into the chimney, and often an opening below it into which the hot embers and ash were shoveled when the oven was cleared for baking. Ovens were sometimes called beehive for their inside shape: most were round or oval with a dome rising to the center, and had wood or iron doors.

While the more usual practice in the East was to incorporate the oven into the fireplace, in some sections of the Middle Atlantic colonies and the South, colonists built ovens outdoors with roofs over them to protect them from weathering and cracking. In the Southwest, the *horno* introduced by Spanish colonists was open to the elements and was repaired as needed with extra clay when weathering and use cracked the dome. Outdoor ovens did not require chimneys, though the *horno* often had a small vent hole off-center in the roof, and the fire heating it billowed smoke into the air, to be blown away.

Kitchen Furniture

Few colonists immigrating to America, and few settlers moving westward, carried much furniture. For the first few years, a kitchen work surface might be little more than a board on the top of a barrel or a table that doubled as a dining table. Cooking pots and kettles sat to the side of the hearth. The few plates, bowls, cups, eating utensils, and small storage containers such as jars or bottles were kept on shelves. Sacks and bags hung from beams to hold dry foodstuffs. Stools, benches, and occasionally a chair provided seating.

As time went on, shelves and cupboards were added to kitchens. A table might be dedicated to work, and a different table designated for dining. Dressers, combinations of cupboard and shelves similar to what are now called hutches, appeared in some homes. Offering both a work surface and storage, they were sometimes built into the kitchen and sometimes freestanding. Chests holding meals and flours doubled as work surfaces. Some colonial kitchens had a dough box or trough that stored flour and served as a breadmaking workstation.

As in other colonial kitchens, Dutch settlers hung some cooking utensils from overhead beams or from pegs or hooks in walls, or placed them on shelves. Utensils of brass and copper, being more costly, were often displayed when not in use. Food was stored in casks, kegs, barrels, and baskets. Many kitchens had a cupboard, called a *pottenbank*, in which cooking pots and storage jugs were kept. Spoons were stored in a rack. In 1744, Dr. Alexander Hamilton, traveling through Albany, New York, observed that Dutch kitchens were very clean, that their cabinets and buffets were full of china, and that "they hang earthen or delft plates and dishes all round the walls in manner of pictures, having a hole drilled thro [*sic*] the edge of the plate or dish and a loop of ribbon put into it to hang it by."[1]

Throughout the Colonial era, and even after, poor people or the enslaved continued, in their homes, to rely on rudimentary kitchen furniture, perhaps only a table, a meal or flour chest, or a board-covered barrel. Where descriptions or inventories, even from gentry homes, fail to show kitchen furniture with work surfaces, cooks probably prepared food by holding bowls or cutting boards on their lap, perching on a stool, or even kneeling on the floor or hearth.

FUEL AND WATER

Fire and water were as essential to cooking as they were to life itself. In Colonial America, most cooks fueled their fires with wood and hauled water from wells.

Fuel

Open-hearth cooking required fuel. Settlers in nearly every part of eastern North America found abundant hardwood forests for building and for firewood. For some, plentiful fuel was a new experience; parts of England and Europe were denuded of forests. Whereas in the old country, gathering wood or digging peat had occupied much time, or buying fuel had meant out-of-pocket expense, merely clearing land for farming in the first decades of settlement generated much more firewood than most families would need for day-to-day heating and cooking. Further, charcoal making thrived, most of the charcoal intended for ironworks and blacksmiths, though some fueled kitchen stew stoves.

During the Colonial and Federal eras, most farms and plantations maintained wood lots to assure a supply of household firewood. In cities, firewood was carted in and sold in markets along with foodstuffs and hay. Firewood, especially supplies for urban areas, became more costly as the 1700s wore on, and was increasingly drawn from sources farther from the cities. This led to the wide adoption of the more fuel-efficient Rumford fireplaces at the eighteenth century's close, and eventually of cooking and heating stoves in the 1820s and 1830s.

In the Southwest, wood was harder to come by than in the heavily forested East. A sustainable supply available to the Native Americans was overstressed by the Hispanic settlers, and even though most common cookery techniques required only modest fires, by the end of the Colonial era, mule loads of wood were gathered, cut, and brought into the towns and settlements. Native American potters shifted from using wood to fire their pottery to using dried dung.

Water

The water supply determined where both settlements and individual houses were sited. The first settlements often shared a well or spring, around which a palisaded cluster of buildings was erected, and individual households carried water to their homes. Later, when settlement was dispersed, householders built near streams, cleared and enlarged springs, or dug wells close to the house. Most estate inventories from the period list pails and buckets with kitchen equipment, pointing to much water hauling.

In some instances, the house eventually encompassed the well, and while water still might have to be drawn manually, the supply was indoors, and in cold regions was less likely to freeze in winter. In southwestern homes, the courtyard may have been the site of the well, though most people carried water from a nearby stream.

Gradually pumps replaced pails. In some instances, a house might be sited to take advantage of a gravity-fed water supply running constantly from an uphill spring or well through a pipe into a kitchen, and draining out to troughs for animals.

People heated water in large teakettles or in kettles at the side of the fire. Dishwashing today, with plates and silverware immersed in hot, soapy water, was not the norm for most households until later in the Federal era. The appearance of "dish kettles" by name in estate inventories reveals the increasing prevalence of household dishwashing. Before then, platters, plates, and eating utensils were wiped with a damp rag and put back on a shelf. When a great deal of hot water was required—for example, for laundry or during butchering— very large kettles were set up in the side yard with a fire beneath to warm the water. Prosperous households might have a set kettle in brickwork with a firebox beneath it for heating water, but usually it was in a separate space, not the kitchen.

Cities addressed water supply early, establishing reservoirs and maintaining public hydrants or running pipes into cities from which individual homes got their supply. Even so, in many places, within a few decades of settlement, the water was not fit to drink.

COOKING METHODS AND UTENSILS

Colonists came prepared to begin housekeeping with a rudimentary set of cooking and fire-keeping equipment. Not all cooking activity required a specialized tool, and many utensils served more than one purpose. As refinement and gentility increased in importance, and as people prospered, they added more cooking equipment and attempted finer cookery.

Seventeenth-century colonists brought this basic set of cooking equipment with them. Left to right, back row: wrought-iron gridiron for broiling, brass kettle, spider with a long handle, skillet, redware cooking pot with feet, mortar and pestle, and andirons with hooks to hold a spit (seen in the center). Front row: trammel with ratchet, chain trammel with hook at each end, S-hooks, iron pot, and redware pipkin. (Courtesy of Plimoth Plantation, Plymouth, Massachusetts.)

Earliest Equipment

Colonists embarking from England or Europe for settlement almost anywhere in North America came with the equipment for the most basic food preparation. The Plimoth Company and the Virginia Company recommended or provided for their settlers at least a pot, a kettle, a frying pan, and a gridiron, plus a couple of skillets, a spit, some wooden platters, dishes, spoons, and trenchers. Settlers pressing westward carried a similar set of basic cooking gear and a comparable set of provisions, thus repeating the colonists' experience for nearly 250 years as frontiers were opened and newcomers cleared land, established temporary shelter, and made do until time and cash made improvement possible.

The Fire

Cooking on a wood fire was, and still is, not difficult, but because the fire changes in size and intensity as the firewood is consumed,

hearth cooking requires constant attention. While a large blaze effectively heated a room and the people in it, it was difficult to cook
on, so cooks built a large fire to start, then let it moderate, stoking
it steadily until it burned down to coals and maintained an even heat.
Some early accounts speak of a large backlog, held in place by
andirons, against which a smaller fire was maintained, gradually burning through the log till it was reduced to coals. Cooks used coals to
create smaller "burners" of varying intensities on the hearth. In fact,
large, open hearths were very flexible spaces. Cooks hung pots and
kettles over the fire, baked in reflecting devices at the sides, roasted
in front of or at the sides of the fire, stewed gently or made sauces
on small piles of coals, or set a bake kettle at the side with coals on
top and beneath it. All of this could occur simultaneously.

Boiling, Poaching, Simmering, and Stewing

The most basic cooking method, boiling, called for immersing food
in a liquid and cooking it, usually at a high temperature. Most boiling was done in iron pots, often footed, or in kettles of various sizes.
Equipped with handles called bales, these cooking vessels were hung
from trammels or S-shaped pothooks, which allowed the cook to
move the pot farther from or nearer to the fire, depending on how
high a temperature was needed. A cook changed the temperature
from hard boil to simmer by raising the pot away from the flames or
letting the fire die down. Cooks boiled anything from meats to grains
and vegetables.

Poaching, essentially boiling very gently at a lower temperature,
was considered a good way to cook fish. Prosperous households acquired fish kettles, usually oval-shaped and long enough to hold a
whole fish.

To boil puddings, early seventeenth-century cooks usually stuffed
ingredients into casings made from animal intestines. Later, cooks
tied the pudding in a dampened and floured cloth before immersing
it in water. By the early 1800s, tin containers with tight lids were set
into cooking pots to steam.

When a longer, slower cooking time was needed for stewing—
cooking food in smaller amounts of liquid—the cook set the pot to
one side, or even down the hearth, on a bed of coals. When the coals
cooled, the cook added more, shoveled from under the logs burning
toward the back of the hearth.

In the early seventeenth century, redware pottery vessels were used this way, especially by the Dutch, German, and Spanish colonists. Dutch cooking containers were often footed and were as broad and open as a skillet. They appear frequently in Dutch genre paintings. Enslaved Africans also used a type of pottery called colonoware in this way. Colonoware was made without using a potter's wheel by building a vessel up with coiled strands of red clay, smoothing it, and firing it in an open fire instead of a kiln. Both the Native Americans and enslaved Africans made and used it. In the Spanish Colonial Southwest, Spanish settlers used Indian–made pottery to cook in during the seventeenth and early eighteenth centuries. Toward the end of the eighteenth century, Hispanic New Mexicans, much influenced by the Indians, began making domestic cooking vessels, including micaceous wares. Bean pots and Crock-Pots are the modern applications of this technology.

For making sauce or gravy, or heating small amounts of food, small, sometimes footed, iron or brass pans or posnets or pottery pipkins were used, set directly on a small bed of coals or on a trivet over coals.

Frying

After pots and kettles, the cooking utensils most frequently mentioned as recommended equipment for immigrants and settlers or on estate inventories were skillets. They were used for stewing as well as frying, and also were set over coals. Some were three or four inches or more deep and made of iron or brass. Dutch and German skillets were often made of redware pottery. Some had tight-fitting lids on which hot coals were laid to create a kind of oven. Skillets in the seventeenth and eighteenth centuries usually had three or four short legs.

Frying pans were metal, shallower than skillets, and did not usually have feet, so they rested on a trivet or directly on coals. Many had long handles so the cook could manipulate them at a distance from the fire.

The term "spider," which today is often applied to a cast-iron frying pan, was a kind of skillet with long legs, and often a long handle as well, and almost always was made of iron or sheet metal. Cooks simmered, stewed, or fried in a spider. True deep-fat frying was done in pots or kettles.

Griddles, flat metal pans, were hung over the fire and used for cooking small cakes or breads. When early cooks spoke of "baking" pancakes or bannocks, the process was somewhere between frying over a fire and baking in an oven. Most breads baked on a griddle had to be turned so that heat struck both sides of it, and while the pan might be greased, it did not usually have so much fat that the bread was thought of as fried. Similarly, hoecake, simple bread made with cornmeal, water, and salt, mixed to make thin cakes, implies that a farmer's tool doubled as the cooking utensil. This is almost entirely a southern phenomenon, and while some people, most notably enslaved Africans, may indeed have used their hoes to cook on, there is evidence from a store advertisement in Williamsburg that "baking hoes" were made for the purpose of cooking.[2]

Broiling and Grilling

Gridirons were made of wrought iron, were usually rectangular (though sometimes round), and had legs to hold them above the coals. Cuts of meat, poultry, or fish could be laid on them to broil. They were common except in the poorest households. Today this kind of cooking with bottom heat is called grilling, and when top heat cooks the food, it is broiled. To make top heat in the hearth-cooking era, a cook placed a fire shovel or long-handled iron tool called a salamander in coals until it was very hot, then held it over the food's surface until the food browned. Salamanders were much more common in wealthy households; less prosperous ones made do with fire shovels.

Roasting

Roasting is cooking with radiant heat; it was usually reserved for meat, although other foods, such as apples, also were set before a fire. To be roasted, meat had to be supported before the fire on a spit to which it was skewered, hung from a stout cord on a nail or hook in the chimney face or lintel, or propped up before the fire. Spits were sometimes supported on hooks on the upright shanks of andirons and turned by hand, or were part of a jack mechanism. Meat hung by a cord turned when the cord was twisted, unwinding and then rewinding. Cooks put a dripping pan underneath roasts to catch the fat and juices to make gravy.

Much ingenuity was dedicated to designing roasting devices throughout the Colonial and Federal eras. One device sometimes seen in museums and historic sites looks like a small brass barrel on legs with part of the side cut away. A spit installed vertically was driven by a clockwork device at the top, which was wound up and turned the spit until it ran down.

Roasting required a bright, clear fire—lively flames and no smoke. Roasting instructions always cautioned the cook to make up the fire in proportion to the meat being prepared—as long as or even a bit longer than the roast itself. Roasting consumed quite a bit of wood, another instance of America's early firewood abundance that put a previously less accessible cooking technology in the homes of people who formerly did not enjoy it.

At the end of the 1700s, along with more efficient fireplaces came the use of reflective roasting devices called tin kitchens. They had a curved reflective side and bottom, enclosed ends, one open side, and a spit through the center on which the meat or poultry was skewered inside the device. It was placed with the open side facing the fire. The curved bottom collected the drippings, and some of these devices had spouts at one end for pouring them out for gravy. Tin kitchens were costly at first, being imported from England, but gradually American tinsmiths made them inexpensively enough that by the early 1800s middle-class households could afford them. People considered tin kitchens a great improvement in roasting technology and, by confining the heat, they reduced the time and fuel needed.

Baking

Cooking food by dry, retained heat was done in ovens or devices that worked like ovens. (So-called reflector ovens, which baked by radiant heat, in the manner of roasting, did not appear until later.) A cook baked eggs, potatoes, partially shucked corn, or any food wrapped in something like a leaf by burying it in hot ashes near a live fire.

Breads, pies, cakes, and other pastries needed an oven or a baking kettle (sometimes called a Dutch oven). These devices had tight-fitting lids and were placed over a bed of hot coals laid the hearth, with more hot coals heaped on top or around. When the coals died, more were added until the baking was done.

To heat a brick, stone, or clay oven, the cook built a fire inside the oven, letting it burn briskly for two or more hours, until the oven was covered inside with fine white ash and the floor was thick with hot coals. The cook then shoveled out the coals, or perhaps left behind a few, and swept the floor clean. To prevent scorching, cooks sometimes swished a damp broom around the inside of the oven to cool it slightly. At that point, the bread and baked goods were put inside by hand or with a peel, a long-handled wooden or metal spatula-like tool similar to the ones used by pizza bakers today, and the oven was closed.

Temperatures in the ovens started out very high, gradually declined, and cooled. An experienced cook placed the baked goods in the oven in such a way as to be able to remove items that baked the quickest first. The long, gradual temperature decline was fine for foods that needed lower temperatures, such as custards or pots of beans. An oven with no temperature control baffles cooks today, but early cooks were accustomed to the varying temperatures, and adjusted cooking times accordingly by rebuilding fires or adding hot coals to the oven when a higher temperature was needed again.

How often the oven was heated depended on the household's size or how elaborately it wished to present food. Farm households with several family members and hired help might need to bake twice a week—in the North, usually on Wednesday and Saturday—to provide sufficient yeast bread, pies, and puddings for everyone. Small households baked once a week, often on Saturday. Gentry households that entertained and wished to set their tables with meat pies, fancy baked goods, and fresh bread every day would bake more frequently.

No matter how often they baked, cooks timed their work so that bread was kneaded and formed into loaves, crusts were rolled and pies were assembled, and puddings and cakes were mixed and ready to be baked when the oven was sufficiently heated. Long experience taught how much time was needed to have everything ready at the right moment. It required skill and attention.

Households lacking an oven might arrange to use a neighbor's oven until, if ever, they had one of their own. Some kind of exchange in cash or goods paid for the oven's use.

Toasting

Hardly ever on the list of absolute kitchen necessities, toasting devices appeared after the era of first settlement. Swiveling wrought-iron bread racks mounted on feet at the end of long handles showed up on inventories in the last half of the 1600s. Before that time, cooks impaled bread on long-handled forks and held it before the fire, turning it by taking it off the fork and putting the untoasted side toward the flames. Forks continued to suffice for families not prosperous enough to acquire toasters. Bread could also be laid on gridirons, and flipped over to toast both sides.

Chopping and Cutting

Most cutting and chopping was done with knives. Along with other small utensils hardly ever listed on estate inventories, knives were personal tools that many people carried with them at all times. Some households had chopping knives and wooden trays or bowls in which to use them. The cook put food into the bowl and, grasping the handle on top, chopped the curved blade into the food until it was sufficiently fine. This was how hash, minced meat, and sausage were made.

Nicks and fractures found on bones uncovered in archaeological digs of historic sites reveal that butchers in this era usually used axes and cleavers for cutting up large animals, such as cattle, pigs, sheep, and wild game such as deer. Smaller cuts of meat were prepared in the kitchen by the cook with a heavy knife. Sawn cuts of meat did not appear until the 1800s.

Mixing, Beating, Turning, Skimming, and Straining

Wooden spoons, stirring sticks (some called mush sticks), and bundles of small sticks bound together served for mixing, stirring, and beating. Skimmers—of brass for the well-to-do, of iron for others, and sometimes no more than a clamshell for the poor—allowed cooks to remove boiled food from liquid, and also to remove cream from the top of milk or to skim a boiling pot. Dippers and ladles transferred liquids from one vessel to another. Small peels or spatulas were used for blending ingredients, and possibly for turning as well, although deft cooks loosened a pancake and flipped it over in the air by snapping the frying pan upward. Some households had sieves for sifting flour and meal. For pureeing something like cooked pumpkin, or straining lumps out of a sauce, cooks used pottery colanders.

While poorer households did not have specialized tools for these operations, they accomplished them by using one tool for many things: one spoon can stir, beat, skim, lift food from hot liquid, then serve food at table, and be used as an eating utensil. The more gentrified the household, the more specialized tools became, and the more likely they were to be made of more expensive metals (e.g., brass or copper) than of wrought iron.

Measuring and Weighing

Sometime during the era from first settlement to the early 1800s, many Americans abandoned the long-standing European practice of weighing ingredients and turned to measuring by the cup or tea-spoon. Gentry households, particularly in the South, continued to weigh ingredients longer than northern or western middle-class households.

Scales and weights were used for weighing ingredients. Early inventories show relatively few of them, and those appear mostly in prosperous households. Measures for dry quarts or pecks, and liquid measures for gills, pints, quarts, and gallons, appear in many more instances. Fine cookery requiring the greatest care in measuring did not appear in poorer households, so they did not require measures. When, in the years after the Revolution, more people aspired to finer cooking, they adapted household utensils to the job—cups, teacups, spoons, glasses. Quart and pint measures are mentioned in recipes well into the 1800s.

When a recipe called for butter as big as an egg or a walnut, the cook who often handled eggs and walnuts had a clear idea of how large that was. Other measures, such as "handfuls," "a little," or "enough," implied a cook who had seen what a batter or dough looked like when a handful, a little, or enough flour had been added. Seasonings were added to taste, so amounts were often not specified. Early Americans were apparently unconcerned about the variations in the end product that results from this kind of measuring.

Large scales called steelyards were less common in estate inventories until the 1800s. These were particularly useful for weighing large quantities—for example, calculating how many pounds of meat one had in order to determine the amount of brine to mix to preserve it. Anyone engaged in selling or trading meat weighed it, and since diaries and account books reflect how carefully people kept track of meat they shared and sold, it must be assumed there were more steelyards and weights and scales than appear in the written record.

Brewing

One of the housewife's essential skills from earliest settlement through the early 1800s was brewing beer and ale for family use. As observed earlier, English, Dutch, and German settlers were accustomed to bread and beer with meals. Colonial cities and larger towns had both breweries and bakeries, although some urban housewives continued to brew and bake. Diaries of rural housewives reveal that they baked and brewed on the same day; both activities required yeast, with the brewing generating more. This pair of activities was embodied at Pennsbury Manor, north of Philadelphia, where Pennsylvania Colony founder William Penn ordered the construction of a brew house that had a brick oven for baking.

Brewing depended upon barley, the favored grain for malting (sprouting), and hops, which flavored the beverage and supported proper fermentation. Malt was valuable enough to be listed on inventories with other stored foods, such as meat, cheese, and vegetables. Malting was done both by housewives and by maltsters, who practiced malting as a trade. Housewives kept the yeast for beginning the brewing, tended the beer as it worked, and stored it in barrels or bottles when it was ready. They also harvested yeast from brewing, gathering up the foamy barm, which rose to the top of the fermenting mixture, and the residue at the bottom when the beer had been drawn off. Both were used to begin a new batch of yeast for bread. Because beers and ales were considered appropriate for family use, brewing had to be done frequently enough to maintain a steady supply.

Dairying

The care of milk cows and poultry was considered the housewife's work. To her and her female children or servants fell the twice-daily job of milking and setting out the milk in pans in a cool place, to allow cream to rise.

The women skimmed cream and churned it into butter, using a wooden or pottery churn with a wooden dasher. When the butter had formed solid lumps that separated from the buttermilk, they washed the butter in a wooden tray or bowl, using a wooden tool called a clasher to knead the butter until the water ran clear. The housewife chose at that point whether to salt the butter, to promote preservation. Because making butter was a seasonal activity, following cows' calving and feeding on grass until they were bred and dried off, some provision had to be made for keeping a butter supply when no new butter could be made or purchased. To do that, housewives packed the butter into a wooden container called a firkin or into crocks and covered the top with salt, or else put butter into brine.

Making cheese was another of the housewife's responsibilities. She made soft cheeses, similar to modern-day ricotta, for immediate consumption, and hard cheeses, such as cheddar, to store for aging and later consumption. Soft cheeses required no special equipment beyond perhaps a colander for draining the curds. Brass kettles sufficed for heating the milk, and if she was making hard cheeses, the housewife needed a cheese press and hoops to squeeze excess moisture from the curds.

Making cheese also required the housewife to collect the lining of a calf's stomach, when it was butchered, for a source of rennet. She salted and dried the stomach lining, stretched on a hoop of wood; when she needed to make cheese, she clipped pieces from it and soaked them in water that was poured into the heated milk. Rennet contained the enzyme necessary for curdling the milk to convert it into solids (the curds) and liquid (whey). The whey, drained off, was fed to pigs, though some families might enjoy a meal of curds and whey on cheese-making day. The curds were emptied into a cloth-lined hoop, and a wooden disk placed on top of them was screwed down gradually to press out the whey. Homes lacking a cheese press could substitute a rock or other heavy weight as long as sufficient, even pressure squeezed out the whey (if left in, it would spoil the cheese).

Cheese and butter added variety to the diet and, more important, preserved highly perishable milk and cream. Because dairying was women's work, colonial settlements in which men without families predominated, imported cheese. This was true of parts of the Chesapeake and early frontier areas for a time. Where making cheese and butter was important to a farm's economy, as it increasingly became in the early 1800s in the Northeast, it ceased being women's work alone and whole families were involved in the effort.

Tending poultry and gathering eggs also fell to the women and children. Colonists routinely kept chickens as well as other domesticated fowl, but most were allowed the freedom of the yard; little care went to feeding or attending to them except when snow covered the ground. Hens found their own places to roost: trees, barns, or sheds. Housewives and children learned the hens' habitual laying places and gathered the eggs there, allowing enough hens to set and hatch eggs to continue the flock. When hens ceased laying as the days grew shorter in late October, families used up what eggs there were, and made do without them until the hens began to lay again in February. When eggs were plentiful, they joined butter and cheese as marketable commodities.

PRESERVING

Food preservation is an ancient art, and nearly every kind of foodstuff—grains, legumes, vegetable, fruits, meat, and fish—can have its useful life extended past harvest. For much of human history, people have shown wealth and status by serving great varieties of food, and food out of season. Most people, especially those who live in climates with seasons during which no food can be grown, have sought to eliminate or reduce seasonal scarcity. Most American colonists needed to provide for sufficient food year round, but they also desired the variety that preservation techniques assured.

The other preservation method widely used in colonial America, besides cool storage of fresh foods and preserving milk as butter and cheese, were salting, fermenting, drying and smoking, pickling in vinegar, and preserving with sugar or alcohol. It was possible to preserve most foods more than one way: for example, fruits could be dried; preserved in sugar syrup or in an alcohol such as brandy; or their juice could be fermented into wine or cider. Some foods were subjected to a two-step preservation process: meat could be kept in brine, but it might then be smoked or dried.

Choosing a food preservation method depended not only on climate but also on custom, ingredient availability, and personal taste. Preparing jerked (dried) meat is hard to do in humid climates, where it becomes moldy or rancid before it has dried sufficiently. Salting and smoking might then be the best preservation choice. While cabbage can be fermented into sauerkraut, as the German settlers often did, the English preferred to pickle it. If salt was scarce, less could be used in a brine than in a dry salting process. Where sugar was very costly, a family might rather eat all their strawberries and raspberries fresh, if they grew them at all, or dry them if their climate permitted, and not attempt to enjoy them in another season. When a household could afford sugar, the family might prefer strawberry jellies and jams, or might make strawberry wine.

Keeping Food Fresh

Food was stored or distributed fresh until it was in danger of spoiling. For example, butchering of large animals was done in cold weather. In the North, some of the meat might be allowed to freeze in the frigid winter air until needed, when it would be thawed and cooked. Most families knew how much meat to consume fresh, and brined or salted and smoked the balance. In the South, where there was less chance of relying on natural freezing, more meat was preserved sooner.

In warm weather, farmers butchered smaller animals such as lambs or calves, and shared fresh meat among relatives or close friends, who returned the favor. Diaries and account books reveal exchanges, with entries recording how many pounds of meat were taken and given. Sometimes the exchanges were described as "loans," implying that an equal amount of the same kind of meat was due to be returned. These exchanges provided households with the fresh meat they always preferred. City dwellers obtained fresh meat from butchers who continuously sold enough that preservation was seldom necessary.

Cooking and Potting

Cooking extends the useful life of most foods, particularly meat and fish, and was often the first step in some preservation processes. To pot meat, a cook boiled or baked meat or poultry until it was very tender, pounded it into a paste with a mortar and pestle, mixed it with spices, salt, pepper, and butter or melted animal fat, and then packed it tightly into earthenware or pottery jars, and sealed the top with melted butter or animal fat. Kept cold, this would last for a while, and was easily spread on bread, as canned deviled ham is used today. Sometimes meats were baked in pies, with melted butter poured in to exclude air, and stored until wanted. Caveaching fish was a variation on this. Heavily seasoned mackerel slices or pieces were fried in oil and then stored in a vinegar pickle on which more oil was poured to exclude air.

These were effective short-term storage techniques, although sometimes cookery literature makes more generous claims for probable storage time. And while cookbooks, both printed and manuscript, give instructions for these preservation methods, rarely is there an account of anyone actually eating these foods, so the recipes' actual usefulness is unclear. An exception is mincemeat which was enormously popular. Mincemeat combined cooked meat (often beef or venison) with suet, apples, currants or raisins, citrus peel, and brandy or cider. It was packed in earthenware jars from which quantities were scooped when needed, or baked into pies and kept cold to be reheated later.

Salting and Brining

Meat, fish, and some vegetables were preserved by salting or brining. Most bacteria responsible for food spoilage will not grow in a salty environment. Salting food replaces the water in meat and fish with a salty brine, and also begins a drying process by extracting moisture from the food.

Salt was so essential for food preservation, particularly for meat and fish, that new settlers brought salt with them and looked for nearby sources. Hardship was often expressed in terms of "meat with no salt."

Light salting was termed corning, and merely required the cook or butcher to rub the exterior of the meat or fish with salt. This preserved meat for up to a week or more in cold weather, and a shorter time in warm weather. The longer the storage time required, the longer the salting process.

Dry salting, used to make bacon, for example, required cooks or butchers to spread salt, sometimes mixed with brown sugar and saltpeter, over the meat's surface. (Saltpeter, sodium nitrate, maintained the meat's red color and boosted preservation somewhat.) This work was sometimes done in a staved container, called a powdering tub, that held the salt while the meat was placed in it to be rolled and rubbed all over before it was put in a barrel. The salt drew out the meat's moisture, which was allowed to drain away. Meat, mostly beef, pork, and mutton, was also salted heavily all over the outside and put into barrels. As the salt drew water from the meat or fish, it formed brine, in which people sometimes continued to keep the meat. Salt, sugar, and saltpeter were also dissolved in hot water, and when the water cooled, it was poured over the meat in the barrel. This process was sometimes called pickling, but should not be confused with the pickling that used vinegar.

Which of these procedures was used depended on how fatty the meat was, how the meat was to be used, how long it would be stored, and whether drying or smoking would follow. Pork, including hams, bacon, and sausage, was more often salted than beef because its saturated fat readily absorbed salt. Some cuts of beef, however, such as the fatty brisket and beef sausages made with lean and fat meat, took salt well and were even improved by it. Under some circumstances, such as salting beef for export or for army use or aboard ships, nearly all the beef animal was salted, which rendered some cuts particularly tough.

Fishermen very often salted fish aboard their fishing vessels as soon as they caught the fish. When alewives, shad, and salmon ran up rivers to spawn, fishermen cleaned and salted them nearly as soon as they were caught. The salt both began dehydrating the fish and changed the chemistry of the natural liquid in the fish that would otherwise be prone to spoiling. White-fleshed fish such as cod were taken ashore for drying on racks called flakes, a practice that hardly changed from the late Middle Ages up to the mid-1800s. Oilier fish such as mackerel, shad, and herring were stored in barrels in the brine that formed when they were salted. Occasionally these fish were smoked.

A few vegetables could be and were salted, cucumbers in particular. Although cookery literature provides instructions for salting green beans and peas, there is scant mention in diaries or narratives of anyone doing so.

Smoking and Drying

Smoking and drying extended the life of meat or fish even longer than salting or brining. Most English or European settlers preferred to smoke their salted meats if they wished to keep them for use later, particularly if they lived in more humid sections of the country.

Before smoking, meat and fish was salted or brined. Smoking dried the meat slightly, further diminishing chance of spoilage, and the smoky exterior discouraged insects, particularly flies. Meats, especially hams and bacon, were subjected to longer and more thorough smoking and drying in warmer regions. In fact, any threat of spoilage, such as prolonged heat and humidity, called for a new smoky fire to be kindled and a fresh layer of smoke to protect the meat as the gentle heat further dried it. Attending to the condition of stored meat was another household task.

Native Americans were accustomed to drying meat, a process termed jerking, more easily done in drier regions. In the Southwest, it was possible to dry meat without salting it at all.

Well-cured meats and fish required soaking and boiling to prepare them for consumption, both to rehydrate them and to remove excess saltiness. Today salting and smoking are not absolutely necessary for meat preservation, but meats are still processed in these ways because their flavors are pleasant and they add variety to diets. This is also true of making pickles and fruit preserves.

Simple Drying

Meat and fish were sometimes dried or partly dried after salting. Other foods were simply dried, most notably peas, beans, and grains. Certain fruits and vegetables lent themselves to slicing and drying, particularly apples, squash, and pumpkins, although they were also kept whole and fresh for a few months. Drying guaranteed their usefulness from harvest well into the following summer. Work bees to pare and cut apples for drying, together with shucking corn and making apple butter, were social occasions.

Whether any other fruit was dried depended largely on the climate and the cost or availability of sugar. Highly perishable soft berries—strawberries, raspberries, and blackberries—were rarely dried until more advanced drying technology was developed in the nineteenth century. Grapes could be dried to make raisins, but were more frequently eaten fresh or made into wine, and raisins were imported instead.

Pickling in Vinegar

Vinegar's acidity prevents spoilage of vegetables, fruits, meats, and even shellfish. From earliest settlement through the 1800s, pickling was an important form of food preservation, and vinegar was as necessary a staple as salt. Cookery books offered instructions for making vinegar, and many people made their own from apple cider or wine. Homemade vinegar varied in acidity, which affected both its preservative qualities and the favor of pickled food.

As salting was the usual way to preserve meat, pickling was the usual way to preserve vegetables, particularly the more perishable vegetables that could not be dried or effectively stored cold, such as cucumbers and green beans. Some fruits, including peaches, apples, and plums, were pickled, as were oysters, mussels, and clams. Few pickling instructions call for vinegar alone, but incorporate salt, sugar, and/or spices as well. Pickled food was stored in earthenware jars and crocks, or in wooden casks or kegs, in cool parts of the house. Few inventories fail to mention these kinds of containers.

Fermenting

Some foods were preserved by controlled fermentation. Clearly, wine, cider, perry (fermented fruit juice), and even beer, ale, and other alcoholic beverages, are a way of capturing valuable carbohydrates by fermentation and of adding value to an otherwise lower-value grain. Cheese, as fermented milk, is a way of saving milk for another season. Some vegetables, especially cucumbers and cabbage, also can be fermented and result, respectively, in sour pickles and sauerkraut. The process requires salting the vegetables and allowing them to remain at a fairly warm temperature until they begin to work. When the process was over, the vegetables were stored in a cold place.

Making sauerkraut was common among German settlers, but caught on slowly with their English neighbors.

Sweet Preserves

As with other food-saving processes, preserving was done only seasonally, usually once a year when the fruit was harvested. Making sweet preserves is often described in cookbooks and manuscript recipe books of the era. The generic terms "preserves" and "sweetmeats" described a way to store fruit for out-of-season use, usually as whole as possible, the way modern canned fruit is processed. The simplest method, often referred to as pound-for-pound, called for equal weights of fruit and sugar boiled together until jellying was observed. (The word "jelly" for most of this period referred specifically to a dish made with gelatin and served as part of dessert.) Other preserves included marmalades and, later, jams. Apple butter evolved among German settlers as a replacement for their accustomed plum butter. Apples grew better here than plums, but both fruits formed a smooth, thick preserve when cooked for a long time with sugar and their juices.

The sugared fruits were placed in jars and glasses, which were covered with paper soaked in brandy and sometimes sealed further with a dampened bladder stretched over the mouth of the jar and allowed to dry and shrink to fit tightly. If mold formed, it was merely scraped off.

Sugar's cost meant the well-to-do were most likely to make preserves, and to a certain extent, preserves were reserved as food for invalids. Tinned copper and brass kettles were considered the best utensils for making preserves, and their relatively high cost was another factor in limiting preserves mostly to prosperous households.

Brandying

Archaeological digs have revealed a fair amount of evidence for brandying as a way of preserving fruits. Whole cherries were dropped into a bottle and covered with brandy, as bottles with cherry pits in them reveal. Peaches also were brandied, then preserved in sugar syrup.

COOKS AND COOKING

During the Colonial and Federal eras, white society tended to divide all work along gender lines. There are notable exceptions, and the occasional female blacksmith or soldier emerges from the historic record, but most women tended house and men pursued trades or business, the military, and farming.

Women's Work

Women contributed to their household economy both by the judicious management of their farms' products and by working for cash in some craft, and sometimes by supplying food. Women took in boarders, and ran taverns and inns where travelers and others bought meals.

Few widows or widowed men still in middle age remained unmarried for very long. One reason for this was that women's work formed half of the subsistence equation. Men in colonial America, even if they had a trade, often farmed as well. They raised livestock and planted field crops of grains and fodder for animals, but once the food was harvested and brought into the house, it was the woman's responsibility to turn it into a meal or store it for use another time. A woman might, under straitened circumstances, perhaps with the help of male relatives, attempt to operate a farm, but generally the work needed at least two people, with help from children and/or servants if all they hoped for was survival. Prospering required much more help.

In early Colonial America there were regional characteristics to this equation. Many New England colonists immigrated to North America in family groups, husbands and wives with children, with the intention to build communities and to farm. Because New England did not have a successful single cash crop, there was less need for servant labor there. Farms had diversified products, and housewives produced part of them.

In the Colonial Chesapeake, however, many colonists were men arriving alone to obtain land and grow tobacco. A cash crop such as tobacco created a market for food and food products produced elsewhere. Raising tobacco was labor-intensive, and was considered a male activity until slavery was established, whereupon field work was done by men and women alike. Young men were recruited by agents in England to work in the Chesapeake, and for most of the seventeenth century the immigrants to the region were men. The women who did migrate, particularly in the first half of the century, were usually married. Toward the end of the seventeenth century and the start of the eighteenth, more women migrated to the Chesapeake, many as indentured servants whose domestic work was valuable enough, although sometimes their indenture periods were slightly shorter than those of male servants. Upon gaining her freedom, a woman could anticipate marriage and an opportunity to have a home and family of her own.[3]

Thus the average white woman almost anywhere in the Colonies cooked; milked cows and made butter and cheese; baked bread and pastries; brewed beer, made wine and cordials; took care of poultry; cultivated the kitchen garden (vegetables used in daily cooking); prepared remedies and special food for the sick; and assisted with butchering, particularly preparing meat for preservation and what is called secondary butchering, which turned large pieces of meat into cuts ready for the table. All the household was called on to help with harvesting grain, and women and all capable children worked in the fields with men, cutting wheat and rye.

Housewives also monitored the family's food supply to check for signs of spoiling, to determine when a food should be used, and to keep storage spaces clean. Failure to do any of this might put a family's food supply at risk, sometimes with dire results if there was no alternative supply or sufficient cash to buy it. The housewife's attention had economic value.

Enslaved Cooks

Among enslaved people, the line dividing gender-appropriate work was blurred by the requirement that some women work as field hands. Slave cooks in the North or in the South, however, were usually women. Clearly not all households could afford slaves, and owning slaves usually implied relative wealth. The implications for food are that in households where slaves cooked, a higher-style gentry cookery, with its concomitant increased effort, was supported by the labor-supply. This helps explain, in part, how labor-intensive traditional cookery lasted longer in the South than elsewhere—for example, the continued use of yeast or beaten egg whites in making cakes when cooks elsewhere in the country turned to chemical leaven.

Black women cooks were valuable as skilled practitioners. Combining their own knowledge with the instructions given them by the mistress of the household, they were responsible for what was served on the owner's table and also for feeding their own families. Slave cooks were sometimes isolated from other slaves by the requirement of living in the or near the master's house, to be handy to the kitchen.

Their work put them at risk for violence if they failed to meet the master's or mistress's expectations. Cookery skill enabled some women slaves to become street vendors. Travelers in Charleston, South Carolina, New Orleans, and Philadelphia in the late Colonial era observed and described black women food vendors. Some women purchased their freedom and became caterers or bakers.

Food Professionals

Towns of any size had commercial food businesses. Millers, bakers, and butchers were the most common, with brewers, maltsters, and confectioners found in larger towns and cities. Millers were essential to flour production and ground the grain brought to them by individual farmers. As part of the fee, or toll, they retained a portion of the flour for sale elsewhere. Bakers usually made bread of various kinds, including fine white and coarser rye or blends; rolls and some pastries might also be part of the baker's offering. Some bakers rented space in their ovens for the use of households lacking them. Butchers in towns bought animals driven in on foot, and slaughtered to provide a constant supply of fresh meat; some also salted and smoked meat. Other butchers traveled from farm to farm in butchering season to help with the slaughtering of cattle or pigs, receiving meat or cash in payment.

Brewers were found in larger towns and cities, making beer and selling yeast for household use. Maltsters sprouted grains such as barley, and roasted them for making beer. As a more specialized trade, they were most likely in cities where a large population demanded malt for making beer. Distillers were in larger cities, making rum or whiskey. Confectioners made a variety of sweets: small to larger cakes, pastries, candies, and ice cream.

NOTES

1. Carl Bridenbaugh, ed., *Gentleman's Progress: The Itinerarium of Dr. Alexander Hamilton 1744* (Chapel Hill: University of North Carolina Press, 1948), 72.

2. Greenhows Store advertisement, *Virginia Gazette* (Purdie & Dixon), September 29, 1768, p. 2, col. 3; image of page online at http://www.past portal.com/cwdl_new/VA_Gazet/Images/PD/1768/0159hi.jpg.

3. Alan Taylor, *American Colonies: The Settling of North America* (New York: Viking, 2001), 143.

CHAPTER 4
EATING HABITS

Eating habits include everything concerning daily food. In recent years "foodways" has been applied to their study because it is an all-encompassing term that comprises agriculture, food production and distribution, cooking technology, customs and beliefs, and daily, seasonal, and occasional habits. The term "culinary history," which sheds particular light on the development of recipes over time, is sometimes used to describe food habits. Other people use the word "cuisine" to describe a group's cooking and eating habits. In French, *cuisine* means "kitchen," and so cuisine is what happens in kitchens, and describes where food comes from, and how it is cooked and served year round.

HOW TO KNOW WHAT PEOPLE ATE

It cannot be known for sure what anyone ate in past times. Food is ephemeral; as soon as it is eaten, it disappears. A student of Colonial furniture can actually see, measure, touch, even sit in a chair from an earlier time. Learning what people ate requires turning to a variety of incomplete sources.

Archaeological Evidence and Material Culture

With food, what little material is left consists of archaeological evidence—largely bones, shells, pits from fruit, seeds, and pollen. Archaeology is growing in technological ability to analyze the chemical traces of oil, wine, and grain that lodge in cracks of jars and containers, and these can reveal a little more.

There are also the cooking utensils and tableware that were used to prepare and eat the food. Tools show wear that reveals how they were used. Some historians re-create meals, using cooking equipment and recipes from the past, in order to understand how people cooked then, and to discover what the food tasted like.

Paintings and Drawings

There are paintings and drawings of food and meals. For example, many Dutch still-life paintings show baked goods, fruits, vegetables, meat, and fish, all carefully rendered in colorful detail, that reveal what was eaten by the wealthy Dutch during the period when such paintings were fashionable. There are not similar paintings of, for instance, African American food of the seventeenth and eighteenth centuries.

Written Descriptions

Written descriptions of meals tell something, but not everything, about food habits, and it is hard to know what is missing. People often recorded special meals, or wrote down their complaints about a bad one. Sometimes they named the main ingredient without describing how it was prepared. They might write, for instance, "We had beef and bread and nice strawberries." But the reader is left to guess whether the beef was roasted, cut into steaks, stewed, or prepared like a pot roast. If there was bread, there was probably butter or cheese, though that cannot be known for sure. There may also have been potatoes, other vegetables or pickles, and a beverage, all unmentioned.

The food of the wealthy classes was more carefully documented by both themselves and their guests because the elite were usually literate and had leisure time in which to record their daily activities. Protestant women in the Northeast were often educated enough to read the Bible, and they were much more likely to keep diaries.

Travelers often described the food they ate, but it must be kept in mind that they often ate in taverns and inns, where the food was somewhat different from home fare. Foreign visitors, very curious about this new country, often traveled to early America. Not all were pleased with Americans' habits and manners or what they ate, and so their accounts make the food sound a good deal less appetizing than it was for the people who ate it all the time. On the other hand, some people wrote about this country in order to encourage immigration to America or migration to newly opened lands. They often exaggerated the good that they saw. The truth lies somewhere between the harsh criticism and the extravagant praise.

More is known about some parts of the country because they have been the subjects of more scholarship and historical exploration. New England and the Chesapeake have been very well studied; much historical documentation has been uncovered and examined, and archaeology has revealed a great deal. This is not as true of the upland South or the Spanish Southwest. Exciting opportunities exist for students of food history in parts of America where little historical work has been done on food. For now, in many places, there is only scant evidence of what people ate in the Colonial and Federal eras.

Regional Foodways

Most people have experienced going to a new place and encountering a dish they had never before eaten. If they go into a grocery store in a different part of the country, they find foods different those in hometown grocery stores. For example, in the South cornmeal choices are greater than in New England, and in New England, the seafood selection is wider than in Wisconsin, where there is an impressive selection of German sausages. In the Southwest, freshly made tortillas are sold in packages of two or three dozen, but in the rural Northeast, consumers more usually buy packages of a dozen (sometimes frozen).

These are examples of regional variations in foodways. Because the United States is such a large place and has so many different climates, and because it was settled over time by many nationalities and ethnicities, eating habits are different from one part of the country to another. In the recent past many nationwide eating habits have emerged as commerce and industry have made it possible to distribute food all over the country. There are not only nationally recognized fast-food restaurants but also national brands of everything from beverages to frozen broccoli to breakfast cereal. Now, no matter where in the country they live, people eat beef produced in the West and fresh produce from Florida and California.

Long before this development, however, most foodways were regional, with both many similarities and distinctions among different parts of the country. With a few exceptions, most of the food people ate was what they themselves grew or obtained close to their homes. They cooked it much as their parents had cooked it. Change came gradually but steadily. Of all people's habits, eating habits are among the hardest and slowest to change. While certain aspects of eating habits were and are subject to fashion's influence, changes are not usually abrupt.

THE CONTRIBUTING NATIONALITIES

This chapter discusses regions of the country, who lived there, and what they ate. First, however, the foodways that colonists from various nations brought with them will be considered. Some food historians have seen American foodways as a great length of cloth, formed largely of an English warp into which have been woven the threads of many countries and ethnicities. If one steps back a bit, however, a different pattern emerges. American foodways begin to look like a striped warp of many contributing food habits, into which many more were woven to create the bright, textured cloth of today.

The Native Americans

There were many nations of Native Americans living on the land that European settlers occupied, and they were the object of much curiosity. Something is known of their foodways at the time the Europeans came to America because explorers, naturalists, and travelers often commented on the Indians, describing what they ate, how they dressed, how they sheltered themselves, and what they hunted or grew for food.

Native American tribes across the country lived in different ways, but most grew corn, beans, and squashes, and hunted both large and small animals. They gathered wild fruits, nuts, seeds, roots, and plants. Obviously, the wild foods they used depended a great deal on where they lived. They developed grinding and pounding technology to make flour from grains, seeds, and nuts, and to extract oil. They had cooking containers that allowed them to heat foods in liquid, and they had methods of roasting and baking. They also had food preservation techniques and developed portable foods for traveling.

The Natives hunted deer, elk, buffalo, and bear; they caught raccoons, opossums, rabbits, even skunk. They fished. In coastal areas they gathered in summer to dig clams and gather oysters, which they ate on site and also dried and smoked for later. Salmon in the Northwest and alewives in the Northeast were important sources of food. Natives hunted and ate turkeys and other wildfowl. The meat from large animals was cooked and eaten, and also preserved by drying with smoke, or jerked by simply drying. When the Natives took bears, they used the fat in many dishes, much as Europeans used butter or olive oil.

Their primary grain, corn, was cooked and eaten "green" (ripe but not dry). Green corn was also dried, and in the Southwest, it was boiled and then dried, which produced very sweet kernels. When corn had ripened, it was left to dry naturally on the stalk, and the Indians stored it on the cob. This corn was removed from the cob and used whole, soaked and boiled; pounded into grits or flour to make into bread, to thicken soups and stews, or to form into dumplings; or steamed in the husks, as tamales are.

Dry corn kernels were also parched, roasted until the kernel swelled slightly and dried. It was then ground and carried on trips; Indians added water to it to make a nearly instant food. (This product should not be confused with true popcorn, which appeared after the colonial period.)

The Native Americans also grew beans, which, like corn, were used, both fresh and dried, or sometimes combined with corn and other ingredients in stews. Beans were also cooked, mashed, formed into cakes, and dried for use later. Indians grew pumpkins and squashes, ate them fresh, and dried them. Wild roots and greens, berries, groundnuts (not to be confused with peanuts), pokeweed, persimmons, strawberries, wild legumes, and many other foods were included in the Native American diet.

Native Americans gathered nuts, including hickory, walnuts, chestnuts, and others, as well as acorns. The nuts were eaten, dried and pounded into flour or meal, and added to other dishes. Acorns, which are nut, needed processing to make them edible. They were pounded, and then water was leached through them to carry away the tannin. Though they were labor-intensive to prepare, acorns were an important part of the diet for Indians living in hardwood forests.

Although there are no accounts written by the Native Americans themselves of what they ate before the arrival of Europeans, a few descriptions of Indian dishes were recorded by travelers and newcomers, and these make it possible to visualize the Native American dishes through white men's eyes.

The Dutch settler Adriaen Van der Donck, near what became Albany, New York, wrote in the early 1600s that the Native Americans there commonly ate meat and fish: "Their fish or meat they usually boil in water, without salt or [oil] and nothing more than the articles yield." For bread they used maize, "which the women pound fine into meal . . . of which they bake cakes. . . . They also use pounded maize, as we do rice, and samp, with their boiled meat." He also reported that the Native Americans' most common food, eaten daily by young and old, and always served to guests, was cornmeal cooked in a mush, which the New Netherlanders called *sapaen* or *suppawn*. The *sapaen* was frequently cooked with dried and pounded meat or fish.[1]

In 1700, the English naturalist John Lawson, led by a Native American guide, traveled from Charleston, South Carolina, into the interior and arrived again on the coast at New Bern, North Carolina. He and his party ate a number of meals with Native Americans along the way. Near the Yadkin River, among the Waxsaw people, "The Fire was surrounded with Roast-Meat, or Barbakues, and the Pots continually boiling full of Meat, from Morning to night." Another time he wrote that the Indians he saw cooked most animals without gutting them, and that in one place they had a fawn cooked in the doe's bag (inside the mother). Another time, his party was served an ungutted country hare cooked with its skin on, which some of his fellow travelers refused to eat.[2]

In 1811, the naturalist John Bradbury explored the Mississippi and Missouri rivers, and met with many Native American nations along the way. In June, among the Arikara, as the guest of one of their chiefs, he reported on "a feast of sweet corn, prepared by boiling and mixing it with buffaloe grease. Accustomed as I now was to the privation of bread and salt, I thought it very palatable." He also described a Native woman who "prepared something for us to eat; this consisted of dried buffaloe meat, mixed with pounded corn, warmed on the fire in an earthen vessel of their own manufacture; some offered us sweet corn, mixed with beans (*Phaseolus*)."[3]

These foods were both similar to and very different from European food. Sometimes the circumstances of eating among the Native Americans was as exotic an experience as the food itself. But, as Van der Donck observed, stewed meat with pounded corn added (used as the Dutch used rice) was not very different in essence from similar dishes in cultures worldwide.

Spanish Foodways

By the time the Spanish reached the territories that would eventually become part of the United States, they had already adjusted their foodways to the New World. Before departing Europe, Spaniards had been strongly influenced by the centuries-long Moorish occupation of the Iberian Peninsula, which introduced Arabian ingredients and cooking methods, as well as the foodways of the many Jews who had lived there since Roman times.

Many kingdoms made up Spain and Portugal before the Moors were driven out and the Jews were expelled or required to convert to Christianity. The country today called Spain did not emerge until the beginning of the sixteenth century, at about the time Queen Isabella sent Christopher Columbus to the New World. Columbus's explorations resulted in what has become known as the Columbian exchange, in which New World foods such as corn, tomatoes, peppers, turkeys, chocolate, and potatoes were introduced to Europe and swine, cattle, sheep, wheat, and melons were brought to the Americas.

Spanish cuisine still included some medieval characteristics when Spain began colonizing Mexico. It used eggplants, spinach, chickpeas, pork, mutton, rice, wheat (in bread), olives and olive oil, and a great variety of fresh fruits, including citrus, melons, and peaches, as well as dried fruits such as raisins, currants, figs, and dates. Most Spaniards drank wine. As a Catholic nation, Spain adhered to patterns of church fasts that preserved the use of almond milk in lieu of cows' milk and required the use of fish, including a great deal of (salted) cod caught in the Atlantic and sardines from the Mediterranean. The Spanish used coriander leaves, garlic, onions, and saffron as flavorings.

The native Mexican people whom the Spanish conquered used corn for a staple grain; ate tomatoes, squash, beans, and avocados; and seasoned their foods with several sorts of peppers. The corn, after an overnight soaking in lime water, a process called nixtamalization, was ground daily by the women and patted into thin, flat breads baked on a griddle. The Spanish called these flatbreads tortillas. Using them for eating as Europeans used bread, the natives wrapped cooked beans or meat in the tortilla. The Mexicans made a kind of cornmeal dumpling, called a tamale, to which seasonings and other ingredients were added. It was then wrapped in corn husks and steamed similarly to the European use of cabbage leaves. A sauce of ground chili peppers seasoned the food. Natives made a simple gruel of cornmeal called *atole* thin enough to be a beverage, and they drank unsweetened chocolate.

After about a century of Spanish occupation of Mexico, the use of tomatoes, corn, peppers, and chocolate gradually increased in Spain and rest of Europe, and spread into Africa, more often among the poorer people than the gentry. By this time, Spaniards living in Mexico had absorbed many food habits from the Indians, including the extensive use of corn as a primary grain, squashes, New World beans, and chocolate as a beverage.

English Foodways

The earliest colonists in New England and Virginia were first and foremost Tudor-era English. Their cookery showed remnants of late medieval characteristics, largely in seasonings. They valued meat, bread, and ale. The gentry and all who imitated them particularly valued beef, mutton, and venison, though pork and a variety of domestic poultry, such as turkey, geese, ducks, and chicken, were prized. Hunting as a sport among the gentry put a high value on all sorts of wildfowl that are no longer eaten, including herons, cranes, and even songbirds. The favorite bread was of wheat, which the gentry always ate and which the middling and poorer sorts ate whenever they could, settling for rye, oats, or barley when they could not. They made beer from barley and hops.

The colonists ate peas and beans, and made porridges from them or from grain. They enjoyed root vegetables such as parsnips, carrots, and turnips, as well as cabbage, and onions, and knew the sweet potato. They grew salad vegetables that included many plants now called herbs (e.g., parsley). They grew caraway and mustard for their seeds. The Tudor English kept dairy animals and made cheese and butter; their chickens provided eggs. Orchard fruits abounded.

The Protestant Reformation greatly reduced the number of fast days on which the faithful ate fish, but Lent, Fridays, and Saturdays were still fish days, and occasionally Wednesdays were added. Salmon, cod, eels, herring, haddock, flounder, and many other fish were considered good.

English cooking had simplified in the Tudor era as the number of the noble elite declined and the middle classes emerged, so that many of the complex medieval dishes began to fade away, replaced by roasted or boiled haunches of meat. Venison, as a meat restricted largely to the gentry, had special status. Simple desserts such as custards or strawberries and cream, and little cakes, the precursors of cookies, gained favor. On special occasions, when there might be guests, more elaborate foods might be called for, with great variety in meats particularly being the way to show hospitality. The wealthy who could afford it used citrus fruits, spices, dried fruits, wine, verjuice (usually the juice of unripe grapes, though there were substitutes), and flower waters such as orange water and rosewater.

These preferences formed a baseline of expectation among the colonists. They would be the food habits that the English would attempt to preserve or re-create—or, if they were of the lower classes, emulate.

Dutch Foodways

Bread, meat, and fish were the basis of the diet that the Dutch colonists brought to America in the seventeenth century. The Dutch were accustomed to using wheat flour even though they had had to import it from the Baltic. They had a strong baking tradition and made bread in a great variety, pastries, waffles, and pancakes. They also made bread from rye. The Dutch liked beef, mutton, and veal as well as poultry and game (e.g., rabbits and venison), and favored a list of wildfowl very similar to that of the English. Meat was roasted, stewed in *hutspots*, and cooked with vegetables. The Dutch, as a maritime nation, enjoyed fish, and their paintings show a great variety of them. The gentry ate a wider variety of fresh fish than the poorer classes, who consumed salted and dried fish.

A wide variety of vegetables appeared in Dutch markets and gardens, and are portrayed in still-life paintings: cabbage, onions, asparagus, beets, carrots, cauliflower, spinach, turnip, and many others. Peas and beans were cooked in porridges, as was barley. The Dutch drank beer. They enjoyed orchard fruits and berries. They were, at the time they settled in America, a wealthy nation, importing spices, currants, citrus fruits, raisins, wine, pine nuts, and capers from the Mediterranean. Although, as in England, much of the medieval seasoning was fading, those who could afford them used these exotics in their cooking. Importantly, Holland was also a center for sugar refining. Dutch colonies in the West Indies and South America grew sugar that was taken to Holland and made into the refined form needed in baking and confectionery.

French Foodways

The French lived in parts of the country destined to become the United States, but they had lived in Canada for nearly two centuries before the Louisiana Purchase. Like the Spanish, many of them had already adjusted to New World foods and conditions.

In Europe the French had observed a couple of centuries of great change from a mixed agriculture of grains, dairying, and animal husbandry to one increasingly dependent upon grain. Many French who immigrated to America grew up relying on bread as the staple food. If they knew anything of the court, they were aware that variety and wild game were fashionable, and they may also have known that medieval sauces thickened with bread and sharp with vinegar and heavily spiced, had given way to sauces thickened with roux (flour and butter cooked together) and seasoned with herbs. French cookery for fast days was well developed.

Like other Europeans, the French adopted new foods and beverages in this era, including coffee, which caught on more strongly than tea. Some American foods had arrived in France by the Colonial period, including corn and potatoes, which were adopted only slowly, and the turkey, which, because it was a large bird, fit into the elite menu with other large birds: swans, cranes, and herons.

Dessert, consisting of fresh and preserved fruits, had become part of the French bourgeoisie's eating habits. In the middle of the seventeenth century, French cookery became very stylish among Europeans, and even some English, though there was a backlash in the eighteenth century against what some British cookery writers called French extravagance. A major contribution of the French was the order of the meal, which began with soups and appetizers; the second course followed, with roasted meats and side dishes; if there was a third course, it had a variety of dishes; last was dessert of fruit and sweetmeats. Fashionable English and Americans adopted this order of the meal, and by the end of the Federal era, even middle-class Americans began their meals with soup and ended with a sweet dessert.

African Foodways

Africa contains many nations and foodways, a number of which are similar continentwide. Africa's involuntary contribution of foodways to the Americas was not evenly drawn from the whole continent, however, because most slaves were captured and shipped from the

West African coast. Slaves knowledgeable in growing rice, in particular, came with well-developed rice cookery skills. Like other settlers
they adopted and adapted Native American foods to their cookery;
like other settlers, succeeding waves of new slaves brought fresh re-
minders of the old ways, a process that seems to have kept African
foodways more vigorous in the South longer than in the North. Further influences came from some slaves' experiences in the Caribbean
islands.

When Africans found themselves captured and bound for America
as slaves, the main foodways they carried were their cooking skills and
cultural information about ingredient combinations, but even that
was at risk. Because young men were the most valued and most readily acquired in the early days of slavery, foodways information, particularly preparation, stayed behind with the women until the
mid-eighteenth century, when gender balance was regained in the
British colonies. While there are some claims that slaves "brought"
seeds or certain foodstuffs with them, the circumstances of their un-
planned, forced emigration worked against their being prepared to
bring favorite food seeds or plants with them. Some slave merchants
and shippers, however, observed the slaves' refusal to eat unfamiliar
food and soon comprehended the necessity of providing familiar fare
to feed slaves en route to America or the West Indies.

In addition, enslaved blacks working as sailors, translators, and
body servants traveled with their white owners to and from Africa
and other places. These people were culture bearers, often trading
and bartering with the urban slaves with whom they had contact.
These slaves had an opportunity to procure familiar and desired
foods—okra, sesame, black-eyed peas, hyacinth beans, pigeon peas,
and eggplants—and introduce them into the colonies.[4]

Some other foods (e.g., sweet potatoes, greens, peanuts, and cassava) widely eaten in Africa had been introduced to that continent in
relatively recent times, carried there by the Portuguese from the New
World or tropical Asia. Some, but not all, were reintroduced to America as part of the slave diet.

In Africa, cooks boiled the staple starch—rice, millet, cassava—in
a large pot; in smaller cooking vessels, often pottery ones, they prepared savory mixtures of vegetables, meat, or fish. Most African cultures from which slaves were seized retained the ancient practice of
eating with their hands from a communal vessel, as Europeans had
before they adopted eating utensils and individual plates. The main
dish was served in a large bowl or on clean leaves, and the savory

stews were served in smaller bowls set around it. People helped themselves to a piece of the starch and used it to scoop up some of the stew.

German Foodways

The section of Europe now known as Germany did not become a nation until the later nineteenth century, so German colonists coming to America hailed from many regions that often had distinctive food habits not necessarily shared by all. Some German colonists were Protestants; others, Catholic. Generally all ate a great deal of meat and had a strong tradition of producing smoked hams and a variety of sausages, although residents of the regions bordering on the Baltic Sea also ate fish. They made sauerkraut, dumplings, and noodles, and used potatoes. They preferred beer as a beverage; ate bread of wheat, rye, or spelt; and enjoyed orchard fruits. Until the seventeenth century and later, they continued the medieval practice of cooking meat with fruits and spices, and had a sweet-and-sour tradition. They brought all these culinary habits to America.

Other Contributors

While most of colonial America's food habits were based on those of England, Germany and Spain, other groups who came to the colonies also brought their foodways with them. Jewish, Swiss, Irish, Welsh, and Swedish immigrants in many instances were quickly assimilated, retaining only a few, often holiday, dishes. These and other immigrants had more of an impact on American food habits when they came in larger numbers in the nineteenth century. (For more about Jewish food habits, see chapter 5.)

REGIONAL FOODWAYS

Each region will now be explored to see what, when, and how people ate in each. The discussion follows the chronological order of settlement, beginning with Spanish Colonies, then the Chesapeake and New England, and other Colonies.

Spanish Southwest

Beginning in 1513, Spaniards were among the first to explore and claim the parts of North America that later became the United States.

The first permanent settlements were in Florida in 1565 and in New Mexico in 1598. These two parts of the country were vastly different—the Southeast, from Florida toward the Mississippi, with its low-lying land and humid, warm climate, and the Southwest, on the other side of the country, from the California coast to Texas, with its higher elevation and hot and dry climate. The other important influence on food in the Southwest was the village-dwelling Native Americans, whom the Spanish called Pueblos. The Southwest has had strong connections to its Hispanic and Indian roots ever since, and if modern Americans eat tortilla chips and refried beans, it is because of Spanish colonists and their continuing migration from Mexico, and the Native Americans who survived and continued their foodways.

In 1598 Don Juan de Oñate established a colony in New Mexico on the site of a commandeered Native American pueblo, which the Spanish named San Gabriel. Like colonists everywhere, the 500 setters and a handful of Franciscan friars brought with them familiar food and seeds, in this instance a combination of European and Mexican foods. European ingredients that they brought included wheat and barley, cattle, sheep, goats, pigs, lentils, and chickpeas.[5] Foods of Mexican origin were chile peppers, a new variety of corn, tomatoes, and Mexican beans.[6] By 1602, although the colonists had abandoned Oñate and returned to Mexico, the process of introducing new food to the Pueblos had begun, and with it the changes that European livestock left on the landscape. Also, the Franciscans had begun building missions to convert the Indians to Christianity and a Spanish way of life, which meant that they insisted the Indians adopt European dress, manners, and (presumably) foodways.

By 1609, Santa Fe was established as the new capital of the province, although the Spanish abandoned it for twelve years following the Pueblo Revolt of 1680. Spanish authorities founded Santa Fe some distance from the pueblos to prevent further conflict with the Indians, which often flared when Hispanic colonists seized food supplies the Pueblos stored, and required Hispanic colonists to grow their own crops.

In the seventeenth century, however, New Mexico experienced a combination of drought and the intense cold experienced by eastern colonists. New Mexico was a challenging place to grow food in the best of circumstances, even after the Hispanics took over the better farmland and irrigation systems of the Pueblos. In the face of adverse weather, the settlers butchered their cattle for food, including those they needed for breeding. They were seldom able to grow more food

This corner fireplace in a house at the Acoma Pueblo in Valencia County, New Mexico, shows Spanish influence. Before colonization, the Pueblos cooked on open fires vented through a hole in the roof. In a small fireplace like this, a cook could prepare long-cooked dishes of meat, grain, and vegetables. (Courtesy of the Library of Congress, Historic American Buildings Survey, HABS, NM, 31-ACOMP, 1-15.)

than what they needed for subsistence, and continued raiding the Pueblo supplies. In addition, no market incentive existed to improve agriculture beyond subsistence level because New Mexico was so remote from potential markets in Mexico; the supply caravans' round trip between Mexico City and New Mexico took three years to complete. All these factors meant that the colony had the poorest standard of living of other colony in seventeenth-century America.[7] The circumstances led to some of the more complex food adaptations and adoptions anywhere in the country.

The Pueblo Indians had raised turkeys and dogs for a meat supply, and traded with Plains Indians for dried buffalo, called by the Hispanics, who adopted it, *carne seca* (dried meat). But the colonists were not about to eat dog, except in extremity, and relied heavily on mutton from the churro sheep, which tolerated New Mexico's climate well, or goat. In time, the Indians would raise sheep as well, and devise dishes using it. Cattle, never quite as important to Spaniards as to others in Europe, were raised and eaten, but not in great quantities, as in the eastern Colonies or in Spanish Texas and Arizona. Because most of the Southwest provided little forage, pigs were not widely raised. Poultry provided eggs and the occasional roast. Archaeological evidence for consumption of deer, rabbits, squirrel, and bison appears in one mission archaeological site, but, like most colonists elsewhere, seventeenth- and eighteenth-century New Spanish preferred to rely on domestic animals.

As in eastern Colonies, large animals were slaughtered in the fall. The New Spanish relied heavily on drying meat to preserve it. Smaller animals were killed year round and eaten soon after butchering.

Most of the Southwest, like Mexico, had less firewood than eastern Colonies. Cooking was skewed toward using as little of it as possible. Wealthier colonists in New Mexico brought spits for roasting and could afford the relatively scarce firewood. They also could afford the spices and dried fruits for the Spanish-style forcemeat stuffing for chickens or turkeys. Roasts were, however, a special-occasion dish.

Probably the most common way of preparing almost any meat was to stew it slowly in pottery cookware, which the Hispanics tended to rely on the Indians to make. The Hispanics drew on their Spanish heritage for some of these dishes, making *estofados, cocidos,* or *ollas* When meat was cooked with chile in the Mexican tradition, the dish was called *guisados* or *temole. Carne adobada* was meat that had been marinated in chile sauce, then dried. It was stewed for eating.[8]

Spanish colonists in the Southwest were no different from other people of the seventeenth and eighteenth centuries in their consumption of organ meats and traditional blood puddings; *morcilla* was the name given to the sausage made from sheep and goat blood. The Spanish in Mexico made a pork sausage called chorizo, as they did in the Southwest when they had sufficient pork. Tongue, kidneys, and tripe were prepared and eaten.

Most New Mexican colonists lived near the Rio Grande, and consumed fresh fish besides importing dried fish. Most of the colonists, however, relied on meatless bean dishes with tortillas or egg dishes rather than fish for fast days.

Corn and wheat were the primary grains of colonial New Mexico. The indigenous Pueblo corn crossed naturally with the corn introduced from Mexico, yielding more productive strains. Corn fared better than wheat, but wheat was needed by the missions for making the Eucharist wafer. In Colonial Texas little wheat was grown, and most of what was consumed there was brought from Louisiana or Mexico. In Arizona, as in New Mexico and Mexico, wheat flour also appeared in tortillas.

The chief virtue of the thin bread was that it cooked quickly on the *comal*, which needed only a small fire beneath it. The relative scarcity of firewood made heating an oven a costly proposition. The Spanish had brought with them to Mexico the Moorish-style freestanding *horno*, heated, as eastern beehive ovens were, with a fire inside. They also brought a taste for yeasted loaves. In Colonial New Mexico, archaeological evidence for *hornos* appears in missions and pueblos, and it may be concluded that as long as there was sufficient wheat flour and firewood, colonists made yeasted bread. It, like roasting, was the privilege of the prosperous.

Everyone else, from New Mexico to Texas, relied on corn tortillas, and women had the daily responsibility for making the *nixtamal* (alkali-soaked corn), grinding it into masa harina, and baking tortillas. Masa harina was seasoned with meat and chile for tamales, a festival dish. When Tennessee native Josiah Gregg, who traveled the Santa Fe Trail in the 1830s, described tortilla making thus: "The thinness of the tortilla is always a great test of the skill in the maker," and the tortilla, no matter how "wholesome, substantial, and well-flavored, when newly made," was unpleasant when cold.[9]

Nixtamalized corn was also boiled, then cooked with meat and chile to make a dish called posole, or dried for use later. Sweet corn was steamed, then dried on the cob for use later, and called *chicos*. Rubbed off the cob, *chicos* were stewed with beans to make a dish reminiscent of succotash, or were eaten as a vegetable. Dried corn also was ground or pounded to thicken stews, or to make a porridge or *atole*. Dried corn was sometimes roasted or parched before grinding.

The Native Americans of the Southwest relied for vegetables upon domesticated squash, both summer and winter types, pumpkins, and beans, to which they added wild food such as prickly pear, wild potato, and purslane and other wild greens. Hispanics colonizing along the borderlands brought with them familiar European vegetables. Oñate and his colonists brought onions, garlic, cabbage, lettuce, and radishes into New Mexico, along with some of the vegetables they had adopted in Mexico, such as chiles and corn. Carrots, peas, tomatoes, cucumbers, garbanzos (chickpeas), and tomatillos were brought later.

The vegetable that has come to characterize Southwestern cookery is the chile. Useful green and fresh or ripened and dried, the chile was stewed with meat or ground into a sauce. It was sometimes picked green, roasted, peeled, and subsequently dried. If used fresh, it was roasted, peeled, and stuffed with cheese or meat. The dried red chiles, strung for storage in *ristras*, were stewed and then made into a sauce with water. Meat was added to make chile con carne.

Among other seasonings, the Hispanics substituted safflower, or *azafrán*, for the preferred saffron, and used coriander seed and its leaves (cilantro) and oregano. Cinnamon, pepper, and true saffron had to be imported. Sugar was scarce: the friars and governors had some; a limited supply of honey was available to others.

The Spanish brought fruits to America, and the watermelons, cantaloupes, and peaches thrived so well that they preceded Spanish colonists into the borderlands east and west, where Native Americans grew them. Wherever Spanish colonists in the Southwest pursued agriculture, they grew apples, grapes, apricots, plums, pears, and quince. However, Josiah Gregg reported in the 1830s that "Famous as the republic of Mexico is for the quality and variety of its fruits, this province [New Mexico] considering its latitude is most singularly destitute in this respect. A few orchards of apples, peaches, and apricots are occasionally met with."[10]

At missions in New Mexico, grapes were cultivated at first for sacramental wine, though additional wine was imported from Mexico. Gradually, the New Mexicans were able to produce table wine and vinegar as well as table grapes. A thin grape jelly called *arrope* was made. Figs were grown successfully in El Paso. Cantaloupes were cut into strips and dried. Piñons (pine nuts) gathered from cones of the piñon pines were like the Italian pignoli that the Spanish were familiar with. These were exported to Mexico.

Spanish colonials certainly arrived in the New World with a preference for wine. Grapes were hard to grow in Mexico, and over time settlers adopted the local beverages, which included pulque, *atole*, and chocolate. In the Spanish Southwest, chocolate became a great favorite even though it was an import (as were sugar, spices, almonds, and delicacies such as dried oysters). Most beverages, aside from water, were thin cornmeal mixtures such as *champurrado* (*atole* with chocolate added); *hormiguillo* (a gruel made with bread crumbs, sometimes sweetened), or *pinole* (a sweetened drink made from toasted cornmeal and milk). *Atole* was so common that American travelers nicknamed it "the coffee of the Mexicans."[11]

Water sufficed as a beverage for many. Josiah Gregg wrote that the New Mexicans observed "a very singular custom of abstaining from all sorts of beverage during meals." Each person was given a large cup of water at the start of the meal but, he reported, "Should anyone take it upon his hand while in the act of eating the host is apt to cry out, 'Hold, hold! There is yet more to come.'" Gregg concluded that the New Mexicans regarded drinking while eating to be "unwholesome." Those who could afford it, drank wine. Gregg observed that most New Mexican used "but little wine at meals, and that exclusively of the produce of the Paso del Norte."[12]

Dairying was limited to milking goats and sheep until the nineteenth century, when Americans came to settle in the Southwest. There is little evidence of an aged cheese tradition, though in the eighteenth century there is evidence of pressed cheeses. However, fresh cheeses were made and used in cooking, or sometimes served with syrup as a dessert. Milk was used in custards.

Documentation is very sparse for descriptions of meals in the Southwest. The common settlers certainly would have eaten more simply than the wealthy or the governing classes. In New Mexico even the Franciscan missionaries ate more simply than they would have in Spain or longer-settled parts of Mexico, saving their resources for ornate church furnishings. Given the remoteness of the region, we can assume a slow pace of change until the lands were annexed by the United States and new settlers poured in from the north and east. A handful of descriptions from early nineteenth-century travelers to New Mexico give us glimpses into the daily fare.

In all likelihood there were two meals a day, with possibly a third among the prosperous; the biggest meal of the day was eaten at noon. Most people, especially poorer ones, ate meals based on stews of grains and legumes—in the Southwest, tortillas and stewed beans seasoned with chile, with meat (if they had it), eggs, or stewed chunks of squash or pumpkin. People still cooking in the Spanish fashion would eat soups and prefer wheat bread, but stews and tortillas were more the Hispanic style.

Gregg described some New Mexicans hunting for buffalo. They sliced the meat thin and dried it in the open air, or jerked or barbecued it over a fire if the weather was too damp for drying meat. He reported that the poorer New Mexicans "virtually breakfast, dine, and sup" on *atole*, and it, together with frijoles and chile, "consists their principle [*sic*] food." The red chile pepper, Gregg observed, was ground into a sauce. "*Chile verde* (green pepper,) not as a mere condiment, but as a salad, served up different ways, is reckoned by them one [of] the greatest luxuries."[13]

James Josiah Webb, who engaged in the Santa Fe trade in the mid-1840s, described a meal eaten by New Mexicans that consisted of baked pumpkin, wheat *gordos*, and *atole*. The *gordos*, he wrote, were made by "grinding wheat on the metate, wetting the meal with water sufficient to pat it into cakes about the size and rather thicker than our buckwheat cakes, and baking them on a flat stone without the addition of soda or yeast and frequently with out salt." Elsewhere, among Americans living in New Mexico, he reported, "Our bill of fare was the usual dishes of *chile colorado*, beans, *atole*, tortillas, etc. . . ." The *chile colorado* is defined as "a compound of red peppers and dried buffalo meat stewed together."[14]

The manner of dining in the early Southwest among the rancheros and ordinary people had probably changed little when Josiah Gregg visited. He wrote that women seldom ate with the men, but ate by themselves in the kitchen. Further, the rancheros seldom used tables, and served food on plates that people balanced on their knees. "Knives and forks are equally dispensed with, the viands being mostly hashed or boiled so very soft as to be eaten with a spoon. This is frequently supplied by the tortilla, a piece of which is ingeniously doubled between the fingers, so as to assist in the disposal of anything be it ever so rare or liquid . . . each fold of the tortilla is devoured with the substance it conveys to the mouth."[15]

Among the well-off, however, elegance and plenty were more usual. On March 4, 1807, U.S. Army officer Zebulon Pike met with the governor in Santa Fe and reported in his journal, "The dinner at the governors was rather splendid, having a variety of dishes and wines of the southern provinces and when his excellency was a little warmed with the influence of cheering liquor, he became very sociable."[16]

The Chesapeake

Coastal Virginia, Maryland, and Delaware touch on the great Chesapeake Bay around which so much of colonial America developed, including the first permanent English colony of Jamestown. From here, the rest of Virginia was settled westward into the piedmont and Kentucky. Low-lying and tidal, it had abundant wildlife and a mild climate, but also harbored diseases such as malaria, which made life difficult for the earliest settlers. Tobacco was king for a while, but this region ultimately produced more corn and wheat. The English who settled here were able to indulge their taste for oysters, wildfowl, beef, and pork, and learned how to make good bread with cornmeal. Modern Americans who like country ham and cornbread owe their availability in part to the English who established colonies around the Chesapeake Bay.

The Marquis de Chastellux, an American ally in the War of Independence, traveled into Virginia in 1782 and observed that the "Virginians are still English in many respects."[17] This was revealed partly by their food choices, and helps explain why the first cookbook to be printed in America was an English one, *The Complete Housewife; or, Accomplish'd Gentlewoman's Companion*, by E. Smith, printed at Williamsburg, Virginia, in 1742. How closely the Virginians clung to their English culinary roots depended quite a bit on their economic status, however. The wealthy planters, who had slave cooks, access to a variety of food, and frequent enough communication with England to know what was fashionable, maintained or aspired to a gentrified way of life more easily than did small planters or former indentured servants. These latter, trying to make a home in Virginia or Maryland, relied more on local produce and had little time to dine fashionably.

As nearly everywhere in the Colonies, once the first period of settlement was past, the heavy use of wild food ceased, and dependence on domesticated animals increased substantially. While the actual amount varied, depending on a person's economic standing, age, and gender, scholars have estimated that in the last half of the seventeenth century, Chesapeake colonists annually consumed 45 to 200 pounds of meat, compared with people in England, most of whom never ate meat more than once a week.[18]

Beef topped the list in the Chesapeake wherever people owned enough land for cattle grazing. Pork, as elsewhere in the colonies, followed in importance except in the case of poorer people, who were often tenant farmers and did not have adequate grazing land, and therefore relied more heavily on swine, chickens, and wild meat. Unlike parts of New England and old England, however, there was relatively little mutton or lamb eaten in the Chesapeake in the seventeenth century.[19] The care required to protect sheep from predators made them impractical for most of the Colonial Chesapeake. Wildfowl and game provided variety on wealthy tables and subsistence for poorer people and slaves. A hunting tradition continues in parts of the Chesapeake today.

Chesapeake Bay yielded oysters, the favored shellfish in the seventeenth and eighteenth centuries, whose shells abound in archaeological remains. Colonists probably also ate crabs, which do not typically survive in archaeological remains unless they have been burned. Recipes for crab dishes provide evidence of their being taken for food. The relative abundance of fish provided more food, and the archaeological record shows that the most frequently consumed fish were sturgeon, sheepshead, black drum, red drum, striped bass, perch, and catfish. Planters with access to streams where alewives ran in the spring were very likely to send slaves to net and salt them for the slaves' own consumption later on.

Corn often preceded wheat as a grain crop in the Chesapeake. Following Native American practice, settlers felled trees and hoe-cultivated corn among the stumps until the stumps could be pulled and the field plowed, whereupon they planted wheat. Tobacco was such an important cash crop, however, that it often took precedence over wheat, and in the first hundred years or so, new land was cleared for the corn on which many subsisted until the mid-eighteenth century, when farmers found that wheat grew on tobacco-exhausted soil.[20] This firmly established corn in the Chesapeake diet, but like most English settlers, people there returned to using wheat flour as soon as they could. Farmers on the long peninsula of the Eastern Shore grew a great deal of wheat during the American Revolution. The gentry ate wheat bread, and the poor and slaves ate cornmeal in various forms.

The Chesapeake is famous for hoecake, a plain cornmeal, water, and salt bread baked on a griddle or on a hoe. The name has given rise to the assumption that field workers literally made hoecakes for their midday meal, using their cultivating tools and a small fire built in the field. While this may have happened, the premise is compromised by a Williamsburg, Virginia, newspaper advertisement for "bake hoes" of various sizes, which certainly sounds as if one could purchase a hoe specifically for baking hoecakes.

Elsewhere in the Colonies from north to south, the same combination of ingredients was also baked buried in ashes, on griddles, and on boards propped up before the fire. As a vernacular dish of the seventeenth and eighteenth centuries, the recipe went unrecorded until later. Elizabeth Ellicott Lea's cookbook *Domestic Cookery*, printed in Baltimore in 1853, reported that Virginia Hoe Cakes used to be baked on hoes, but she instructed cooks on how to use a barrelhead, which is identical to the method described in the 1800s by Rhode Islander Thomas Hazard.[21] Mrs. Lea instructed her readers to make a stiff mixture of meal, water, salt, and a little butter, then have ready a board about the size of a barrelhead "(or the middle piece of the head will answer,) wet the board with water, and spread the dough with your hand; place it before the fire; prop it aslant with a flat-iron, bake it slowly; when one side is nicely brown, take it up and turn it, by running a thread between the cake and the board, then put it back and let the other side brown."[22]

The New Englander Amelia Simmons gave a recipe for a more elaborate version of this dish, which called for flour, milk, and molasses, in the 1796 *American Cookery*, but named it "Johny Cake or Hoe Cake" and instructed, "bake before the fire."[23] Travelers in Virginia and other southern parts commented on being served "cakes." For example, in 1782 the Marquis de Chastellux, at Steel's Mill, north and east of Waynesboro, Virginia, wrote that since bread had only just been kneaded up and was not yet baked, "A few cakes, however, baked over the coals, excellent butter, good milk" was what the travelers received.[24] Another time, on the same trip, he noted that at a farmer's house "He gave us cakes and milk, for he had neither bread nor biscuit."[25] Another name for these cakes was bannocks, and a similar kind of simple bread of the same name was made of oats in England, particularly in the north and in Scotland.

Hominy was another form of corn used largely in the Chesapeake and other southern areas; in the North it was usually called Indian. The simplest preparation of hominy, once it was pounded or ground, and sifted, was in a mush. The coarser bits of corn were called grits, and the finer were termed meal. They were boiled into a porridge, and formed a basic dish for breakfast and supper for poorer people and slaves, though even wealthy planters ate them. Whenever a foodstuff is prominent among a group of people, there are usually many variations for its use—for instance, in the Chesapeake as elsewhere in the corn-growing south, in puddings. The now-famous spoon bread was a nineteenth-century development.

Wherever in this region the prosperous could afford enough wheat for baking, and combined it with slave labor, more labor-intensive traditional English baking survived; there is a lasting tradition of great cakes and evidence of cookie-like baked goods such as Naples biscuits, seed cakes, jumbles, Shrewsbury cakes, and wafers.

English settlers in the Chesapeake planted seeds of familiar vegetables—parsnips, carrots, cabbages, turnips, lettuce, onions, mustard, and garlic.[26] To these were added, because of the hot summers, warm-weather vegetables such as sweet potatoes, tomatoes, okra, and eggplants, which caught on there sooner than they did to the north. Okra, eggplants (also called Guinea squash), and field or black-eyed peas were associated with the slave trade and slave agriculture, but the gentry consumed them as well. Squashes, pumpkins, beans, fresh corn, white potatoes, asparagus, and other vegetables were found throughout the region, the greatest variety of them among the wealthy. Besides being eaten plainly cooked, sweet potatoes, squash, and pumpkin were made into puddings and eventually into pies, or the pulp was mixed with cornmeal or with flour for biscuits and breads.

Chesapeake settlers imported English fruit trees—apple, pear, cherry, and plum—grapevines, and gooseberry, currant, and strawberry plants. They found wild versions of domestic plants—bramble fruits such as raspberries and blackberries, strawberries, and grapes—that they recognized, and others, such as persimmons, that they did not. As everywhere in the Colonies, the wealthy established orchards and plantings for a variety of fruits, while the lesser sorts made do with less variety and smaller plantings, or gathering wild fruits when time permitted. Everyone ate much fruit fresh as it came into season, and during the early years, the wealthy, who could afford sugar, made preserves or fruit cordials or wines. Preserving fruit in brandy, which preserved the fruit and flavored the brandy, is revealed by the archaeological dig in Williamsburg, Virginia, which turned up a bottle with cherry remains in it. Cooks used some fruits, particularly berries and small, perishable fruits such as peaches and plums, in sweet baking—tarts, for instance. People stored apples for out-of-season consumption and made cider.

This region's proximity to the West Indies and to the coast meant readier access to citrus fruits than in more northerly regions. Lemons, limes, and oranges were more available. Among the gentry the eighteenth-century fad for serving pineapples or at least presenting them as a centerpiece, which had caught on in England, found its way to Chesapeake and other southern elites as well.

Throughout the Chesapeake, as elsewhere in the plantation South, the wealthy imported wines, brandies, and sherries and laid them down in cellars, as did the well-off in England and Europe, and other Colonial cities. Most English settlers also drank beer and cider, and the region became a center for the making of rye whiskey. One of the earliest distilleries was built by George Washington at Mount Vernon. Rum was imported. The southern gentry entertained in as high a style as they could afford, and wines with meals and punch after meals, with much toasting, were important expressions of hospitality. At the Carter family plantation on the Northern Neck of Virginia, tutor Phillip Fithian reported in his diary that the company sat at the table after dinner (which would have been in the afternoon) until sunset, and drank three bottles of Maderia and two bowls of toddy.[27] There is some evidence that by the late eighteenth century, this convivial after-dinner drinking had gotten a little out of hand, and when the ladies left the table, the men stayed behind, often drinking to excess.

A French military officer, the Marquis de Chastellux, came to this country as a supporter of the American cause in the Revolution. He visited what he described as a middling Virginia plantation in 1782 and observed of the meals of the day: "An excellent breakfast at nine in the morning, a big dinner at two o'clock, tea and punch in the afternoon, and an elegant little supper, divided the day most happily, for those whose appetites were equal to it."[28]

Breakfast in the Chesapeake, as everywhere, was largely determined by what social class and economic status. Many of the middling and poorer farmers ate a breakfast of hominy and milk or bread and milk. The more prosperous had eggs and meat, but personal taste, being the basis of all food choices, meant that in the early 1700s even the wealthy planter and diarist William Byrd reported that he "ate milk" daily for his breakfast, varying it occasionally with chocolate; when there was company, milk and rice or hominy, sometimes strawberries and milk, seldom bread and butter, rarely any meat.[29] John Bernard, an English comedian traveling in Virginia at the end of the eighteenth century, reported that one Virginia planter breakfasted at ten in the morning on coffee, eggs, and hoecake.[30]

A description of breakfast with the Virginian George Washington in Philadelphia on June 6, 1794, was recorded by Henry Wansey, a retired English clothier traveling in America, who joined the Washingtons at breakfast: "Mrs. Washington herself made tea and coffee for us. On the table were two small plates of sliced tongue, dry toast, bread and butter, etc., but no broiled fish, as is the general custom." Wansey noted relative simplicity: "Only one servant attended, who had no livery [uniform] and a silver urn for hot water was the only article of expense on the table."[31] Clearly Wansey had been served enough broiled fish to conclude it was a common breakfast—which, given the time of year, it probably was, alewives being in season and ideal small fish for broiling.

Dinner was the main meal of the day, and was served at midday, although as the eighteenth century progressed, it was moved later in the afternoon among the Chesapeake gentry, as it was among the fashionable in England. Many descriptions of the meal show that the well-to-do put a great variety of dishes on their tables: soup, large joints of meats (both roasted and boiled), fish, smaller dishes of fricassees and ragouts, vegetables, and pies. That cleared, a second course might follow with both savory and sweet dishes, and after that, with the tablecloth removed, dessert consisting of nuts, apples, raisins, and wines or punch. Obviously the meals of the less well-off did not display such variety and required simpler preparation, but meat as a main dish, or made into a stewlike dish, accompanied by vegetables or a pudding and bread was usual.

Supper occurred later in the day and was often a warm meal, with a variety of choices, especially among the gentry. The Marquis de Chastellux ate a refined supper in Petersburg, Virginia, in 1782, at the home of a Mrs. Spencer. Supper "was not long in coming, for scarcely had we time to admire the cleanliness and beauty of the tablecloth before it was covered with plenty of good dishes, particularly some monstrous-large and excellent fish."[32] Poorer people made do with boiled hominy mush, or bread and cheese, for their supper, and middling sorts might add a small fried fish or piece of meat. In some households, by the end of the eighteenth century, tea had become a small, supperlike meal, but more often featured cold food to go with the tea.

An evening party might feature a few small savory dishes of meat or fowl, an array of sweetmeats—preserved fruits—jellies, small cakes, and fresh fruit served with wines. How much and how elaborately it was presented depended entirely on the household's wealth and the importance of the occasion. Smaller gatherings of family members or close friends might feature cake, wine, and fresh or preserved fruits and nuts.

In Colonial era Chesapeake, Christmas and New Year's were more likely to be celebrated than in the northern Colonies settled by Puritans and Quakers. Christmas was largely a religious holiday, but the season up to Twelfth Night (January 6) featured much entertaining among the more prosperous, with traditional Christmas puddings, mincemeat pies, and, for those with strong ties to the English holiday traditions, possibly a Twelfth Cake on Epiphany. Thanksgiving was not observed as it was in New England.

New England

Along the Atlantic coast from Long Island Sound northward to the coast of Maine and into nearby New Brunswick, colonizers attempted several settlements from 1604 until the permanent settlement at Plymouth in 1621 was established. For most of the early years of colonization, it was English settlers who came and established homes in a daunting climate with, at best, a five-month growing season and rocky, thin soil that nevertheless proved fine for animal husbandry. From coastal southern New England, settlers spread to the northern coast toward Canada, and into western and interior New England, parts of upstate New York, and Ohio. New Jersey and some southern Colonies absorbed colonists who did not

The Farrar-Mansur House in Weston, Vermont, was a tavern, built in 1797, where travelers could get a meal and stay the night. (Courtesy of the Library of Congress, Historic American Buildings Survey, HABS, VT, 14-WEST, 2-1.)

find land in New England or who wished to avoid theocracy. New Englanders shared with their fellow English colonists elsewhere in North America the taste for beef, wheat bread, peas and beans, and beer and cider.

From one end of colonial New England to the other, there were a few minor regional differences and a few pockets of ethnic food habits. But taken as a whole, New Englanders ate similarly region-wide, with differences more pronounced between classes than geographic areas. English foodways were reinforced with succeeding English immigrants who brought gradually changing English cooking and eating habits, as well as new dining fashions.

Colonists came from English regions with distinct food habits, and many of those distinctions depended on English regional agricultural practices. Those differences diminished considerably once the colonists were established in New England and adjusted their agricultural practices to the climate. A notable example was the use of oats and wheat. Oats were associated with the north of England and were regarded as countrified. Wheat was associated with the south and East Anglia, considered England's bread basket, and there were no oat bannocks in London when colonists left for America. But all New England settlers, no matter what English region they hailed from, turned eventually to corn, and made bannocks of it, as they would elsewhere in the Colonies.[33]

New Englanders ate beef, pork, and mutton as well as veal and occasionally lamb. They preferred their meat fresh, but salting was useful for preservation, so they corned beef, dried beef, salted pork, produced hams, and bacon, and occasionally salted mutton. Small animals such as calves and lambs were usually eaten fresh. If the meat was a fresh large joint, it was very likely to be roasted. Smaller cuts, such as steaks, were fried, and other pieces were stewed or put into pies. Salted meat was most often boiled, and leftovers of any meat were hashed—chopped fine, mixed with gravy, and served on bread or potatoes.

New Englanders kept domestic fowl, including chickens, turkeys, ducks, and geese, and ate them both roasted and boiled whole, as well as cut up for fricassees, stews, and pies. Wildfowl were shot in season, and were so well liked that they were hunted virtually to extinction.

Wild meats appealed to many New Englanders: primarily venison, and moose in frontier parts of Maine, New Hampshire, and Vermont. Generally, however, once New Englanders were established in an area, they depended more on domestic meat than on wild.

Tavern kitchen inside the Farrar-Mansur House. The unusual double fireplace made it possible for the tavern keeper to cook food for large numbers of people. Only one fireplace, the one on the left, has an oven, which may have been heated daily. The cooking utensils are typical of late 1700s and early 1800s, and belong to one of the families who lived here. The half-round device in front on the left is a tin kitchen, used for roasting. Just to the left of it is a flat-topped bake kettle in which a cook could bake a pie or piece of meat. The lip on the lid held hot coals. (Courtesy of the Library of Congress, Historic American Buildings Survey, HABS, VT, 14-WEST, 2-4.)

The most favored seafood included cod (both fresh and salted), salmon, and oysters. Other fish were caught and eaten, particularly alewives and shad in the spring. Vendors sold fresh haddock, flounder, stripped bass, mackerel, eels, and lobsters in coastal towns. People inland ate freshwater fishes such as trout and, like many in the region, had salt cod for Saturday dinner. The Scottish-born Annapolis physician Dr. Alexander Hamilton reported that in Boston on July 21, 1744, "I was invited to dine with Captain Irvin upon salt cod, which here is a common Saturday's dinner, being elegantly dressed with a sauce of butter and eggs." The salt fish, soaked overnight, was simmered until done; the sauce Hamilton described was made by melting butter and mashing hard-boiled eggs into it.[34]

English settlers planted wheat, and for a while it succeeded well enough for the grain to be an export commodity. By the middle of the seventeenth century, however, it became apparent that wheat was subject to a mildew rust, and New Englanders began to shift from wheat bread to a combination of rye and cornmeal as their daily loaf, which they called "rye 'n' Indian." This was a coarse bread that did not rise as readily as wheat bread, but was quite flavorful. Wealthier New Englanders continued to eat wheat bread, but for the next 150 years, rye 'n' Indian predominated among the majority.

From time to time, when wheat was available, some housewives combined it with rye and cornmeal to make a mixed loaf; if they used only wheat, they were likely to refer to it as wheat or flour bread, and the rye 'n' Indian was sometimes called brown bread. (This brown bread should not be confused with the sweet steamed bread of the mid-nineteenth century.) Otherwise, wheat was reserved for finer baking, such as pastry crusts or the occasional cake.

Indian meal proved very useful as a porridge grain, called mush or hasty pudding (the same dish as *suppawn* in other regions). It was also made into bannocks, called jonnycakes in Rhode Island, which consisted of meal, hot water, and salt mixed to form a thick dough and spread on a board or griddle to bake before the fire or over it. There were also Indian meal dumplings, and by the end of the Colonial era, pancakes made of it as well. The following recipe for Indian meal mush appeared in Hannah Glasse's 1805 edition of *Art of Cookery Made Plain and Easy.*

To make Mush

Boil a pot of water, according to the quantity you wish to make, and then stir in the meal till it becomes quite thick, stirring all the time to keep out the lumps, season with salt, and eat it with milk or molasses.[35]

By the mid-eighteenth century, cooks mixed grains, as well as starchy vegetables and dried peas, with some combination of milk, water, eggs, shortening, and seasoning to make a pudding boiled in a cloth. This served as a starch at the meal. Another version of pudding was baked in a crust like a pie. The word "pie" was applied to a sweet dish, often served as a dessert, by the mid-1700s, but in early New England pie was often a raised crust of rye or coarse wheat flour in which meat or fish was baked, the crust serving as a baking and serving dish while the contents were scooped out to be eaten. Poorer households could hardly afford to throw out an empty crust, but crusts made from coarse grains were not necessarily intended for consumption.

In the late seventeenth and early eighteenth centuries, most fine baking followed the English model very closely. In 1706, for instance, merchant and witch trial judge Samuel Sewell, of Salem, Massachusetts, wrote in his journal that he took a Banbury cake to an ill friend.[36] This rich cake, filled with raisins and currants and well-spiced, was very popular among the gentry in the seventeenth and eighteenth centuries. Later eighteenth-century New Englanders were more likely to offer pie as a sweet than fine cakes. Nonetheless, until the very end of the Colonial era, New Englanders made cakes with yeasted and enriched dough.

Particularly famous is election cake, which townspeople made in large quantities to serve country company who came into town to vote. This cake often contained dried fruit and was sometimes frosted.

Gingerbread of the Colonial era was more similar to what are today called cookies or bar cookies than a soft cake. During the Federal era, the use of the chemical leaven pearlash (potassium carbonate, an alkaline derived from wood ash) yielded a softer, more cakelike gingerbread, giving rise to the distinction in cookbooks between hard gingerbread and soft gingerbread.

As the Federal era progressed, New Englanders made more cake and cookielike baked goods that were referred to as "cakes." Popular recipes included sponge, pound, loaf, cup, and tea cakes. There were also seed cakes, flavored with caraway, and Naples biscuits. These fine cakes were largely found in more prosperous households until the Erie Canal was completed in 1825, opening eastern markets to less costly wheat and putting the price of flour within reach of less wealthy households. "Cookies" found their way into New England via the Dutch connection along the western edge of New England, and Amelia Simmons's 1796 cookbook gives a couple of recipes for cookies as well as the English cakes, which were quite similar in many respects.

Another Dutch sweet, doughnuts, also found favor in New England; many households, even less well-off ones, fried a batch of these each week. In the late 1700s and early 1800s, doughnuts were small balls of fried dough (today called doughnut holes). The ring-shaped doughnut had not yet become common. This doughnut recipe is from Glasse's 1805 *Art of Cookery*.

Dough Nuts

To one pound of flour, put one quarter of a pound of butter, one quarter of a pound of sugar an two spoonfuls of yeast; mix them all together in warm milk or water of the thickness of bread, let it raise, and make them in what form you please, boil your fat (consisting of hog's lard), and put them in.[37]

Vegetables found their way to the New England table plainly cooked as a side dish. In the seventeenth century, many vegetables were described as potherbs, meaning that they were cooked with meat and sometimes with grain, as distinguished from salad herbs, which were eaten raw. Most of these plants came with the settlers from England, and like most colonists, New Englanders embraced squashes and pumpkins, corn and beans, adding them to the familiar cabbages, onions, leeks, parsnips, turnips, peas, and lettuces.

Solid and fleshy vegetables, such as squash and many root vegetables, were likely to be boiled and served as a side dish. Much garden produce was called "garden sauce" or "sass," at this time, which showed its role as an accompaniment to meat. Sarah Kemble Knight, the daughter of a Boston merchant and businesswoman, traveled from Boston to New York in 1704. The diary of her trip shows that in Stonington, Connecticut, she ate "roast beef and pumpkin sauce for supper."[38]

Today pumpkin is largely regarded as the filling for a sweet pie. Fruit pies, preceded in New England by fruit tarts, were made of fruits that grew in the region, predominantly apples, which were also chopped and added to chopped meat, raisins, spices, and suet to make mincemeat. Apple, pumpkin, and mincemeat were probably the most common pies in the Colonial era. This recipe for pumpkin pie is from Amelia Simmons's *American Cookery* (1796).

Pumpkin Pie

Pumpkin No. 2. One quart of milk, 1 pint of pumpkin, 4 eggs, molasses, allspice and ginger in a crust, bake 1 hour.[39]

Strawberries, blueberries, raspberries, and cherries were eaten fresh, with or without cream. Cranberries were baked into tarts or made into sauce to accompany fowl. The greatest variety of fruits grew on the property of the wealthiest New Englanders, but wild fruit was gathered by children and adults for fun as well as fresh food. Some berries were made into wine.

Most New Englanders preferred ale or beer as a common daily drink, and housewives often brewed beer when they baked bread,

Tavern bar. In one corner of the Farrar-Mansur House
is the bar from which the tavern keeper sold alcoholic
beverages. Men from the town probably gathered here
in the barroom to drink and discuss politics and town
and personal business. Ladies used a parlor in the house.
(Courtesy of the Library of Congress, Historic American Buildings Survey, HABS, VT, 14-WEST, 2-3.)

using malted grain. These grain-based beverages were joined by fermented hard cider, which preserved apple juice for use later. Even
children drank these mildly alcoholic beverages. The wealthy imported and drank wines and made rum punches. Tea was widely
adopted throughout New England by the early eighteenth century
and during the Revolutionary War. When tea was subject to British
tax, many people switched to coffee, which became a favorite bever-

age for most of the nineteenth century. Chocolate was served mostly among the wealthy in the earliest years, and never was as popular as either tea or coffee.

English settlers in the seventeenth century ate three meals a day, as they had in England, and by the end of the Federal era, a fourth meal appeared in some households. How much and what was served depended, of course, on the relative wealth of the family.

For most people, breakfast consisted of bread, cornmeal mush and milk, or bread and milk together, and tea. Even the gentry might eat modestly in the morning, although they could afford meat or fish. By the end of the eighteenth century, however, many travelers to America noted that Americans ate meat as often as twice or three times a day. Beefsteak was by no means uncommon on breakfast tables, along with other meat, such as venison (reported by Samuel Sewall for breakfast in October 1697, when he also had chocolate).[40]

Dinner, as elsewhere in the colonies, was at midday, though the wealthy were likely to do as their peers in England did, and have it in midafternoon. As in the Chesapeake, New England's gentry had a great variety of food on the table, especially when they entertained. In January 1698, for example, after the birth of one of Judge Samuel Sewell's children, he noted, "My Wife Treats her Midwife and Women: Had a good Dinner, Boil'd Pork, Beef, Fowls; very good Rost-Beef, Turkey Pye; Tarts."[41]

An everyday meal might feature only one or two meats with a pudding, tarts, and vegetables. In 1744, when Dr. Alexander Hamilton visited a Mr. Lechmere in Boston, had beef and pudding for dinner.[42] The difference between the more prosperous households and more modest ones might be in the quality and quantity of the meat served. Martha Ballard reported that one Sunday in late May 1789, she had pork, veal, and greens for dinner, and in August 1790 she had baked lamb, green peas, and cucumbers.[43] The less well-off ate salted meat— for example, a simple boiled dinner of salt beef or pork with vegetables or beans.

Supper was a smaller meal, often similar to breakfast: bread, cheese, mush or hasty pudding, or warmed-over meat from the noon meal. Supper among the gentry was also a sociable meal, and might have warm food, meat or shellfish, such as oysters, in season. By the end of the eighteenth century, in some homes tea was served in the late afternoon, with bread or toast, perhaps some preserved fruit, or cold meat. When tea was shared with company, the food might be nicer, with bread and butter, cold meat, pastries, and even wine.

New Englanders did not generally celebrate Christmas until the nineteenth century. They did observe New Year's with visiting, and tea type refreshments were served. Thanksgiving often featured a substantial meal, more like a gentry-style meal with a variety of roasted and boiled meat, vegetables, and pies. The Fourth of July did not have a specific meal associated with it at this time.

The Middle Colonies

From New York south to New Jersey, Pennsylvania, Delaware, and parts of Maryland, a mix of nationalities established colonies and immigrated to ones where they were confident of finding a welcome and freedom to worship without governmental interference. Dutch, Swedes, and English colonized here. Germans, Scotch-Irish, Welsh, French, and Africans all subsequently settled there, ranging in religious beliefs from Quakers to Presbyterians to Catholics. In 1744, Dr. Alexander Hamilton, staying in the region's major city, Philadelphia, recorded: "I dined att a taveren [sic] with a very mixed company of different nations and religions. There were Scots, English, Dutch, Germans, and Irish. There were Roman Catholicks, Church men, Presbyterians, Quakers, Newlightmen, Methodists, Seventh day men, Moravians, Anabaptists, and one Jew. The whole company consisted of 25 planted round an oblong table in a great hall."[44]

The eastern area of this region enjoyed a warmer climate and longer growing season than New England or the western reaches of New York and Pennsylvania, but it was cooler and less likely to breed disease than the Chesapeake and low-lying regions to the south. From this region, the Shendandoah valley in western Virginia and portions of Ohio, Indiana, and Kentucky were settled. It took a while for these varied ethnic groups to mix, but when they had, the Dutch left a legacy of coleslaw, cookies, crullers, and doughnuts. The Germans, who also settled elsewhere, left a great variety of apple dishes and sauerkraut, and added to the array of sausages. Successful wheat growing helped entrench the eating of white bread.

Because this region was settled by an ethnic mix, it tended to develop subregional characteristics and contained more pockets of ethnic foodways than neighboring New England.

Dutch New York. Like most Europeans, the Dutch brought cattle and hogs with them. They subsequently bought beef cattle from New Englanders, who, according to Adriaen Van der Donck, bred cattle able to withstand the absence of shelter in hard northern winters.

(Van der Donck in 1641 came to Rensselaerswijck, now the counties of Albany and Rensselaer, to serve as sheriff for the patroon Kileaen Van Rensselaer.) Similarly, there was a hardy English hog, though the Dutch preferred their Holland hogs, whose fat was thicker. Hogs were allowed to run in the woods and root for acorns and other food, but might be finished on corn. With a strong dairying tradition, the Dutch counted on good milking animals, and new settlers and others "who possess small means" kept goats for milking. Goats, according to Van der Donck, were preferred in New Netherland over sheep, which required labor-intensive tending.[45]

The Dutch made sure to have "every kind of domestic fowls . . . such as capons, turkeys, geese and ducks."[46] Chickens and pigeons rounded out the list. Wild animals provided some food, particularly venison and more rarely bear, buffalo, and raccoon. About the latter Van der Donck reported, "When their meat is roasted, it is delicious food, but when stewed, it is too luscious, on account of its fatness." The Dutch appreciated wild turkeys, which, "well-cleaned and roasted on a pit, then they are excellent, and differ little in taste from the tame turkeys; but the epicures prefer the wild kind." Wildfowl such as pigeons, quail, and waterfowl (swans, geese, ducks of many sorts) provided sport and food for a while. Van der Donck observed, however, "After the increase of our population, the fowls will diminish."[47] Wherever colonists and settlers went, wild animals suitable for food were hunted until they were gone or had moved farther from encroaching settlements.

The Dutch appreciated fish a bit more than the English settlers did, catching familiar saltwater fish such as salmon, cod, flounder, eels, mackerel, herring, and halibut. American striped bass, shad, and drums were new to them. Sturgeon were plentiful in the Hudson River, and Van der Donck reported in the mid-seventeenth century that it was not as esteemed. Later it was sometimes called Albany beef, possibly a derisive term, but had become a more valued food. The Dutch caught freshwater fish such as trout, pike, perch, and carp. They ate oysters, clams, lobsters, and, unlike many New Englanders, mussels.

Hulled and coarsely broken rye, oats, barley, and buckwheat had been made into porridges in Holland; in America, the Dutch used corn. Corn, the Dutch found, was best suited to almost any type of soil, and Van der Donck commented on the cultivation of corn and its suitability for man and beast. Cornmeal cooked and eaten with milk was called *sapaen* or *suppawn*. It was essentially the cornmeal mush eaten elsewhere in the Colonies.

Wheat was the preferred grain for bread in Holland and in America, although, as in other parts of northern Europe, rye was common for the poorer people. In New Netherland, wheat flour was usually plentiful, and bread baked from it was available in bakeries in New Amsterdam and Albany. In fact, the supply was protected by an ordinance which stipulated that bakers could not sell pastries to Native Americans in exchange for beaver pelts because it diminished the supply of wheat, making it scarce the rest of the year. In addition to the common round and oval loaves seen in still-life paintings, there were rolls, rusks, and other baked goods.[48]

Waffles, pancakes, deep-fried cakes called *oleykoeks* (today known as doughnuts), pretzels, various sorts of gingerbread, and other small cakes were part of early Dutch cuisine in America. The use of pearlash, a chemical leaven and the precursor of baking soda, may very well have been a gingerbread baker's guild secret in Holland and America until an observant cook learned about it and tried it herself.[49] Simmons's cookbook gives the first published recipe for the use of pearlash, the earliest chemical leaven in America. Pearlash was used in cookies and gingerbreads at first, but eventually was an ingredient in many other baked goods. Following is Amelia Simmons's cookie recipe:

Cookies

One pound sugar boiled slowly in half pint water, scum well and cool, add two teaspoons pearl ash dissolved in milk, then two and a half pounds flour rub in 4 ounces butter, and two large spoons of finely powdered coriander seed, wet with above; make roles half an inch thick and cut to the shape you please; bake fifteen or twenty minute in a slack oven—good three weeks.[50]

Van der Donck listed in his *Description of New Netherland* nearly twenty kinds of vegetables, including the carrots, turnips, parsnips, onions, leeks, and cabbages often portrayed in the still-life paintings and found in Dutch gardens, together with many more salad lettuces, spinach, and herbs, and "various other things on which I have bestowed no attention." Dutch settlers brought most of these to America, but they also adopted pumpkins, which Van der Donck reported were stewed, as were apples.[51] Like other Europeans, the Dutch adopted the Native American manner of growing beans on cornstalks and letting pumpkins run in the corn patch. Cucumbers, green peas, beans, beets, asparagus, and many other vegetables fill out the list. The Dutch also learned to eat fresh, young corn, roasted in the ear, as a vegetable.

Like European settlers everywhere, the Dutch brought fruit trees and plants to America: apple, and pear, cherry, peach, apricot, plum, persimmon, almond, fig, currant, gooseberry, and bramble fruits. Adriaen Van der Donck, perhaps too optimistically, thought that olives would grow well in America, too.[52] The Dutch adopted cranberries and used wild blackberries. A wide variety of preserves were made from these fruits, and they were eaten in pies and other dishes. Melons and watermelons also grew well, and Van der Donck said, "If the fruit is sound and fully ripe, it melts as soon as it enters the mouth, and nothing is left but the seeds."[53]

Currants, raisins, lemons, capers, bitter oranges, sugar, and spices such as cinnamon, nutmeg, mace, pepper, ginger, cumin, and cloves were imported by the New Netherland Dutch, along with wine. Many of these came, at least for a while, from other Dutch colonies.

Grapes, Van der Donck observed, grew wild in New Netherland, though they did not always ripen properly for eating or winemaking, but he thought that with cultivation and care, they could be tamed. The Netherlanders, whose preference for beer edged out wine, had relatively little of experience in winemaking. Subsequently, some wine was made, but it would be a couple of hundred years before New York State wine became famous.

Like most Europeans, the Dutch preferred beer with most meals, enjoyed imported wine, and, by the end of the seventeenth century, had adopted tea, chocolate, and coffee. By the early 1800s, the American Dutch were, like their English neighbors, making cider from apples.

In early seventeenth-century Holland and in America, the Dutch were accustomed to three meals daily, sometimes four, as were most Europeans of the time except for some of the elite. The day's first meal was breakfast, usually bread and cheese, curds and whey, or porridge, and beer (and, on farms, buttermilk).[54] Some Dutch still-life paintings portray breakfasts with ham, mussels, or other shellfish and glasses of beer or wine.[55] Peter Kalm observed of the Dutch in 1750, "Their breakfast is tea, commonly without milk," taken around 7:00 in the morning. But he also says, "About thirty or forty years ago, tea was unknown to them, and they breakfasted either upon bread and butter or bread and milk." From that one may deduce that in the very early 1700s, the New Netherland Dutch were still eating breakfast similar to the ones they ate in Holland. Kalm further says, "Along with the tea they eat bread and butter with slices of dried beef."

The main meal of the day for ordinary people in early seventeenth-century Holland and in New Netherland was midday dinner, consisting of hot food, usually two or three dishes. Soups or broths, and *hutspots* (stewed dishes of meat or fish with vegetables), peas or beans, or plain boiled salt meat or fried meat were served, as well as, sometimes, *pasteyen*, pies with fillings of meat or poultry. Pancakes, which were sold on the street in Holland, might be served. Bread, butter, and cheese followed. A dinner for some farm families might be porridge, meat, and bread.[56]

Among the more affluent, the meals were similar but the *hutspots* might be made of mutton, beef, veal, or poultry, well seasoned and slowly cooked with vegetables. Where imported dried fruits such as prunes, currants, and raisins were available, they were cooked with the meats or incorporated into sauces. Salads of cooked or uncooked cold vegetables with dressings of oil and vinegar, and sometimes melted butter, were more likely to precede the meal; warm cooked vegetables followed the meal.

Few seventeenth-century descriptions exist of the main meal in America, though one from Jasper Danckaerts, from September 1679, describes a roasted haunch of venison: "The meat was exceedingly tender and good, and also quite fat. It had a slightly spicy flavor. We were also served with wild turkey, which was also fat and of good flavor, and a wild goose, but that was rather dry."[57]

English influences and adaptation to local foods certainly had their impact by this time. Dr. Alexander Hamilton, who ate dinner on Staten Island at the Narrows Ferry, wrote in his journal: "The landlady spoke both Dutch and English. I dined upon what I never eat in my life before—a dish of fryd clams, of which shell fish there is abundance in these parts." Hamilton's landlady served the clams with rye bread and butter, and beer.[58]

There was in Holland, and probably in America, sometimes another small meal in the afternoon, consisting of bread, butter, and cheese, and in the evening the same, or perhaps porridge, might be served. Toward the end of the eighteenth century, among the prosperous, the later afternoon meal became tea. Meat generally marked well-being, so a meal of bread and butter or cheese, or porridge with milk, might have had to suffice for poorer families at all times of day.

Holiday breads and pastries among the Dutch were particularly significant, and several holidays had a particular bread baked for the occasion. For St. Nicholas Day, *speculaas*, a small spiced cake, was made. New Year's had *nieuwjaarskoeken*, originally a thin, waferlike cookie, later rolled and cut. It was an ancestor of the American "cookie" that appeared in Amelia Simmons's *American Cookery* in 1796.[59] On Twelfth Night, or Epiphany, a cake with a bean baked in it was sometimes served. The English version of this was Twelfth cake.

By the Federal era, Dutch cooking had become more American, through adoption of some English ways and American ingredients.

Dutch sovereignty in this region ended in 1664, when the British took over and named the place New York. Yet the Dutch continued to live and cook in Dutch ways for another century. By the early nineteenth century, Dutch foodways had much in common with English and Yankee eating habits.

The Swedes. The Swedes who attempted to establish a colony on Delaware Bay in what is now southern New Jersey and Wilmington, Delaware, were displaced by the Dutch, although a few settlers remained under subsequent governments. When Peter Kalm visited there in 1749, he spoke to an old-timer, who remembered that in his youth they ate a great deal of "white" cabbage (cabbage in heads), winter cabbage or kale, and rutabagas, and that they brewed beer of barley malt. Some Swedes also owned distilling equipment that they shared among themselves. At the time of Kalm's visit, many Swedes, like other Americans of the era, drank cider. They relied upon swine who foraged in woods and raised cattle, which they sold to English settlers who came later. Kalm also reported that the Swedes grew a plentiful supply of wheat, rye, barley, and oats.[60]

The Swedes had largely adopted English ways by the mid-eighteenth century. Kalm observed that they breakfasted upon bread and butter, and drank tea, coffee, and chocolate, as did the English. He saw no hard, "crackerhole-bread," which Swedes made in the old country, but he saw "great loaves." They had also given up many of their Christmas customs, such as lighting Christmas candles, and holiday dishes, such as special breads and porridge, that they had made in New Sweden in the early days.[61] They still celebrated Old Christmas, January 5.

Some of this was confirmed by Rev. Israel Acrelius, the pastor of Holy Trinity Church in Wilmington, Delaware, who came from Sweden to serve at the church and wrote a history of New Sweden. He commented that breakfast consisted of tea or coffee with "long thin slices of bread with thin slices of smoked beef in summer." In winter the bread was "roasted," then soaked in milk and butter; Acrelius said it was called toast. This is essentially what the English called cream toast or milk toast. In the winter, he reported, the Swedes ate mush and milk or milk porridge, or hominy and milk—much as other colonists did—or light buckwheat pancakes. A similar meal was served as supper.[62]

The main meal of the day was at noon, as elsewhere in the colonies, and consisted of soup, followed by meat and vegetables. Acrelius reported that meat was both fresh and salted, and might include ham, beef, tongue, roast beef, fowls, mutton, veal, a pasty of chickens, partridges, or lamb, beefsteak, veal cutlets, mutton chops, turkey, or goose. He said that no one ate fish, and soup was regarded as ordinary household fare. Among vegetables were potatoes, peas, beans, cabbage, turnips, "all kinds of roots," and various kinds of squashes and pumpkins. Sometimes baked or boiled puddings or dumplings were served, which were called "Quaker" food because the Swedes had learned to make them from the English Quakers. In towns, yeasted wheat bread made from fine white flour was usual, but in the country the flour was dark and coarse. Acrelius also reported that there were pancakes of buckwheat meal and wheat flour. Pies of apples, peaches, cherries, or cranberries might form a course, and he said, "When cheese and butter are added one has an ordinary meal."[63]

The English. The English in the Middle Colonies took advantage of their climate's similarity to that of England in order to have a diet more similar to what they were accustomed to. Here, too, relatively greater prosperity put wheat bread and beef on most tables, and this region supplied wheat to other colonies and packed beef and pork for export. The greatest differences in diet among people in this region had to do with their wealth and whether they lived in long-settled and urban centers or on the frontier. In more remote locations, a simpler variation on the menus of the coastal or urban places was usual.

It took relatively little time for a cattle market to develop, particularly in New York, Philadelphia, and Baltimore. Beef animals and pigs were driven to market; some wild game was brought in as well. Some families obtained meat from relatives living on farms. Fish markets were established and sites along rivers, especially the Schuylkill in Pennsylvania, were assigned to inhabitants for shad fishing. The English and others in the region consumed oysters from Chesapeake Bay. Kalm observed in 1749 that cartloads of oysters were sold in Philadelphia, and that "The usual way of preparing oysters here is to fry them on live coals until they begin to open. They are then eaten with a sandwich of soft wheat bread and butter."[64]

Early eighteenth-century fireplace. The Brinton House, built in 1704 by English Quakers in Delaware County, south of Philadelphia, has a broad, deep fireplace. Built into the left jamb is the oven. (Courtesy of the Library of Congress, Historic American Buildings Survey, HABS, PA, 23-DIL, V, 1-8.)

The Brinton House oven, close up, shows the slight curve of its beehive shape. (Courtesy of the Library of Congress, Historic American Buildings Survey, HABS, PA, 23-DIL, V, 1-9.)

Once families established farms, they provided for themselves an abundance of meat that foreign travelers frequently commented on, contrasting American meat consumption with that in England and Europe. In 1817 William Cobbett, who lived for a year on a Long Island, New York, farm, observed the great number of pigs a neighbor planned to slaughter for a year's use, and recorded that there were "fourteen fat hogs, weighting about twenty score a piece, which were to come into the house next Monday,"—roughly 400 pounds each.[65] Some pork was eaten fresh, including the organ meats; much was salted and brined for smoking and made into sausages and head cheese.

Similarly, beef was produced on farms for family use, usually slaughtered in the fall or winter to take advantage of natural cold for preservation, so that much was available for use fresh. Some portions of beef were salted and smoked, and there are accounts of thin-sliced dried beef served with bread for breakfast or tea. The English did not make the array of beef sausage that the German settlers did. Mutton, sheep's meat, was favored among the English, though mutton consumption always depended on the value of wool; when it was high, a sheep was more valuable alive.

Wheat grew so well in the Middle Colonies that it was a major export crop. Even in this center of wheat production there were times during the Revolutionary War when there was no flour to be had in Philadelphia, nor meat and vegetables.

The Newport, Delaware, native Oliver Evans developed what was called an automatic mill in 1782; it cleaned and, with a system of conveyor belts, moved the grain and flour through the mill with less human labor required. This technology was spread through a book, *The Young Millwright and Miller's Guide*, published in 1795 and written by Evans. Particularly useful in the Middle Colonies, the invention increased production of flour, especially fine flour.

The English generally favored wheat bread over others, though in Philadelphia, Peter Kalm observed that buckwheat cakes were sold in the streets, especially in winter.[66] The English also used cornmeal, but less often in cornbread than in mushes or puddings. However, when wheat was costly or scarce, more people turned to cornmeal.

In 1820 John Woods, an English settler, recorded his observations as he and his family traveled through Baltimore on their way to English Prairie, Illinois. They stayed for a while in Fell's Point, Baltimore, and he described what was available in the market in July:

Mid-eighteenth-century Pennsylvania house. In 1765 Peter Wertz built this simple vernacular home for his sister Christianne Lashee in York County, Pennsylvania. The house has a basement kitchen. (Courtesy of the Library of Congress, Historic American Buildings Survey, HABS, PA-67, DAVBU, V, 1-2.)

"flour, meal, meat, fish, butter, cheese, vegetables, and fruit, consisting of pine-apples and cocoa-nuts from the West Indies. Sweet and water-melons, apricots, peaches, prunes, plums, limes, lemons, oranges, cherries, currants, whortleberries, blackberries, fox-grapes, apples, pears, earth-nuts, and walnuts. The fruit in general good and reasonable; and vegetables the same, with the exception of cabbages, and they were very dear, owing to the dry season."[67]

As he traveled toward Illinois, Woods saw American vegetable gardens, which he, like other observers, found generally to be ill kept. Among the vegetables grown he recorded "peas, parsnips, carrots, onions, shallots, sweet, and other potatoes, lettuce, and a large flat sort of cabbage, with a few sorts of herbs."[68] Earlier, cabbages, turnips, onions, radishes, parsnips, carrots, cauliflower were grown in the Middle Colonies by the English, and asparagus appeared in gentry gardens. Potatoes appeared in Pennsylvania in 1685.[69] Peas, a popular English vegetable, were widely grown in mainland New York and on Long Island; Peter Kalm observed, however, that by the mid-1700s, farmers in Pennsylvania had given up cultivating them because of a pest that attacked them. Kalm also observed red beets and sweet potatoes in Pennsylvania, and remarked that the English and Swedes ate pokeweed when it was young.[70]

Peter Kalm frequently commented on the abundance of fruit trees—apple, peachs, cherry—and the fact that they were planted so that passers-by helped themselves to fruit, which the growers seemed not to object to. There were in addition the bramble fruits and melons grown by the Dutch in New York.

As among the English in New England, the meals of the day were breakfast, dinner, and tea or supper in the Middle Colonies. By the

Mid-eighteenth-century basement kitchen hearth in the house Peter Wertz built near Davidsburg in York County, Pennsylvania. This fireplace used a lug pole set into the chimney throat from which the pothooks could be hung. Above the fireplace opening on the left side is a clock jack mechanism for roasting. (Courtesy of the Library of Congress, Historic American Buildings Survey, HABS, PA-67, DAVBU, 1-3.)

end of the eighteenth century, among the elite dinnertime had moved to midafternoon, as it had in England and elsewhere in the colonies. In some affluent households where dinner was earlier in the day, tea was added in the late afternoon. It may or may not have been substantial, depending on the presence of company. Breakfast still began the day and often consisted of bread and cheese or butter, or a porridge. Kalm said that the English liked toast and butter for breakfast with their tea or coffee. Toast at this time was also toasted bread served with hot milk or cream on it.

John Woods recorded that the breakfasts he and his family ate at taverns between Baltimore and West Virginia in 1820 consisted of "several of the following articles: chickens, hams, veal-cutlets, beefsteaks, roast pork, and several sorts of fish; various kinds of hot bread, viz. wheat and corn bread, buck wheat cakes, and waffles, a sort of soft cake, said to be of German origin; butter, honey, jelly, pickles, apple-butter, and the following dried fruits: peaches, cherries, apples, &c." The breakfast included tea or coffee.[71] Tavern meals were no doubt more plentiful than an average home meal, but the list illustrates the variety of foods available at the end of the Federal period in parts of the Middle Colonies where people had been settled over a hundred years.

In his travels from Maryland to New Hampshire in 1744, Dr. Alexander Hamilton described many meals he ate along the way. He often reported chocolate as a breakfast beverage, and once, when it was poorly prepared, he had a porringer of milk instead. At Jamaica, Long Island, he wrote, "We stopt at the Sign of the Sun and paid dear for our breakfast, which was bread and mouldy cheese, stale beer and sower cyder."[72]

During Hamilton's time in New York City, he recorded several dinners, including one in mid-June 1744, at Robert Todd's establishment, a well-known meeting place, where he was served veal, "beef stakes," green peas, and raspberries for dessert. He described a summer meal in a more domestic setting, near Oyster Pond on Long Island: "The family att King's were all busy in preparing dinner, the provision for which chiefly consisted in garden stuff. . . . and att one a'clock dined with the family upon fat pork and green pease."[73]

Supper, a smaller meal in Colonial America for many, consisted at least in part of meat or fish. Travelers almost always found a substantial supper at inns and taverns. For example, in 1744, "near Joppa, Maryland, Hamilton "supped upon fry'd chickens and bacon" at Treadway's Tavern. In Trenton, New Jersey, in July that year, he wrote, "I put up att one Eliah Bond's att the Sign of the Wheat Sheaf. . . . We supped upon cold gammon and a sallett." Oysters were suitable supper fare, and Hamilton ate them pickled near Brunswick, New Jersey. Another time, near Spuyten Duyvil, New York, he wrote, "I supped upon roasted oysters, while my landlord eat roasted ears of corn att another table."[74]

Hamilton also observed that New Yorkers were great "toappers." "To drink stoutly with the Hungarian Club, who are all bumper men, is the readiest way for a stranger to recommend himself, and a sett among them are very fond of making a stranger drunk."[75]

In the northern reaches of the region, Kalm reported in 1749 that better-off French Canadians living near Crown Point, New York, began a meal with clear soup with bread in it, then cooked beef and mutton (almost always fresh) and squabs or fowl, followed by, the summer he visited there, peas, and a dessert of fresh milk with berries. They ate wheat bread, with a little butter, and for a beverage had wine, wine and water, or water alone, or spruce beer. The suppers he saw had "two dishes of meat, both fried, sometimes a fricassee or fried pigeons, also fried fish, and Now and then Milk with berries. The third course in the evening was almost always a salad." The less well-off, often veterans, lived in "wretched cottages," but they were seldom hungry and had wheat bread. Soldiers still in service kept a cow, had kitchen gardens, and hunted to augment rations of meat, as people on rations (slave or free) did everywhere.[76]

Connecticut educator and minister Timothy Dwight, of Yale University, traveled from New England to Niagara Falls in 1804 and stopped for a night at a log home, "not more than half built," near Tonawanda Village in western New York State. His brief description gives a glimpse of frontier life. There was neither bread nor flour, but a fellow traveler produced some flour. "With this supply our good landlady very expeditiously placed before us a cup of hyson tea, with loaf sugar, creams, and excellent hot biscuit, and butter." This supper, though found everywhere in decent inns and older settlements, was here unexpected and very highly relished.[77]

Only a few years later, when British traveler and cartographer John Melish visited in the Middle Colonies and points west, he observed the prosperity that many Americans had obtained by the Federal era. He compared poor Americans with poor British, saying that a farmer in the United States could buy 160 acres for $560 and take eight years to pay for it; if he had it cleared by the end of that time, his land, Melish predicted, might be worth as much as $8000, plus the value of the cattle. Melish further noted that artisans and mechanics were well paid for their labor, earning in two days what it cost to maintain a family for a week, and thus could accumulate savings and soon be independent. The implications of this prosperity for the diet were clear: "[Americans tradesmen] have provisions so reasonable, that they have their wheat bread and roast beef or roast pork or fowl everyday, and accumulate property for old age and their offspring." In Britain, by contrast, the wages were, Melish reported, "from a dollar and a half to three dollars per week," but beef and flour were so expensive that few could afford them. "Small indeed is the portion of these that fall to their lot. No, they are doomed to drag out a miserable existence on potatoes and oat-meal."[78]

English colonists, if they were not Quakers, celebrated Christmas by attending church and possibly having a meal with family. If they wished to obtain food for their meal on Christmas Day, they found it in the market, because Quakers brought goods into town on that day as on all others.

Even though the Declaration of Independence was issued in Pennsylvania, the Fourth of July holiday was not widely celebrated until the early 1800s, and then usually with bell ringing, gunfire, and speechmaking. Certain foods were not associated with the holiday until later.

The Germans. Protestant Germans, Swiss, and German speakers from eastern France settled in Pennsylvania beginning in the last quarter or so of the seventeenth century, taking advantage of freedom of worship in William Penn's colony. Because the English tended to call all German speakers "Dutch," a corruption of the word *Deutsch* (German), these people became known in later times as Pennsylvania Dutch. They left a major mark on Pennsylvanian, and subsequently American, food. From Pennsylvania, the Germans spread through the Shenandoah valley into the Carolina backcountry and trans-Appalachia, each new generation adapting more to American conditions. As seen with their fireplaces in chapter 3, the Germans gradually gave up the old country cooking style while retaining some differences. By the time they reached southern and backcountry areas, they shared many foodways with the descendants of English settlers.

Cooking salty meat and sweet fruit together distinguished German from English cookery. Two dishes, *Gumbis,* consisting of ham, onions, apples, and bacon layered and cooked, and *Schnitz und Gnepp,* made of dried apples, smoked ham, and dumplings, probably came to Colonial Pennsylvania with German settlers. Summer sausage made with beef was a typically German dish. German pork sausage was very similar to English sausage. While the English made head cheese, the Pennsylvania Germans made *panhaas.* A butchering day dish, it used the organ meats, cooked and chopped into the cooking liquid, which was thickened with buckwheat and/or cornmeal, then fried in sausage fat after it had cooled. The German Protestant sect of Crefelders brought the dish to Germantown, Pennsylvania, and it eventually evolved into the scrapple associated with Philadelphia. The Pennsylvania Germans also cleaned and stuffed pigs' stomachs as another butchering season dish.

Like their English neighbors, the Pennsylvania Germans ate duck, goose, chicken, turkey, lamb, veal, venison, rabbit, and other meats. They, too, cooked calf's heads and pigs' feet. They cured hams in brine and later smoked them.

Germans in Pennsylvania, observing the value of wheat for sale, often chose to continue growing and eating rye and sold their wheat. The German pastry tradition called for yeast-leavened dough for various *Kuche,* a kind of flat cake covered with fruit or other filling. The Pennsylvania Dutch adopted the America pie tradition by the nineteenth century. Germans also made dumplings and noodles from wheat flour that they added to soups to thicken them.

Germans are generally credited with being more careful vegetable gardeners than other Americans in the Colonial era. They grew beets more than the English did, and pickled them. Making sauerkraut to preserve cabbage was for many years a distinctive German habit not generally accepted by other nationalities until well into the nineteenth century. In the mid-1700s Peter Kalm saw in a German house in Pennsylvania what he described as a "sauerkraut machine," essentially a cutting board with stationary knives in it that was placed over a barrel. The head of cabbage was slid over the knives, which shaved it off the head and into the barrel.[79]

Because there were so many sects of Protestant Germans in Pennsylvania, there was a wide variety of opinions about the celebrations of various holidays. Not all sects observed Christmas or Easter, for example, and the record is scant in its information until the nineteenth century, when Pennsylvania Dutch observed the holidays more widely. Amish and Mennonite settlers, like the Pennsylvania Quakers and New England Puritans, did not observe Christmas. The Moravians, however, did.

Lowland South and Spanish Southeast

The Spanish explored and sporadically settled the parts of the present United States along the Atlantic Coast from the Carolinas to Florida, and along the Gulf of Mexico from Florida to Texas, long before the English established colonies to the north. Few of the earliest settlements were permanent, and many changes of administration occurred in the region as the Spanish, French, and English occupied and then abandoned the area all through the Colonial era. Ultimately America acquired it in the Federal period by occupation and purchase. Thus the foods there reflect influences from these groups plus contributions from Caribbean natives, Africans, and Native Americans.

"Creolization" is the term most modern scholars use to describe the mixing of these many cultures. Because so many households in this region had slaves, including African and Caribbean cooks, the foodways here show not only the owners' preferences but also the foods familiar to Africans. Also, because Spanish and French settlers more readily married Native Americans, the absorption of certain Indian foodways was eased into the communities of non-Natives.

In the Carolinas and Georgia, England hoped to raise the exotic goods for which it relied upon the Mediterranean, Spain, and Portugal having been disappointed when Virginia did not yield silk, olive oil, sugar, grapes, and citrus fruits. But England's West Indian Colonies shifted the major portion of their production to sugar, importing more slaves and buying and clearing more land to grow sugar. Doing so left less land for newly freed indentured servants and new colonists, some of whom settled in Jamaica and then Barbados, and thence the lowland areas of the American South, where they raised cattle and hogs at first, supplying meat to the islands' sugar plantations, and then turned to rice cultivation by 1700. Rice and livestock continued to dominate agriculture in this area; much meat was exported to Britain, Europe, and the West Indies, but rice was, during the Colonial and Federal eras, the most important and valuable crop.

For Spain, Florida was a foothold on the eastern edge of what became the United States, and settlers moving north from Mexico made its western entry path. While Spain's empire crumbled during the eighteenth century, Florida and the rest of the Spanish borderlands toward Louisiana was often in political flux. The English had pushed the Spanish south out of the Carolinas and Georgia; then Spain lost

Florida under the Treaty of Paris at the end of the French and Indian War regained it in 1783, and lost it to the United States for
good in 1819.

On the western edge of this region, Louisiana was settled by the
French, who first arrived in 1699. After much difficulty colonizing
the area, France gave up the territory to the Spanish in 1762, who
held it until 1803. Then it reverted to the French, who shortly afterward sold the young United States the territory known as the
Louisiana Purchase.

The Carolinas. The area now divided into North and South
Carolina had different settlement experiences though it began as one
colony. The eastern seaboard and its backcountry similarly differed
from one another, and from Virginia to the north. The Spanish
explored what is now called the Albemarle but had little interest in
settling it. They did establish a colony, Santa Elena, on what is now
Parris Island, South Carolina. Eventually it was abandoned, and later
was claimed by England.

In the northern part of Carolina, settlers, some moving from Virginia, established small farms on which they raised cattle and grew
corn. There were slaves on plantations there, but not usually on the
scale found in southern Carolina. This colony was established in the
later seventeenth century, became identified as North Carolina in
1691, and was a colony on its own in 1712. Newly freed indentured
servants and colonists from England found land here; established
small holdings; brought with them familiar vegetables, fruits, and livestock; found the usual array of wild foods, such as persimmons, paw-
paws, and whortleberries (a kind of blueberry); and fished for an array
of fish similar to that found in the Chesapeake.

Among the eighteenth-century North Carolinians, as elsewhere in
the colonies, wealth determined how lavishly one lived and entertained. The English foodways of the region closely resembled those
of Virginia. Less archaeological work has been done in the Albemarle
or Cape Fear regions than around the Chesapeake, so there is less
confirmation from remains of the meat-eating habits of Carolinians
than of Virginians.

The Irish native John Brickell, who lived in Edenton between 1724
and 1731, described the region favorably, commenting that the
people there ate beef, pork, mutton, venison "in abundance," domestic fowl and wildfowl, and fish, along with salad and root vegetables. He also reported that there was good bread, butter, and

cheese, and that people made hasty puddings from rice and from Indian meal.[80] With the exception of the rice, this diet closely resembles that of other southern British colonies.

Travel literature seldom fails to mention pork, but since the English generally showed a proclivity for beef, we can assume that would be true here as well, at least among the better-off. The lesser sorts ate more salted meat, and much of that was probably pork, with vegetables and hominy.

For example, when John Bernard traveled into the Carolinas at the end of the eighteenth century, he wrote a description of a Carolina ordinary, a public place to eat and drink. While a bit exaggerated for humorous effect, it is probably a fairly accurate snapshot. He reported that a traveler recognizes the ordinary by finding a house with a jug suspended from a pole. "As to edibles, whether you called for breakfast, dinner or supper the reply was one, eggs and bacon; but the meal brought not a gratification but a task. . . . Ten to one you had to cook the meal yourself, while the landlady was searching for a trencher; and when it was before you, you were sure of only one thing—to pay for it."[81]

Most of Carolina's low country, particularly the part that became South Carolina, was settled by English colonists from Barbados, who had, like Hispanics in the Southwest, already adjusted to the New World through life in the West Indies. They arrived accustomed to the cooking of African slaves from the islands who were valued highly for their skill. French Huguenots escaping Catholic persecution also settled in the low country in large numbers before the Revolution, many retaining the French language.

When rice became the major cash crop of the area, many West African slaves were imported to grow it, and by the early eighteenth century, blacks outnumbered whites there. The large population of Africans, and the task system imposed on rice plantation laborers, combined to help preserve more traditional black foodways than was usual elsewhere in the South. In the task system, the slaves, assigned a particular task, were allowed—indeed, expected, once the job was done—to tend their own garden plots, hunt, fish, and forage to supplement their rations. In addition to cultivating rice for themselves, the slaves grew okra, black-eyed peas, eggplants, greens of various sorts, and other African garden crops.

Because it was famous for its rice cultivation, rice cookery became a defining characteristic of the region among white and black, free and enslaved, beginning with the knowledge of how to boil it. White settlers in Carolina did not have a tradition of rice cookery, and thus learned from their slave cooks, who had relied on rice as a staple in Africa. Those cooks customarily cooked the rice so that each grain was perfectly tender and separate, a method subsequently identified as the Carolina method.

Regional dishes that incorporated rice included pilaus, jambalayas, and hoppin' John; the following recipe for hoppin' John appeared in Sarah Rutledge's *The Carolina Housewife or House and Home by a Lady of Charleston* (1847).

Hoppin' John

One pound of bacon, one pint of red peas, one pint of rice. First put on the peas, and when half boiled, add the bacon. When the peas are well boiled, throw in the rice, which must be first washed and graveled. When the rice has been boiling half an hour, take the pot off the fire and put it on coals to steam, as in boiling rice alone. Put a quart of water on the peas at first, and if it boils away too much, add a little more hot water. Season with salt and pepper and, if liked, a sprig of green mint. In serving up, put the rice and peas first in the dish, and the bacon on the top.[82]

Recent scholarship on these dishes shows multilayered influences traveling through time, from abroad (often through Africa) to the low country. Rice was also used in yeasted bread, pancakes, and other breads.

Georgia. Like the Carolinas, Georgia had a low-country seacoast where rice was grown on large, wealthy plantations with African slave labor, and an interior frontier where settlers, depending more on cattle raising, established themselves on smaller holdings, often without, or with only a few, slaves. The colonizing company's dreams of wealth from silk, wine, and indigo cultivation for export gave way to corn, beans, squash, cattle, and hogs raised by independent settlers or freed indentured servants.

In 1743, the minutes of the meeting of the trustees of the Colony of Georgia, held in London, shows that they heard testimony from Lt. Col. Alexander Heron of General Oglethorpe's regiment. Heron reported that on St. Simon's Island and other southern parts of Georgia, Indian corn, peas, beans, cabbage, turnips, carrots, onions, and other garden stuff grew as plentifully as anywhere else in the colonies, and that the Palatine German settlers raised enough food for themselves, and thus "had no other dependence but the produce of their lands." Others reported that there were cattle, hogs, poultry, plenty of fish, and bees. Some even suggested that if soldiers there had their own plantations, they would be better off than if they were merely paid.[83]

Although Georgia proved to be a good place to live, it was no more able to return great sums of money to its investors than other Colonies had been, and the colony was committed to the protection of the crown in the mid-1700s.

Florida. As in the Southwest, the Spanish created both secular and religious settlements in sixteenth- and seventeenth-century Florida. Florida's Native Americans seemed, to the missionaries who tried to live among them and convert them, more warlike and less settled. Their agriculture, like that of Native Americans elsewhere, depended heavily on corn, beans, and squash; the rest of their subsistence came from hunting and fishing. Spanish in La Florida established the system of *repartimiento*, which obligated the Indians to work for the mission in exchange for military protection, Christianizing, and what the Spanish regarded as the benefits of Western civilization. Part of their labor involved raising food, including some European grains and enough corn, to supply the friars, the garrisons, and the Indians themselves. In the earliest days, however, the missionaries living among the Indians seem to have adopted many of their foodways, or at least foods, until they could rely once again on primarily European fare. Remains of deer, turtles, and the occasional alligator, as well as small animals such as raccoons and squirrels, are found in archaeological digs at mission sites. Where missions were near estuaries and rivers, fish such as catfish and drums show up as well. Willingness to accept Native American foods certainly helped Spanish survival in the earliest years.

La Florida was not a particularly profitable colony for the Spanish; there was no one crop such as sugar, or resource such as precious metal, that generated wealth. They valued it more for its strategic locations, supporting it with ever less reliable allowances of money and food supplies.

Like other European settlers, the Spanish had brought to Florida seeds for familiar crops, grapevines, and cattle, hogs, and poultry. Neither their preferred grains nor sheep, their preferred meat animal, thrived. In its earliest years, St. Augustine relied on corn, wild game, and fish. The archaeological record shows domesticated animals including pigs, cattle, and poultry, but in small numbers.

Essentially a military colony, St. Augustine had relatively few European women among its inhabitants. The soldiers married Indian women, as Spanish and French did all across the borderlands. Indian women certainly had to learn to cook European-style food, but they also cooked, as they always had, any wild food that came into their kitchens. These cooks understood what to do with persimmons, cabbage, palm berries, palmetto, groundnuts, sunflower seeds, prickly pear, and even acorns, which some of the Indians were accustomed to eating. The archaeological remains of early St. Augustine show chili peppers, lima beans, and *moschata* squash, which may have been imported from other colonies or have been grown there. Hickory nuts were used, as were peaches and watermelons. (As in the Southwest, the latter two fruits preceded the Spanish settlers; Indians had grown them, spreading the seeds in trade.)

Although the Spanish often had enough to eat, during the early years there were, as in other places, the danger of insufficient food and times when the supply was very short. Many colonists greatly missed wheat, olive oil, and wine. Subsisting on fish and cornmeal, some scholars observe, may have seemed to the Spanish colonists more like peasant life than the wealthy life they hoped to gain by immigrating to the New World.[84]

Eighteenth-century Spanish colonists established farms and ranches, and by the mid-1700s were engaged in a mixed agriculture depending mostly on American native crops such as corn, beans, and squash. By 1700, St. Augustine was an established fortified city, with a grocery store, butcher shop, fish market, gristmill, and slaughterhouse. Orchard fruits such as pears, peaches, oranges, quince, pomegranates, mulberries, and figs grew there. Vegetable gardens provided beans, squash, sweet potatoes, garlic, peppers, onions, and pumpkins. Grapes and melons grew. Domestic animals included cows, pigs, and chickens.[85]

Trade with Indians included foodstuffs such as dried turkey, sassafras, lard, salt pork, fish, game, corn, bear grease, and nut oil. Wine, oil, and chocolate came via illegal trade routes.[86]

From 1717 to about 1738, Florida grew enough citrus, primarily oranges, to ship them to South Carolina, Rhode Island, Jamaica, and New York. Once western parts of Florida were settled, what is called the panhandle, settlers grew enough wheat to export it to Spain and Havana, Cuba, and to sell in Louisiana.[87] In the late 1700s, tomatoes were an important vegetable in Florida, where more of them grew than elsewhere in America.[88]

By the 1780s Florida had a mixture of Spanish, English, French, and Catalan speakers living there in addition to Native Americans. St. Augustine's population was relatively small, consisting of Minorcans and other Mediterranean families, some of whom had been indentured servants under the English; some free blacks; and British and Europeans and their slaves. More French came during the French Revolution, and others fled Haiti because of the revolution there. Irish were added to the mix as well.

Archaeological sites dating to the late Spanish Colonial era reveal a little about the foodways that emerged at this time. At sites representing wealthy Spanish and Minorcan households, it is clear that they relied primarily on beef and pork, having given up the mutton preferred in the Old World; they also raised poultry and ate wild birds. Poorer Minorcan households continued to eat primarily fish and shellfish, as they had in the Old World and as other poor colonists did elsewhere in America.

Louisiana. The first colonists in Louisiana were the French, who arrived in 1699. As in many other places, they came to establish a trading post to which French traders from the upper Mississippi brought furs. The low-lying land and heat bred disease that killed many colonists in the first decade of the eighteenth century, repeating the high mortality of many other initial settlements in America. Most colonists were soldiers or tradespeople unskilled in agriculture, and for a time the colony was provisioned in part by French settlers living upriver around present-day St. Louis and by supplies brought from France with new colonists. They also engaged in trade with Spanish colonies in Florida and Havana, obtaining brandy, lard, and tobacco. The Spanish would not supply seed wheat.

With the need to find a profitable crop, the French here, like colonists elsewhere, neglected food production in favor of experimenting with indigo, cotton, and tobacco. The political organization of the colony also saw changes that affected its food production, stabilizing somewhat when the Company of the Indies, in charge from 1718 until 1722, stopped trying to recruit reluctant French settlers and turned to Germans, Swiss, and people from the Low Countries. These settlers cleared land and built farms along the Mississippi River, but Louisiana was still not self-sufficient in food, although an abundance of produce was reported in New Orleans. The population grew very slowly, with setbacks from conflicts with the Native Americans.

In a later attempt to settle immigrants in 1751, the French crown sent a shipload of marriageable young women, promising a cow, a calf, seed grain, some chickens, and supplies for three years to newly married couples. France gave up the region and turned it over to

Spain in 1762. The fairly lenient and brief Spanish governance allowed French Creoles to maintain their language and customs. During Spanish rule more settlers came, some encouraged by the offer
of land fronting on a river or bay, a year's supplies, some farm tools,
a young pig, two hens, and a cock. American Loyalists fleeing the
Revolution, some Spaniards, West Florida British, and the French
Acadians expelled from Nova Scotia arrived in this era and made
homes. In 1803, Louisiana reverted to France, and the young United
States purchased Louisiana shortly afterward. The Acadians are credited with introducing roux, the cooked flour and butter mixture used
to thicken dishes such as jambalaya. Following is Mrs. Abby Fisher's
1851 recipe for "jumberlie":

Jumberlie—A Creole Dish

Take one chicken and cut it up, separating every joint, and adding to it one
pint of cleanly-washed rice. Take about half a dozen large tomatoes, scalding
them well and taking the skins off with a knife. Cut them in small pieces and
put them with the chicken in a pot or large porcelain saucepan. Then cut in
small pieces two large pieces of sweet ham and add to the rest, seasoning high
with pepper and salt. It will cook in twenty-five minutes. Do not put any water
on it.[89]

French colonists were not self-sufficient in meat production until
nearly the mid-1700s. From 1700 to 1718, despite an initial supply
of domestic animals brought with the settlers (cattle, sheep, hogs,
and chickens), the colonists relied on wild food—game, fish, and
fowl. They also depended heavily on French settlers up the Mississippi River in Illinois, from whom they bought smoked and cured
beef, pork, and mutton until they were able to produce sufficient
meat.

The wheat-eating French resisted growing corn for a little while
but, finding that Louisiana's semitropical climate did not suit wheat,
they turned to corn. They, like the Carolina low-country settlers, took
up rice growing and imported slaves knowledgeable in its cultivation.
By 1720, rice was as important a crop as corn.

During earliest settlement, when the food supply was low, the
French settlers made cornmeal mush or gruel, called *gru*, to which
they added fat if it was available. They also adopted the Indian dish
sagamite, a meat stew thickened with cornmeal. Parched corn (dried
roasted corn) was pounded and boiled with beans to make a dish very
similar to succotash. The lack of powered mills in the early days required grain to be hand-pounded or ground. Later in the Colonial

era, wheat from the upper South and the interior of the country was shipped down the Mississippi to Louisiana, making possible wheat bread and pastry.

Louisianans, both black and white, ate okra and used it in gumbo. French settlers also used tomatoes in the Colonial era, not only in the low country and Gulf Coast but also in interior areas.[90] They also grew and consumed squashes, corn, and beans, as well as European vegetables. Here are two kinds of gumbo, the first an 1847 recipe from Sarah Rutledge and the second an 1824 recipe from Mary Randolph:

New Orleans Gumbo

Take a turkey or fowl, cut it up, with a piece of fresh beef; put them in a pot, with a little lard an[d] onion, and water sufficient to cook the meat. After they have become soft, add a hundred oysters, with their liquor. Season to your taste; and just before taking up the soup, stir in until it becomes mucilaginous two spoonsful of pulverized sassafras-leaves.[91]

Ochra Soup

Get two double handful of young ochra, wash and slice it thin, add two onions chopped fine, put into a gallon of water at a very early hour in an earthen pipkin, or very nice iron pot: it must be kept steadily simmering, but not boiling: put in pepper and salt. At 12 o'clock, put in a handful of lima beans, at half past one o'clock, add three young cimlins cleaned and cut in small pieces, a fowl, or knuckle of veal, a bit of bacon or pork that has been boiled, and six tomatas [*sic*], with the skin taken off when nearly done; thicken with a spoonful of butter, mixed with one of flour. Have rice boiled to eat with it.[92]

New Orleans relied upon cisterns, wells, and the Mississippi River for its water supply. Early accounts claim that the sediment-laden river water, if left standing in a jar, would clear sufficiently to be drunk. For other beverages, Louisianans traded with the Caribbean islands, importing sugar, rum, coffee, and cocoa. Even early, they consumed a great deal of wine and other alcoholic beverages, including whiskey brought down the Mississippi River from Kentucky.

As in other Colonies, Louisianans, unless they were very poor, ate three meals a day: breakfast; a main meal at noon including soup, meats, and vegetables; and supper, a light meal consisting of leftovers or a soup or stew.

African American Foodways. In American or island colonies, African slaves, usually women, cooked both for themselves and their families, and for their owners. As enslaved cooks, their first responsibility was to please their owners, which primarily required them to cook European dishes, following directions from the housewife, who may have merely described the desired outcome, or may have read aloud a recipe from a cookbook or manuscript recipe notebook. While her personal safety too often relied on her success at meeting the owners' expectations, the cook based her work on years of habit and experience that were communicated to the flavor of the food. The dishes that the slaves prepared for themselves were observed by their owners, and no doubt sampled. A number of these were adapted from the slave diet into plantation cuisine.

The African cooks, using African, European, and Native American ingredients, mixed foodways, preserving some of their familiar dishes and altering others to create variations on traditional dishes. They also absorbed some European dishes into their cookery. Cross-adaptation like this is generally called creolization, and the process resulted in modern low-country cookery, and a strong influence on all of southern and modern African American cooking.[93] Because slaves were brought to

This simple hearth sufficed for the kitchen of The Oaks, a late Federal era Alabama plantation. (Courtesy of the Library of Congress, Historic American Buildings Survey, HABS, ALA, 17-LEIT, V, 1-8.)

America from various African cultures, they forged new foodways out of remnants of the old ones. When importation of new slaves ceased, and the growth of the American slave population depended on natural increase, the gap between new and old practices grew.

Black cooks who worked in the plantation house or in urban homes were skilled and valuable workers generally acknowledged to be of the highest caliber. The character of southern cookery is attributed to them. To cook for their own families, however, women slaves often had to overcome exhaustion to pull together a meal from the weekly rations supplied by the master. If time and circumstances allowed, the cook included ingredients grown in her own garden plot or foraged from the wild by men in the slave community. Because of the nature of the institution of slavery, certain conventions and even regulations in providing food for slaves blurred subregional distinctions. The greatest determinants of slave food habits was whether they were owned by a small planter or an urban dweller, whether they were one of a handful of slaves or whether they were part of a large plantation workforce. In the case of the latter, their foodways depended on whether they were assigned work according to a task system or whether they labored for a specified amount of time.

In the task system, much used on the rice plantations of the Carolina and Georgia low country, slaves were encouraged to grow a great deal of their own food, particularly rice, and were allotted land on which to do it. They were free to work this land once they had completed each day's specified tasks. Accordingly, less food was rationed to them. On plantations where work was governed by the rising and setting of the sun, many slaves also had garden plots near their cabins where they grew vegetables to provide a little variety to their rations of corn, salt pork, and molasses.

Besides salt meat, plantation owners distributed salt herring, shad, or codfish—dried fish was usually cheaper than meat. Some fresh beef was distributed at Christmas; sweet potatoes and molasses were also purchased for slave rations. There is evidence that slaves grew food or raised chickens for eggs beyond their own needs to sell to their owners or to general stores, and at market days. The income from such sales could be applied to buying food, drink, or clothing. Food, fabric, an occasional ribbon, pots and pans, blankets, rum, and sugar were among the commonest items bought with slaves' earned income.

In addition, slaves fished, and hunted and trapped small animals. Archaeological remains show the lengths to which slaves went to procure additional food. In some cultures, including the American Colo-

This slave cabin on the late Federal era The Oaks plantation in Alabama was still occupied, probably by tenant farmers, when it was photographed early in the twentieth century. Some slave quarters were a bit better than this, and some were worse. (Courtesy of the Library of Congress, Historic American Buildings Survey, HABS, ALA, 17-LEIT, V, 1-11.)

nial southern elite, a great variety in food, particularly meat, demonstrated wealth. But the great variety revealed in the faunal remains of slave cabin sites shows hardship and slaves' persistence in providing a sufficient and varied diet with wild game.

While most slaves lived on medium-to-large plantations in the South *and* North, small planters and urban dwellers were less likely to allow their slaves to live in separate households. Indeed, slaves in those settings were usually relegated to sleeping in a loft or attic. The smaller a master's household, the more likely that slave servants ate food similar to that of the white family, although not at the same table. The cook who prepared the family meal was almost always black. These slaves had less opportunity to cook in distinctively African ways.

Backcountry and Upland South

Deeper into the South, away from the coast into the piedmont uplands of Virginia, Carolina, and Georgia, was wilder land where "long hunters" and cowpen keepers lived until the middle 1700s. Thereafter it was settled by many Scotch-Irish and German Protestant Moravians who traveled there, via the Shenandoah valley, from Pennsylvania, seeking less expensive land and milder winters. "Long hunters" stayed in the woods for a long time, collecting skins for trade. Cowpen keepers allowed their cattle to range on largely unsettled land, then herded their animals into cowpens for driving to market. These ways of life allowed considerable independence but also resulted in social isolation. Many of the most remote backcountry people lived without as much access to material comforts as they would have had in more settled parts, and were certainly not as refined in their cookery or other manners.

The Virginia backcountry was connected to both the Chesapeake and Philadelphia markets, and wheat was the predominant crop for most of the eighteenth century. Some settlers in North Carolina's backcountry raised livestock, grew wheat, and made butter, as well as nonfood goods, for other colonies because access to ports was so difficult. Poor market opportunities slowed the development of North Carolina's backcountry for much of this era, and led some people to decide to move to South Carolina's backcountry, where they might reach better markets. There they were joined by Scotch-Irish and German settlers accepting bounties offered to help increase the population of white people there, in response to growing fear of the majority black population. Others from the backcountry moved into adjacent sections of Georgia.

Backcountry people broke through the line, established by royal decree in 1763 along the Appalachian Mountains, that was intended to keep colonists and Indians apart, and settled in western Pennsylvania and eastern Kentucky and Tennessee. These settlements were dispersed, often remote from commercial centers, and vulnerable to Indian attack. Most backcountry agriculture was done without slave labor; families cleared and worked the land, planting for their own subsistence, grazing animals, and hunting wild game.

At any time from early settlement until the Federal era, the backcountry was likely to show substantial contrasts in the quality of life. Some people lived at first in small, very rough shelters, had poor food, drank too much, and had rough manners that gave rise to the image of the uncivilized backwoodsman. In towns and in areas longer settled, there were prosperous farms, people practicing trades, schools, churches, and familiar European foodways being adapted to American conditions.

After the Revolutionary War was over, Americans turned to settling land west and south of existing colonies. Everywhere they turned, they displaced Native Americans, and eventually challenged Spanish and French claims to land, particularly along the borders of Spanish Florida. Settlers from the southern states seeking a similar climate for southern crops, increasingly cotton, moved into the areas that eventually became Mississippi, Alabama, and Louisiana. On land ceded by Virginia and North Carolina to the new federal government, Tennessee and Kentucky were settled by farmers growing corn and wheat, and some nonfood crops, as well as grazing livestock as they had in the backcountry. Tennessee farmers supplied food to Alabama and Mississippi, and Kentucky converted corn and wheat into the higher-valued whiskey and flour to sell after floating it downstream to New Orleans. Some food products from the upland South were sold in the Northeast and even in Europe.

The amount of pork, particularly in the form of bacon, reported by travelers and others in the early South may be attributable to its ubiquity rather than the actual quantity consumed. It was a lower-value salted meat, on hand even in warm weather, and easily and quickly prepared by remote country people for travelers. Flavorful country ham and fat bacon were good additions to the gentry table, where fresh domestic and wild meat also appeared. Most of the Scotch-Irish who settled here had arrived with a preference for mutton and beef, but the country was too wild for sheep raising, so beef and pork became the primary meats. Beef had value in the market when it was driven to a port town or of more populated center, so some people may have preferred to eat pork and sell beef.

Where families kept milk cows, the traditional Scotch-Irish made a dish called "bonny clabber," or clabbered milk, which was an important part of some people's diet. In warm weather, milk naturally soured, and formed curds that were eaten as yogurt is today.

Corn was a primary grain, pounded and sifted into grits and meal, the grits being cooked in a mush as oat grits had been in the British Isles; the finer meal was used to make simple bannocks or hoecakes, or mixed with wheat to make cornbread. Settlers here also grew wheat and rye. The German Moravians who settled in the Carolina backcountry planted corn, wheat, rye, oats, buckwheat, and spelt.

The Moravian settlers in the backcountry brought with them peas, celery, asparagus, cabbage, carrots, turnips, onions, radishes, beets, and Irish potatoes, and added to them American squashes, beans, pumpkins, corn, and sweet potatoes. Many of these were boiled to accompany meat.

The hardship of some of the Carolina backcountry is portrayed by Rev. Charles Woodmason, an itinerant Anglican minister who traveled through the area around Camden, South Carolina, in 1767 and 1768. He lodged wherever he could, sometimes without refreshment, commenting that the poor people there had nothing but Indian cornbread and water, though later in the spring he observed wheat, rye, Indian corn, and "all kind of Grain and Fruit Trees" growing near Rocky Mount. In 1768, in the Waxsaw area south of present-day Charlotte, North Carolina, he observed—although some of his experience surely was colored by his being among fervent Presbyterians who were not interested in entertaining an Anglican minister—that there was "nothing but Indian Corn Meal to be had Bacon and Eggs in some Places—No Butter, Rice, or Milk—-As for Tea and Coffee they know it not." Many of the people there were Irish, who, he said, "live wholly on Butter, Milk, Clabber." On the other hand Woodmason also found, on Wateree Creek, "a fine farm, and neat decent People. Here . . . I got some Milk, and a fowl broil'd—the 1st fresh Meat [I] had tasted for some time."[94]

It took time for the refinements in dining that Woodmason preferred to become commonplace in the poorer parts of the backcountry. As he traveled, he carried with him cups, knife, spoon, plate, towels, and linen, in addition to tea, coffee, sugar, chocolate, cheese, a pint of rum, and biscuits. This was, he reported, because "As in many Places they have nought but a Gourd to drink out off [sic]. Not a Plate Knife or Spoon, a Glass, Cup or any thing,"[95]—not unlike similarly situated hardscrabble people elsewhere in the colonies.

The meals of the day in the backcountry were largely as they were elsewhere in the Colonies. Breakfast consisted of mush or hasty puddings; hoecakes, ashcakes, johnnycakes, sometimes accompanied by meat and/or eggs; and, depending on the household's prosperity and the beverage's availability, cider, coffee, tea, or chocolate.

The Marquis de Chastellux traveled into the Virginia piedmont in 1782, and described some of breakfasts he ate in remote taverns and homes. At Boswell's Tavern, not far from Charlottesville, he was served ham, butter, eggs, and coffee with milk, and reported that by this time he was "perfectly accustomed to the American habit of drinking coffee as a beverage with meat, vegetables, or other food."[96]

The largest meal was usually at midday, called dinner, and when there was meat, it was served at this meal. As they had in Pennsylvania, the Germans here cooked dried apples, called *Schnitz*, with pork to make a main dish. Dumplings, vegetables in season, or vegetables stewed with salt pork made a meal for middling farmers. The wealthy, as they did elsewhere, had a greater variety of meat and fowl on the table with side dishes of vegetables.

Supper was another small meal, sometimes as big as breakfast and consisting of similar food, sometimes a smaller meal of bread and milk, or bonny clabber, or cold leftovers.

The Old Northwest

Many states, including Connecticut, Massachusetts, New York, and Virginia, ceded their western lands to the new federal government. That permitted development of new towns and states to accommodate the ever-larger American population, growing by birth and continuing immigration. In 1787, the area that became Ohio, Indiana, and Illinois by 1820 (and the Michigan Territory, yet to be formed) was called the Northwest Territory. Neither slavery nor primogeniture (the eldest son inheriting all the father's property) was allowed in these new lands, so small farms generally were the rule.

Many settlers there came from the Northeast and Middle Atlantic states, bringing with them food habits from those regions. This area also attracted settlers from many other countries. John Bradbury reported that west of the Alleghenies one found English, Irish, Scotch, Dutch, Swiss, German, French, and other Europeans, a mix similar to that found in Pennsylvania half a century before.

French Canadian settlers also arrived in this area from the north, settling in the early 1700s around the Great Lakes and spreading southward along the Mississippi, Miami, and Illinois rivers toward present-day St. Louis. Many of the French came first as fur traders, some of whom married Native American women. Others followed and established what the naturalist John Bradford called in 1811 a distinct colony in Upper Louisiana, land that had been recently acquired by the United States from France.

In 1722 Diron d'Artaguiette, on a trip up the Mississippi from New Orleans, observed about the place where the Kaskaskia River emptied into the Mississippi, in present-day Illinois: "the French village called the Cascakias, which is composed entirely of farmers who live there very comfortably. French wheat grows very well there and of a fine quality, of which they gather a fairly large quantity, which they

sell for the subsistence of the troops. All the other vegetables necessary to life grow very well there. . . . Several inhabitants also have
horse tread mills of their own with which they grind their French
wheat."[97]

John Bradbury later described their agriculture, saying that they
raised corn, wheat, oats, barley, beans, pumpkins, watermelons and
musk melons, and apples and peaches, and grew a large variety of
vegetables. Like settlers to the east, they allowed their hogs, having
marked the ears for identification, to forage for themselves, luring
them back to shelter with corn. Cattle also grazed on the prairie lands,
though the settlers harvested some hay to feed the cattle in winter
when there was a snow cover.[98] Food from French settlers here supplied New Orleans through some of its difficult times.

On the eastern edge of this territory, especially in Ohio, settlers
raised cattle for markets in Baltimore and Philadelphia, fattening cattle and pigs, with the corn that grew well there. Cincinnati was
founded in 1789, and by the close of the Federal era, was nicknamed
Porkopolis because of the extensive pork packing business carried on
there.

In the early years wild food was important here and, as in other
frontier areas, was replaced by domestic animals. Native Americans in
the territory killed deer and sold the venison to settlers. Among the
Catholic Canadian French, fish from the Great Lakes and the many
other freshwater lakes of the region was important food, and included
sturgeon, walleyes, and perch. There was (and is) among the French
the westernmost reach of Lake Erie a tradition of eating muskrat.
While the explanation that muskrat was permissible as food on fast
days because the animal lived in water may be apocryphal, the modern preparation of the dish, which calls for corn in a stew of muskrat
meat, points to a Native American borrowing. John Bradford, ex-
ploring along the Missouri River in 1811, noted that the Canadian
French trappers and traders he encountered considered skunk to be
a delicacy.[99] Beaver, particularly the tail, was also considered good
food. In the part of the Old Northwest that is known today as the
Upper Great Lakes, there is till a strong tradition of hunting and fishing for wild food.

As d'Artaguiette observed, wheat grew here well from early settlement, and bread made from it predominated. Settlers from the East
who came in the later 1790s and early 1800s also brought with them
a taste for wheat, brown, and corn bread. The paucity of mills in the
earliest settlement period meant that settlers hauled their corn or

wheat great distances to be ground, or that they used large mortars and pestles to pound the meal, Indian-style, often with the pestle tied to a tree branch to help raise it. They then sifted flour by hand.

By the time this region was settled, the meals of the day had settled into the familiar breakfast-dinner-supper pattern that would endure for a long time to come. The British traveler John Melish recorded a breakfast offered him in what was backwoods Ohio, between Coshocton and New Philadelphia, during the period 1806–1811. Melish's landlady was prepared to wring the neck of a chicken for his breakfast. When he told her all he wanted was egg, toast, and tea, she declared he was the "most extraordinary man" she had ever seen, and asked if he wouldn't prefer some ham or stewed pork. Ultimately she laid the table with "a profusion of ham, eggs, fritters, bread, butter, and some excellent tea. All the time I was at breakfast she kept pressing me to eat." Though Melish ate only the eggs, bread, and tea, he paid the same amount as he would have for the larger meal, and noted, "I mention the circumstance to show the kind of hospitality of the landlady, and the good living enjoyed by the backwoods people." The landlady may have been accustomed to feeding hungry farmers, or perhaps she felt that, as a hostess, something more was called for.[100]

From the hardships and starving times of first colonial settlement to the generous meal served John Melish in the later Federal era, Americans of all regions had established a plentiful diet with more meat than many Europeans of the time enjoyed, with wheat or corn breads, butter, cheese, and a variety of vegetables and fruits, washed down with beer or cider, coffee, tea, or chocolate, or even American-made whiskey.

NOTES

1. Adriaen Van der Donck, *A Description of the New Netherlands*, edited by Thomas F. O'Donnell (Syracuse, NY: Syracuse University Press, 1968), 75, 76.

2. John Lawson, *New Voyage to Carolina*, edited by Hugh Talmage Lefler (Chapel Hill: University of North Carolina Press, 1967), 42, 58.

3. John Bradbury, *Travels in the Interior of America*, March of America Facsimile Series, no. 59 (Ann Arbor, MI: University Microfilms, 1966), 113, 117.

4. Leni Ashmore Sorensen, telephone interview, July 14, 2004.

5. Dr. Cheryle Foote, personal interview, May 7, 2004.

6. Marc Simmons, *Coronado's Land: Essays on Daily Life in Colonial New Mexico* (Albuquerque: University of New Mexico Press, 1991), 66–67.

7. Alan Taylor, *American Colonies: The Settling of North America* (New York: Viking, 2001), 82.

8. Foote.

9. Josiah Gregg, *Commerce of the Prairies*, edited by Max L. Moorhead (Norman: University of Oklahoma Press, 1954), 109.

10. Ibid., 111.

11. James Josiah Webb, *Adventures in the Santa Fe Trade, 1844–1847*, edited by Ralph P. Bieber (Lincoln: University of Nebraska Press, 1995), 65.

12. Gregg, 110–111.

13. Ibid., 110.

14. Webb, 65–66.

15. Gregg, 110.

16. Zebulon Pike, *The Journals of Zebulon Montgomery Pike with Letters and Related Documents*, edited by Donald Jackson, 2 vols. (Norman: University of Oklahoma Press, 1966), vol. 1, 396.

17. François-Jean, Marquis de Chastellux, *Travels in North America in the Years 1780, 1781, and 1782*, rev. trans. by Howard C. Rice, Jr., 2 vols. (Chapel Hill: University of North Carolina Press, 1963), vol. 1, 387.

18. Virginia DeJohn Anderson, "Animals into the Wilderness: The Development of Livestock Husbandry in the 17th Century Chesapeake," *William and Mary Quarterly* 3rd ser., 59, no. 2 (2002): 377–408.

19. Henry Miller, "An Archaeological Perspective on the Evolution of Diet in the Colonial Chesapeake," in *Colonial Chesapeake Society*, edited by Lois Green Carr et al. (Chapel Hill: University of North Carolina Press, 1988), 176–199.

20. John Solomon Otto, *The Southern Frontiers, 1607–1860* (Westport, CT: Greenwood Press, 1989), 12–18.

21. Thomas Robinson Hazard, *The Jonny-cake Papers of "Shepherd Tom," Together with Reminiscences of Narragansett Schools of Former Days* (Boston: for the Subscribers, 1915).

22. William Woys Weaver, ed., *A Quaker Woman's Cookbook: The Domestic Cookery of Elizabeth Ellicott Lea* (Mechanicsburg, PA: Stackpole Books, 2004), 81.

23. Amelia Simmons, *American Cookery; or, the Art of Dressing Viands, Fish, Poultry and Vegetables* (Hartford, CT: Hudson & Godwin, 1796), facs. repr. with essay by Mary Tolford Wilson (New York: Dover, 1984), 34.

24. Chastellux, vol. 2, 403.

25. Ibid., 412.

26. Wesley Frank Craven, *The Southern Colonies in the 17th Century, 1607–1689*, vol. 1, *A History of the South*, edited by Wendell Holmes Stephenson and E. Merton Coulter (Baton Rouge: Louisiana State University Press, 1949), 94, 95.

27. Hunter D. Farish, ed., *Journal & Letters of Phillip Vickers Firthian,*

1773–1774: A Plantation Tutor of the Old Dominion (Williamsburg, VA: Colonial Williamsburg, 1943), 29.

28. Chastellux, vol. 2, 383.

29. William Byrd, *The Secret Diary of William Byrd of Westover, 1709–1712*, edited by Louis B. Wright and Marion Tinling (Richmond, VA: Dietz Press, 1941). I analyzed the breakfast, dinner, and supper mentions in entries from February 6, 1709, through January 31, 1710.

30. John Bernard, "Retrospections of America, 1797–1811," in *American Social History as Recorded by British Travelers*, compiled and edited by Allan Nevins (New York: Henry Holt, 1923), 37.

31. Henry Wansey, "An Excursion to the United States of North America in the Summer of 1794," in *American Social History*, edited by Nevins, 55, 56.

32. Chastellux, vol. 2, 420.

33. Kathleen Curtain, personal interview, April 12, 2004.

34. Carl Bridenbaugh, ed., *Gentleman's Progress: The Itinerarium of Dr. Alexander Hamilton, 1744* (Chapel Hill: University of North Carolina Press, 1948), 108.

35. Hannah Glasse, *Art of Cookery Made Plain and Easy* (Alexandria, VA: Cottom and Stewart, 1805); facsimile with historical notes by Karen Hess (Bedford, MA: Applewood Books, 1997), 137.

36. Samuel Sewell, *The Diary of Samuel Sewell, 1674–1729*, edited by M. Halsey Thomas, 2 vols. (New York: Farrar, Straus and Giroux, 1973), 1:557.

37. Glasse, 138.

38. Howard H. Peckham, ed., *Narratives of Colonial America, 1704–1765* (Chicago: R. R. Donnelley, 1971), 47.

39. Simmons, *American Cookery*, 28.

40. Sewell, vol. 1, 380.

41. Ibid., 460.

42. Bridenbaugh, 110.

43. Martha Ballard, *The Diary of Martha Ballard, 1785–1812*, edited by Robert McCausland and Cynthia MacAlman McCausland (Camden, ME: Picton Press, 1992), 127, 169.

44. Bridenbaugh, 20.

45. Van der Donck, 41–42.

46. Ibid., 42.

47. Ibid., 47, 50, 53–54.

48. Rusks are slices of sweet bread that have been dried somewhat, similar to biscotti.

49. Sandra Oliver, "Early Chemical Leavenings: Part I," *Food History News* 4, no. 2 (1992): 2.

50. Simmons, 35.

51. Van der Donck, 67, 67–68.

52. Ibid., 24.

53. Ibid., 70.

54. Peter Rose, ed. and trans., *The Sensible Cook: Dutch Foodways in the Old and the New World* (Syracuse, NY: Syracuse University Press, 1989), 8.

55. Donna R. Barnes and Peter Rose, *Matters of Taste: Food and Drink in Seventeenth-Century Dutch Art and Life* (Syracuse, NY: Syracuse University Press, 2002), 91, 122.

56. Rose, 6.

57. Jasper Danckaerts, *Journal of Jasper Danckaerts*, edited by Bartlett Burleigh James and J. Franklin Jameson (New York: Scribner's, 1913), 37.

58. Bridenbaugh, 39, 40.

59. Barnes, 25.

60. Peter Kalm, *Peter Kalm's Travels in North America: The America of 1750*, edited by Adolph Bensen, 2 vols. (New York: Dover, 1964), vol. 1, 267.

61. Ibid., 273.

62. Israel Acrelius, *A History of New Sweden*, translated by William M. Reynolds (Philadelphia: Historical Society of Pennsylvania, 1874), 158.

63. Ibid., 158–159.

64. Kalm, vol. 1, 91.

65. William Cobbett, *A Year's Residence in the United States of America* (London, 1818), 193.

66. Kalm, vol. 2, 184.

67. John Woods, *Wood's Two Years' Residence in the Settlement on the English Prairie—June 25, 1820–July 3, 1821* (London: Longman, Hurst, 1822), repr. in vol. 10 of *Early Western Travels, 1748–1846*, edited by Reuben Gold Thwaites (Cleveland, OH: A. H. Clark, 1904), 192–193.

68. Ibid., 209.

69. Percy Wells Bidwell and John Falconer, *History of Agriculture in the Northern United States, 1620–1860* (New York: Peter Smith, 1941), 16.

70. Kalm, vol. 1, 91, 95, 104.

71. Woods, 199.

72. Bridenbaugh, 186, 90.

73. Ibid., 48, 96.

74. Ibid., 7, 31, 37, 171.

75. Ibid., 88.

76. Kalm, vol. 1, 383, 379–381.

77. Timothy Dwight, *Travels in New England and New York*, edited by Barbara Miller Solomon, 4 vols. (Cambridge, MA: Belknap Press of Harvard University Press, 1969), vol. 4, 41.

78. John Melish, *Travels in the United States of America in the Years 1806 & 1807, and 1809, 1810, & 1811* (Philadelphia: Thomas and George Palmer, 1812), 76.

79. Kalm, vol. 1, 163.

80. John Brickell, *The Natural History of North Carolina* (Dublin: J. Carson, 1737; repr. Murfreesboro, NC: Johnson, 1968), 38.

81. Bernard, 43.

82. Sarah Rutledge, *The Carolina Housewife or House and Home by a Lady of Charleston* (Charleston, SC: W. R. Babcock & Co., 1847), 83.

83. Allen D. Candler, comp., *The Colonial Records of the State of Georgia* (Atlanta: C. P. Byrd, 1904), 445–448.

84. C. Margaret Scarry and Elizabeth Reitz, "Herbs, Fish Scum and Vermin: Subsistence Strategies in Sixteenth Century Florida," in *Columbian Consequences*, vol. 2, *Archaeological and Historical Perspectives in the Spanish Borderlands East*, edited by David Hurst Thomas (Washington, DC: Smithsonian Institution Press, 1991), 343–354, 352.

85. Kathleen Hoffman, "Cultural Development of La Florida," *Historical Archaeology* 31 (1997): 26.

86. Ibid., 26, 27.

87. Donna Rhule, "Oranges and Wheat: Spanish Attempts at Agriculture in La Florida," *Historical Archaeology* 31 (1997): 36–45, 41–42.

88. Andrew F. Smith, *The Tomato in America: Early History, Culture, and Cookery* (Columbia: University of South Carolina Press, 1994), 27.

89. Mrs. Abby Fisher, *What Mrs. Fisher Knows About Old Southern Cooking* (San Francisco: Women's Cooperative Printing Office, 1851; reprint #67 of 110, by The Sontheimer Foundation, Greenwich, CT, May 1991), 57–58.

90. Ibid., 38.

91. Rutledge, 83.

92. Mary Randolph, *The Virginia House-wife* (Washington, DC: Davis and Force, 1824), 34–35.

93. The word "Creole," which is now often applied to residents of Louisiana, was in the past sometimes applied to first-generation American-born Europeans and Africans.

94. Charles Woodmason, *The Carolina Backcountry on the Eve of the Revolution: The Journal and Other Writings of Charles Woodmason, Anglican Itinerant*, edited by Richard Hooker (Chapel Hill: University of North Carolina Press, 1953), 22, 36, 34.

95. Ibid., 39.

96. Chastellux, vol. 2, 388.

97. d'Artaguiette, Diron "Journal of Diron d'Artaguiette 1722–1723," in *Travels in the American Colonies*, edited by Newton D. Mereness (New York: Macmillan, 1916), 67–68.

98. Bradbury, 258–264.

99. Ibid., 28.

100. Melish, 70.

CHAPTER 5
CONCEPTS OF DIET AND NUTRITION

Food is chosen for many reasons—for example, to be healthy or to have a familiar and safe diet. Foods choices can also reflect belief systems and help people live consistent with their cultures.

The definition of healthful food has changed over time, and the American metabolism has changed as well. Consuming or avoiding certain foods because of religious or philosophical beliefs, and fasting and feasting are ways people have used food to express spiritual convictions. This chapter concerns how Colonial and Federal era Americans viewed nutrition and how they expressed religious and philosophical ideas through their diet.

NUTRITION AND HEALTH

Humankind has always understood the connection between food and health, but the particulars of nutritional theory and recommendations for altering one's diet to preserve or improve health have varied and changed much over the past thousands of years. Nutritional science as known today is only a little more than a century old. Calories were defined in the 1860s, and most vitamins were not discovered until the early 1900s. Although in 1660 the Dutch scientist Anton van Leeuwenhoek had an improved microscope through which he observed and reported on bacteria, the germ theory of infectious disease was not firmly established until the last half of the 1800s by Louis Pasteur. For the duration of the Colonial and Federal eras in America, a good deal of information about health and disease still awaited discovery.

The definition of good nutrition was, for many people, simply enough to eat to do the work at hand, to stay warm in winter, to fend off disease, and not to feel hungry. Colonists valued fatty meat to an extent that baffles people today, but, quickly metabolized, it was absolutely essential to people working strenuously outdoors and living in colder regions of the Colonies. A grain-based, high-carbohydrate diet gave people plenty of energy to clear land, build homes, and plant and harvest crops.

Over the 200 years of American colonization and early independence, a number of significant changes occurred in European thinking about diet and health. Many of these ideas found their way to America and influenced nineteenth-century dietary practices. During the period discussed here, the ancient system of humoral physiology was being abandoned, and the scientific revolution that was under way set in motion the discovery of the causes of disease. It also led to an understanding of how the human body—indeed, all of nature—worked, and fostered the study of chemistry, medicine, botany, and biology. All these sciences affected ideas about diet.

Humoral Physiology

Humoral physiology was a dietary system in use from the early Middle Ages to the early modern period. Its influence was beginning to fade during America's colonization. It was based upon the principle that four elements—fluids or humors—governed the body and characterized plants, animals, and minerals. The four humors were blood, phlegm, yellow bile, and black bile. People believed that in each person one of these humors had more influence than the others: a person was sanguine if blood predominated; phlegmatic, if phlegm did. A predominance of yellow bile led to a choleric condition and black bile led to melancholy. These were considered "natural," intrinsic elements of a person's body or nature. Illness developed when these elements became unbalanced or "distempered." To maintain health, people were advised to eat a diet that supported their basic condition, or "temper," and corrected it if it became unbalanced.

To do this, the cook or doctor needed to understand the characteristics of each humor: blood was considered hot and moist, and so was sweet food. Phlegm was cool and moist, and typified fish, vegetables such as cucumbers, and fruits such as melons. Yellow bile was hot and dry; salt, spices such as mustard and ginger, and bitter foods were considered hot and dry. Black bile was cold and dry, and sour foods such as vinegar and lemon juice typified it.

Certain other influences, called "nonnaturals," came from outside the body. They included a person's age, the season of the year, even air quality, and people believed they affected the humors of the body, as did the kinds of activity people engaged in, including work, sleep, and sexual activity. Clearly, too, the humors created and reflected certain emotions: sanguinity was cheerful; choleric was angry; melancholic was sad; and phlegmatic was slow and calm. A humoral imbalance could be corrected by diet, managing the nonnaturals, or taking medicine. For example, an overly hot and moist condition was cured by bloodletting, a common practice into the nineteenth century, that was even performed on sick animals.

Further elaborations of the humoral system implied class distinctions. For example, farmers and laborers were considered able to eat cabbage, legumes, and whole grains because they were thought to have hotter systems. The relatively idle elite were thought to require more delicate and refined foods: wheat, sugar, poultry, and fowl. Many of these ideas endured even to recent times and attached certain prejudices to foods. White bread and sweetmeats were considered refined and delicate; cabbage and rye bread were regarded as coarse, unrefined fare.

Aspects of humoral physiology have survived to the present, and the system is still used in some parts of Asia. The process of correcting humoral imbalance was termed "tempering." Serving cucumbers with vinegar; putting lemon on fish; adding salt, vinegar, and oil to salad greens; and serving pork or beef with mustard are the slight evidence of old ways of "tempering" the nature of foods.

In the Colonial era, people who had grown up with the humoral system as part of their working knowledge of health still followed its principles when helping their families maintain health, and might more consciously prepare food according to the system when someone fell ill. Although specific aspects of the system faded in practice, some general ideas of balance in the system, of diet's affect on it, and illness as arising from distemper remained part of many people's thinking about diet and health.

An interesting example of this comes from the journal of Colonel William Fleming, who, traveling in Kentucky in 1779 and 1780, fell ill. He submitted to bleeding, and reported that the blood let was "solid like liver and black as tarr dark and thick." He attributed this to the effects of his diet while traveling: "I had lived for a constancy on poor dried Buffalo bull beef cured in the smaok [*sic*] without salt and dressed by boiling it in water or stewing it without any addition but a piece of Indian hoe cake which made my breakfast and the same for dinner—it was owing to this coarse food that I had such a thick vicid [*sic*] and black blood."[1]

Dietetics and Digestibility

The scientific revolution introduced ideas about the mechanics of digestion and is today called metabolism, and laid the groundwork for the later discovery of proteins, carbohydrates, and fat and, later still, vitamins and minerals. The effects of these new ideas began to be detected in eighteenth-century America, particularly the concept of a diet adjusted to an individual's therapeutic needs in various life stages and during illness.

This system, articulated by the late sixteenth-century English writer Thomas Moffett in his book *Health's Improvement* (published in 1655 but written earlier), did not reject humoral physiology completely but combined it with what is called solidism. The system prescribed full, middle, and low diets for the ill. The full diet was designed to build flesh, blood, and humors to promote growth and strength, particularly in young people. This diet called for vegetables and meat (which was considered stimulating food), bread, beer, and a rich boiled pudding. A middle diet was prescribed for middle-aged people to rebuild strength that was lost or expended. A low diet was recommended for old people and for the ill; it was designed to avoid stimulating and taxing the system, so it eliminated meat and offered broth, bread pudding, gruel, and milk porridge. These diets contain the roots of later invalid cookery.[2]

Because solidism focused on the movement of blood and what were thought to be nervous fluids through the body, health was considered to be free movement of these and of other bodily functions, such as urinating and bowel movements. By extension, solidists thought food should move through the body unobstructed, an idea expressed by the term "digestibility." The concept of digestibility had been around for many years, and became a focus of early nineteenth-century nutritional theory. In the late 1400s a physician, Conrad Heingartner of Zurich, wrote about the importance of avoiding a great variety of foods at one meal and the advisability of chewing food very well to promote digestion. This particular idea reemerged in the late nineteenth century when the American dietary reformer Horace Fletcher recommended chewing one's food once for each tooth before swallowing it.

Invalid Cookery

Few cookbooks of the seventeenth and eighteenth centuries failed to omit remedies and directions for cooking for the sick. After the Reformation in England, when King Henry VIII closed many monasteries, the monks' role in preparing and supplying communities with remedies ceased, and the work fell to housewives. Subsequently part of the skillful housewife's knowledge included which plants to gather and grow for medicine, and how to make jellies, syrups, and distillations of various sorts. In the fifteenth and sixteenth centuries, sugar was considered to have medicinal properties, and even in the seventeenth and eighteenth centuries, when sugar became a common household item, delicate and sweetened dishes, many things regarded today as desserts, served as food for invalids. These included calf's-foot and hartshorn jellies, some fruit jellies, and marmalades. Wines and cordials also had a role in the sickroom.

E. Smith's 1729 *The Compleat Housewife*, an edition of which was published in 1749 at Williamsburg, Virginia (the first cookbook to be published in the Colonies), also contained recipes for cordials, distilled waters, and remedies, as well as salves and ointments. Seventeenth- and eighteenth-century gentry manuscript recipe books contain many recipes for remedies, some copied from books such as Smith's and Hannah Glasse's 1747 English cookbook, *Art of Cookery*, plus recipes shared among friends. Many remedies called for a distilling process, but not all households could afford a still; if one was prosperous enough to own a still, the housewife likely was responsible for providing physics, as remedies were sometimes called, for her family, household, and neighbors.

Glasse's *Art of Cookery* dedicated a chapter to "Directions for the Sick," which included recipes for mutton broth; "To make a Beef Drink, which is ordered for weak People"; a white caudle, a thin oatmeal-and-water beverage lightly seasoned and sweetened; a brown one made with ale; "Bread soop for the Sick"; and "Barley Water."[3] These recipes call up the principles set forth by the solidists.

Actual practice of the solidist theory and the low diet prescribed for the ill appears in a 1764 letter from John Adams to his then fiancée Abigail, as he prepared for an inoculation against smallpox that would lead to being sick with a low-grade infection with the disease. He writes that the doctor gave him ipecac, which caused him to vomit and thereby clear his stomach. Then, he wrote, "We have had our Breakfast of Pottage without salt, Or Spice or Butter as the Drs. would have it." Three days later he wrote to Abigail: "Both the Physick and the Abstinence [from food] have hitherto agreed extreamly well with me, for I have not felt freer from all Kinds of Pain and Uneasiness, I have not enjoyed a clearer Head, or a brisker flow of Spirits, these seven Years than I do today."[4]

Sufficient Diet

Although there were no widespread, long-lasting famines, people did starve in America, particularly during initial settlement in some locations. Crops destroyed by warfare or weather, such as drought, flood, or early frosts, created acute food shortages from time to time that, combined with destitution, caused most hunger. Without money, hungry people could not purchases supplies to get through hard times to a new planting season, but there were times when there were so few supplies that not even money could buy food.

Frontiers were always susceptible to privation. The adventurer Estwick Evans, who explored the Michigan Territory on foot, observed scarcity of provisions while traveling through the remote parts of western New York in 1812: "There are so many emigrants travelling and settling in that quarter during winter, that want is frequently the consequence. The emigrants, who settle during that season of the year, must be fed, for many months, from the common stock of provisions, before they can, by their labour, add to it. Some of them have money, but money will not save them from want."[5]

The metabolism of the Early American population was very high compared with that of later eras. Much work required physical labor and muscle-powered tools, and people expended many calories merely walking or riding a horse. Only the wealthy could afford wheeled transportation. In cold regions, where in winter fireplaces provided heat to those who sat near them, and bedrooms were frosty, people burned calories merely staying warm. Food powered activity, and grain and meat were the primary sources.

Bread was central to the Colonial diet, as it had been for centuries in the Old World. If grain was not ground into flour for bread, it was boiled whole or at cracked into a coarse meal and cooked into porridge. Though most people preferred porridge with milk or butter—

or lacking that, some other fat such as bacon or bear fat—a simple grain dish provided carbohydrates for energy. Meat, particularly fat meat, was the other important source of pure energy. When the Dutch settler Adriaen Van der Donck, wrote in the early 1600s that hogs in the Dutch colony grew fat a hand-breadth in thickness by feeding on acorns and forage in the woods, or as much as six or seven fingers in thickness if fed corn, he was delivering good news.[6] The fat was an important source of calories for hard work.

Food-Related Illness and Mortality

More premature deaths in past times were caused by contagious disease and accident than by diet-related disease. Malaria, spread by mosquitoes in hot, humid regions, killed many colonists and settlers. Tuberculosis, diphtheria, influenza, and smallpox claimed more lives in colonial America than hunger or famine or poor-quality food. There is evidence that plenty of food and the overall health of the population contributed to a high rate of women surviving childbirth and of children surviving infancy.[7]

What food-related illnesses did exist were often confined to particular populations for limited amounts of time. For example, scurvy, the result of the lack of vitamin C, caused sufferers' gums to swell and bleed, teeth to loosen, and sores to develop, was much more common among sailors and soldiers who were periodically deprived of sufficient fresh foods. Although scurvy surely had occurred many times in the past, it did not emerge identifiably until the era of sea exploration, when sailors developed, and often died, of it on lengthy voyages. By the time of American colonization, it was a familiar malady, and although vitamin C itself would not be identified for another century and a half, the lack of the nutrient and its source in citrus fruits and fresh food had been determined. For a while, some people believed that there were two sorts of scurvy, one sort among land-lubbers and the other among seafarers. Poor people, who often had to rely on a diet of salt meat, peas or beans, and bread with few or no vegetables or fruits for the duration of a winter, were most susceptible to scurvy. The origin of the land scurvy idea may have been the large numbers English urban poor in the seventeenth and eighteenth centuries suffering from scurvy. In America any colonist, free or slave, who ate only a diet of salt meat and grain for a protracted period also suffered from scurvy.

Physician to the Fleet James Lind of British Navy, finally determined that there was one sort of scurvy. With the publication of his *Treatise of the Scurvy* in 1753, he demonstrated that lemons and oranges were the most effective in curing it. It would be some time before all British ships carried lemon juice (lime juice in the nineteenth century) and American ships carried vinegar. For seafarers or landsmen, fresh meat also supplied vitamin C, as did pickles, sauerkraut, or fresh and winter-stored cabbage. Unknown to many, potatoes were a valuable source of vitamin C, and as long as they were carried on ships and people ashore grew and ate them, scurvy could be largely avoided even in winter.

Pellagra, another diet-related disease, is caused by the lack of the B vitamin niacin. It occurred among people who subsisted primarily on corn. The name, translated from the Italian, means "rough skin," and sufferers first show rough red skin. In its advanced stages, pellagra causes depression and mental distress. When maize was introduced to Europe from the New World, part of the knowledge about processing it to make it wholesome food did not travel with the seed corn. The Mexican Indians usually soaked the corn and mixed it with an alkaline solution before grinding it to form the dough from which they formed tortillas. This process, called nixtamalization, released niacin so it could be absorbed by the body. Many Europeans, particularly poor people, suffered from pellagra from the late eighteenth century through the nineteenth and early twentieth centuries.

Black American slaves and others who received rations containing primarily corn and salt pork probably also suffered from pellagra. Slaves who grew or gathered vegetables and hunted for fresh meat could avoid the disease, although barely, because the body can store niacin. In some cases, slaves and poor people deprived of fresh food though a winter may very well have been in a precondition for pellagra.

In a few instances, when corn was soaked in lye, as it would be to make samp, that process released niacin. Clearly pellagra was a disease that primarily affected eastern colonists, whereas the Hispanics in the Southwest had wisely adopted the Native manner of preparing corn.

Because the human body can store many necessary nutrients, the colonial diet did not usually adversely impact people's health. While their diet might have been deficient in some vitamin or mineral at various seasons of the year, most people managed to obtain all the necessary nutrients over the course of a year as long as there were no major disruptions in growing seasons or supplies. For example, because they were open to eating many foods that modern people now reject, their diet benefited by the consumption of nutrient-rich organ meats during the winter when a variety of fresh fruits and vegetables was not available.

Gout, another diet-related disease, afflicted the Colonial wealthy. Caused by a buildup of uric acid in the system as a result of a diet heavy in protein, it gave sufferers painful joints, often the ankles and toes. Declaration of Independence signers John Hancock and George Walton of Georgia both suffered from gout. Generally associated with the prosperous, gout was attributed to a rich diet. In a letter written in 1803 to Benjamin Hawkins, his agent among the Creek Indians, President Thomas Jefferson wryly commented, "I learn you have the gout. I did not expect that Indian cookery or Indian fare would produce that." Benjamin Franklin suffered from gout and complained that it reflected poorly on his good name because he had been for many years vocal on the wisdom of eating abstemiously.[8]

PHILOSOPHICAL AND RELIGIOUS BELIEFS AND DIET

Both secular and religious beliefs motivated people to make certain food choices. Ethical choice could be based on religious convictions or might have no connection to a particular spiritual belief system. Social reform movements such as Temperance and vegetarianism, and an interest in self-improvement, affected some people's food choices. Sometimes religious practices determined what people ate or when they ate it.

Intemperance and Temperance

As seen in the accounts of their eating habits, colonists and settlers were, by modern standards, accustomed to drinking a great deal of alcohol. Beer or hard cider as a daily family beverage, even at breakfast, seems incredible today, yet among the Puritans of New England and the English adventurers in Virginia it was the usual thing. Beer and cider, however, especially as home-brewed beverages, were relatively low in alcohol, beer at about 5 percent and hard cider at 10 percent. Wine, favored by those who could afford it, had about 18 percent alcohol. Drinking these beverages was a centuries-long practice by the time America was colonized, and they provided valuable calories as well as being ways to preserve grains or fruits for out-of-season consumption.

It was the spread of spirits, rum and whiskey in particular, as well as gin and brandy, through most classes that caused the level of alcohol consumption that the Temperance Movement wished to end by the close of the Federal period. While no one in the seventeenth or eighteenth century approved of unalloyed and chronic drunkenness, a certain tolerance for alcohol was expected and accepted.

In New England, few social events or community work parties were without the distribution of rum. House raisings, ship launchings, and even ordinations were marked by the host's generosity with spirituous liquors. In fact, in 1673, Rev. Increase Mather described drink as "a creature of God" that ought to be "received with thankfulness."[9] In the interest of maintaining social control, taverns and public houses where liquor was sold, were customarily licensed, with the intention of making sure only responsible people sold spirits. Private drinking was not, however, subject to that kind of control, and prosperous people, North and South, imported brandy, Madeira and other wine; concocted punches; and toasted one another frequently at table.

Among the gentry, conviviality called for serving alcohol, but some travelers in America observed casual, all-day drinking. The English comedian John Bernard, performing in America at the end of the eighteenth century, particularly in Virginia, described a planter concluding breakfast with "the commencement of his diurnal potations—a stiff glass of mint-sling—a taking disorder peculiar to the South. . . . Between twelve and one his throat would require another emulsion and he would sip half a pint of some mystery termed bumbo, apple-toddy or pumkin flip. At three he dined and drank everything—brandy, claret, cider, Madeira, punch and sangaree."[10]

Georgia native Richard Johnston, writing about his childhood, reported that his father, Malcolm, born in 1788, "used to make a bowl of toddy of mornings before breakfast, have it graced by the touch of my mother's lips, modestly sipped by us children, then drained by himself." The practice ended with his conversion to Christianity in 1823, when he was thirty-five.[11]

After-dinner drinking by the gentlemen, once the ladies were excused to have coffee in the drawing room, became notorious by the end of the eighteenth century. It was humorously depicted in satiric prints that show the imbibers in a sad state: glasses and punch bowls overturned, drinkers with wigs awry and sliding from their seats or out cold. Not all classes were leisured enough to drink all day or to become terribly inebriated after dinner. Many autobiographers of the time, benefiting from hindsight, remark on the writer's wisdom of avoiding drink or overcoming the folly of it. Economically marginal people could ill afford drunkenness.

That most people, particularly men, were accustomed to drinking spirits every day was codified, for example, by the rations given sailors on American ships in the early 1800s. The usual amount was a gill (half a cup, four fluid ounces), based on the practice customary in the British Navy, cut with water. A sailor could decline the spirits and be given additional pay, but most accepted their ration gladly. A ration of spirits, watered as it was at sea, was sometimes distributed to slaves during periods of particularly strenuous activity—for example, at harvest. Slaves with produce to sell, such as eggs or vegetables, sometimes raised cash or obtained credit at a store that enabled them to buy liquor. In many places, storekeepers were eventually prohibited by law from selling liquor to slaves. Similarly, laws were enacted, and often ignored, that forbade the selling of liquor to Native Americans.

Most drinking, however, was done by men, and the era of heaviest consumption was roughly 1790 to 1830, when America was in a fair amount of social upheaval. Some attribute the drinking to post-Revolutionary War social and economic instability. Many people aspiring to land ownership were by no means sure of obtaining it, except by moving to the dangerous frontier; city populations were growing rapidly; newly settled areas often lacked institutions such as churches and schools that exerted some social control.[12] Estwick Evans, during his travels from New England to New Orleans, wrote in 1818: "Still, there is, in the United States, much inebriation, and a great want of economy in the use of spirituous liquors. By the distillery of grain among us, the community are, sometimes, deprived of the necessary quantity of bread; and a substitute is furnished which tends, at once, to beggar, and to depopulate the country."[13]

It is not surprising, then, that heavy drinking in the Federal era resulted in the backlash of Temperance Reform. Physician and artist Benjamin Rush in Philadelphia was among the first, by the early 1780s, to identify alcoholism as a progressive disease. He was also the first to give liquor the name "Demon Rum." His pamphlet *An Inquiry into the Effects of Spiritous Liquors*, published in 1784, argued that, contrary to conventional beliefs about spirits, they did not warm the drinker when the weather was cold, nor did they cool him when the weather was hot. They did, however, cause illnesses ranging from stomach and liver disease to apoplexy. Rush believed that spirits needed to be replaced with beer, light wines, and weaker punches, as well as nonalcoholic beverages.[14]

Rush's work was immediately influential. It was one impetus among many, including a substantial national debt in 1789, for a Federal excise tax on domestic distilled liquors, primarily rum and whiskey, which led to the Whiskey Rebellion of 1794. His work also launched the Temperance Movement, embraced mostly by Protestant clergymen and many of the Federal elite, who regarded drinking as a threat health and drunkenness as a sign of unrefined behavior.

No small part of the impetus behind the Temperance Movement was industry's need for a large, sober workforce. Industrial manufacturing required workers who showed up predictably and on time, and who worked around machinery efficiently, without putting themselves or anyone else in danger. Arguments for the health benefits of sobriety combined with economic motives to drive the Temperance Movement through the nineteenth century.

Early Vegetarianism

Vegetarianism as a dietary philosophy had been known for many centuries by the Colonial and Federal eras, but relatively few people embraced it from the 1500s through the early 1800s. The average person considered vegetarians to be peculiar. Among famous early Americans, at least one, Benjamin Franklin, experimented with vegetarianism.

Franklin began his vegetarianism in 1722, when he was sixteen and an apprentice printer to his brother in Boston, and continued it for several years. Franklin had read, and was much influenced by, *The Way to Health* by Thomas Tryon, who advocated a vegetable diet. Tryon, a famous seventeenth-century vegetarian and the author of several books advocating a vegetable diet, held the view that it was inherently wrong and cruel to kill fellow creatures for food.

The Commonsense Diet

Among Franklin's writings were many years' worth of *Poor Richard's Almanac*, which offered much practical advice for living—what today would be called self-help literature. Franklin often articulated a commonsense approach to diet and nutrition. For example, among his aphorisms is "The poor man must walk to get meat for his stomach, the rich man to get a stomach to his meat"—that is, the poor man may have to walk a way to find food or work to buy it, but the rich man has to walk to build an appetite.

The 1751 edition of the *Almanac* laid out a set of rules for maintaining a good diet. Franklin advised that each person needed to discover what quantity and kind of food was most suitable to his or her constitution, and then "Eat and drink such an exact Quantity as the Constitution of thy Body allows of, in reference to the Services of the Mind." This practice would preserve a person from illness and susceptibility to disease.

Franklin observed that people who "study much," that is, who were sedentary, "ought not to eat as much as those who work hard." He cautioned that different diets are necessary for young people, the elderly, and the ill, and observed that certain foods are digested more easily than others, and thus could be eaten in greater quantity. A bit of exercise, Franklin said, such as "swing[ing] your Arms about with a small Weight in each Hand," was a good idea before eating a meal. And if one overate at one meal, it might be good to eat lightly at the next meal or skip it altogether.

When Franklin wrote "A temperate Diet frees from Diseases [those who] are seldom ill, but if they are surprised with Sickness, they bear it better, and recover sooner; for most Distempers have their Origin from Repletion," he had in mind the old system of humoral physiology, which said that disease arose from a lack of balance, or a "distemper." The best way for a person to discover what a good amount of food was for his or her particular system, Franklin advised, was to observe "If thou art dull and heavy after Meat, it's a sign thou hast exceeded the due Measure; for Meat and Drink ought to refresh the Body, and make it chearful, and not to dull and oppress it." He recommended that if you found yourself with "these ill Symptoms, consider whether too much Meat, or too much Drink occasions it, or both, and abate by little and little, till thou findest the Inconveniency removed." Franklin probably reflected the point of view of many when he wrote, "But when malignant Fevers are rife in the Country or City where thou dwelst, 'tis adviseable to eat and drink more freely, by Way of Prevention; for those are Diseases that are not caused by Repletion, and seldom attack Full-feeders."

Some of Franklin's dietary advice also reflected his prudence with money: "A fat kitchen maketh a lean will."

Kashruth in Colonial America

Of all American colonists, Jewish settlers had the most demanding religiously based dietary guidelines. To meet them, settlers needed supportive communities with trustworthy sources of meat, wine, and, matzo. They also needed strong family life, particularly wives, who by their cooking and housekeeping routines made it possible for them to follow kosher practices (i.e., to maintain kashruth). Men who traveled alone to the colonies were less likely to continue as observant Jews, but it was not easy even for families to adhere to the religion without a community of other observant Jews.

Nearly all major colonial cities—Charleston, South Carolina; Philadelphia; Newport, Rhode Island; New York—had large enough Jewish communities to form a synagogue. By the close of the Federal period, Cincinnati, Ohio, did, too. Jewish people were not usually agricultural, so while some had farms, most lived in towns. Like other artisans and businesspeople, they relied for their food on markets and on their own capacity to pay for it. A synagogue would make every effort to provide properly slaughtered kosher meat, supporting the work of the *shochet*, the slaughterer. Another need was for unleavened bread, matzo, for Passover, which also relied upon the skill of someone knowledgeable about the prescribed process. Again the synagogue and community endeavored to provide this for the congregation.

Isolated colonial Jews were often at risk of losing their Jewish practices. There were never enough *shochets* to fill the demand, and the problem worsened as Jewish immigrants fanned out to western parts of the country in the nineteenth century. Some people ordered kosher meat from distant suppliers, with the meat sometimes traveling by sea to the faithful. At the very least, Jews could avoid pork. The alternative was vegetarianism or a variation on it. Cherokee Indians, for example, called Jewish peddlers "egg-eaters."[15] But being constantly among Christians and other Gentiles, and lacking other Jews to celebrate with, many Jewish people found the patterns of annual holidays disrupted, together with all their culinary associations. It also increased the possibility of intermarriage with non-Jews.

The responsibility for kosher dietary practice lay with the housewife. Kashruth requires separation of meat and milk products, including different sets of storage, cooking, and eating utensils for each, as well as the ritual cleaning of the house before Passover to remove any fragment of leavened food and any grain that could be leavened. A Jewish housewife's care in this ensured that an observant guest could eat at her home in confidence that the food was properly prepared; this, too, contributed to the community's strength. In addition, most Jewish colonial housewives performed all the other tasks that women of the time attended to. They gardened, tended poultry, made butter and cheese, baked, raised children, cleaned, took care of the sick, and made the family's clothing.

Some Jewish holidays had strong culinary traditions. The Passover seder required matzo, wine, the vegetable dipped in saltwater, bitter herbs, and *charoset*, the mixture of apples, nuts, wine, and cinnamon. *Shavu'ot* was marked with a meal of dairy products. The bread challah was served at the weekly sabbath meal. Jewish women were responsible for these meals, and if they did not cook the foods themselves, they were obliged to supervise their preparation.

Fasting and Feasting

Largely abandoned today, patterns of fasting and feasting were very influential in Europe when America was founded. Jews and Christians alike fasted on certain occasions as a way to atone for sin or, by curbing the appetite, to achieve a deeper spiritual state. Jews fasted before Yom Kippur, the Day of Atonement, and before Purim, the celebration of the Jews' deliverance from Haman's plot to massacre them. The fasts were followed by eating, drinking, and making merry. There were also minor Jewish fast days.

Centuries of Catholicism had established annual and occasional fasts, largely defined as abstention from eating meat. Men and women in holy orders traditionally avoided all meat as part of their dedication to monastic and convent life. One result of the Protestant Reformation was abandonment of the frequent fasts and allowance of much more constant consumption of meat.

In colonial America, wherever Protestants settled—whether New England, Virginia, Pennsylvania, the Carolinas, and much of the southern backcountry—there were no regular weekly or seasonal fasts. Nonetheless, occasional fasts were declared for supplication and prayer. Times of war, in particular, or even local disturbances, might result in a governor's calling for a fast day. In New England, there was an annual spring fast, countered by the annual Thanksgiving. (Not all Thanksgivings were autumnal feasts, however; a thanksgiving could be a day of prayer to express gratitude for deliverance from some affliction or for the peaceful settlement of conflict, without feasting associated with it.)

How closely anyone stayed to the literal meaning of fasting as not eating food, seemed to be up to the individual. In the earliest days, when the small, close communities of New England made it possible for neighbors to be aware of each other's activities, attendance at church and abstention from food on a fast day was more probable than later in the eighteenth century, as farms were more dispersed and more was left to the individual's conscience.

Growing up in a prosperous New England farm family, Sarah Anna Emery reported that in late eighteenth- and early nineteenth-century Newburyport, Massachusetts, the annual April fast day was a "bugbear" for children in strictly observant families. Youngsters sometimes squirreled away food to snack on between the morning and afternoon church services. Emery recounted a story told her by one Deacon Hale of a fast day he recalled from his early eighteenth-century childhood. One fast day, Hale accompanied the minister's sons home at noon; there, to his surprise, the boys gave him and themselves a "hearty meal." Then, "Having become fairly gorged with good cheer, they seated themselves quietly in the kitchen. As the hour for the afternoons service approached, the good parson with a regard for youthful stomachs, came into the room and told the boys, 'that if they were hungry, he would permit a slight lunch.' This the young scamps piously declined, 'not wishing to make any infringement on the religious observation of the day.' "[16]

On fast days, once the afternoon church service ended, most families went home for a warm meal. Martha Ballard, however, living on the Maine frontier near Augusta, recorded in her diary on April 6, 1786: "Clear & pleas[ant], Fast Day, mrs Weston here, Doct Coney also & dind. [dined] we had a Legg of pork. . . . I have been at home all day." Similarly, on April 5, 1805, she reported that it was fast day, but she was home all day and had company for dinner.[17]

Among Catholics, observing weekly fasts on Friday, and sometimes on Wednesday, and the Lenten fast from Ash Wednesday through Easter continued. Fast days among the elite in medieval Europe had been characterized by elegant preparations of fish, the use of almond milk to replace cow's milk, and a meal replete with sweetmeats and spices and wine. The poor, who often had little meat anyway, ate legumes, bread, and salt fish.

In the Southwest, though it is poorly documented, there is some evidence that because of the general scarcity of food, fasting requirements were somewhat relaxed. Traditional Lenten dishes included *torrejas* (egg fritters) served with *quelites* (cooked greens); *panocha*, a pudding made with flour from sprouted wheat; and *capirotada* and/or *sopa* (bread puddings).

Wherever the topic of fasting arises, there is a discussion of what creatures qualified as fasting food. Some of the stories may be apocryphal, but claims are made that among French in the Michigan Territory, since fish was acceptable, muskrat was also appropriate fasting food because the creature lived mostly in water. For the same reason, a similar assertion is made about beaver. In Louisiana, a certain duck was considered appropriate because it fed largely on fish. Eating certain sea mammals, such as dolphins and porpoises, was permitted on fast days.

New England Protestants, though they rejected the enforced Friday fast, continued to eat fish as the main dish at least once a week. New Englanders shifted their fish eating to Saturday to distance themselves from Catholics. For example, in Boston, on Saturday, July 21, 1744, Alexander Hamilton reported: "I was invited to dine with Captain Irvin upon salt cod, which here is a common Saturday's dinner, being elegantly dressed with a sauce of butter and eggs."[18] Fish appeared perhaps more often among the Middle Colonies' and Chesapeake gentry, for whom a variety of dishes on the table, including fish and meat, was fashionable. Otherwise, fish was eaten more frequently by poorer people, Catholic and Protestant, as a subsistence strategy.

Feasting was the other side of the fasting coin. As mentioned, the Jewish Purim was a fast followed by an opportunity to eat and drink with merriment. Sukkoth was, and is, an autumnal holiday with some of the characteristics of a modern Thanksgiving. A Catholic holiday could be called a feast without a particular meal being served, though some ethnic groups had customary dishes associated with the observance of a particular feast day. Similarly, a thanksgiving could be observed in early America without the feast we now call Thanksgiving. Many Protestants objected to Catholic feasts as ordained by man, not by God.

Without fasts, feasts have little meaning, quite possibly an unintended consequence of Protestantism that eliminated some holiday observances. And, as America's relative prosperity grew compared with that of the rest of world, Americans found themselves eating well day by day, year in and year out, so that feasting as an opportunity for eating richly and with great variety was not as uncommon as it had been in Europe. With no particular ritual meaning, feasting truly lost its significance.

NOTES

1. Col. William Fleming, "Colonel William Fleming's Journal of Travels in Kentucky, 1779–1780," in *Travels in the American Colonies*, edited by

Newton D. Mereness (New York: Macmillan, 1916), 617–655; American Memory Project, Library of Congress, http://memory.loc.gov/cgi-bin/query/r?ammem/lhbtn:@field(DOCID+@lit(lhbtn09410div19)).

2. J. Worth Estes, "Food as Medicine," in *Cambridge World History of Food*, edited by Kenneth F. Kiple and Kriemhild Coneè Ornelas, 2 vols. (New York: Cambridge University Press, 2000), vol. 2, 1550–1551.

3. Hannah Glasse, *Art of Cookery Made Plain and Easy, Which Far Exceeds Any Thing of the Kind Ever Yet Published . . . By a Lady* (London: 1747), 120–121.

4. John Adams to Abigail Adams, July 6, 1774, in *The Book of Abigail and John: Selected Letters of the Adams Family 1762–1784*, edited by L. H. Butterfield, Marc Friedlander, and Mary-Jo Klein (Cambridge, MA: Harvard University Press, 1975), 24.

5. Estwick Evans, *A Pedestrious Tour, of Four Thousand Miles—1818* (Concord, NH: Joseph Spear, 1819), repr. in vol. 8 of *Early Western Travels, 1748–1846*, edited by Rueben Gold Thwaites (Cleveland, OH: A. H. Clark, 1904); American Memory Project, Library of Congress, http://memory.loc.gov/cgi-bin/query/r?ammem/lhbtn:@field(DOCID+@lit(lhbtnth008_0091)).

6. Adriaen Van der Donck, *A Description of the New Netherlands*, edited by Thomas F. O'Donnell (Syracuse, NY: Syracuse University Press, 1968), 41–42.

7. Edwin Perkins, *The Economy of Colonial America*, 2nd ed. (New York: Columbia University Press, 1988), 7.

8. Thomas Jefferson to Benjamin Hawkins, Washington, Feb. 18, 1803, *Letters of Thomas Jefferson, 1743–1826: From Revolution to Reconstruction*, an HTML project, Department of Humanities Computing, University of Groningen, The Netherlands, http://odur.let.rug.nl/~usa/P/tj3/writings/brf/jefl150.htm; Benjamin Franklin, "Dialogue Between Franklin and the Gout," in *The Oxford Book of American Essays*, edited by Brander Matthews (New York: Oxford University Press, 1914), http://www.ushistory.org/, also Bartleby.com Great books On-Line, http://www.bartleby.com/109/3.html; Rev. Charles A. Goodrich, *Lives of the Signers to the Declaration of Independence, 458–460* (New York: William Reed, 1856), also declaration/signers/hancock.htm.

9. William J. Rorabaugh, *The Alcoholic Republic: An American Tradition* (New York: Oxford University Press, 1979), 24.

10. John Bernard, *Retrospections of America 1797–1811* (New York: Harper & Bros., 1887), 37.

11. Col. Richard Malcolm Johnston, *Autobiography of Col. Richard Malcolm Johnston* (Washington, DC: Neale, 1900), also *Documenting the American South*, http://docsouth.unc.edu/johnstonr/johnston.html.

12. Rorabaugh, 125–146.

13. Evans, 261.

14. Rorabaugh, 41.

15. Hasia R. Diner and Beryl Lieff Benderly, *Her Works Praise Her: A History of Jewish Women in America from Colonial Times to the Present* (New York: Basic Books, 2002), 109.

16. Sarah Anna Emery, *Reminiscences of a Nonegenarian* (Newburyport, MA: William H. Huse, 1879), 60.

17. Martha Ballard, *The Diary of Martha Ballard, 1785–1812*, edited by Robert McCausland and Cynthia MacAlman McCausland (Camden, ME: Picton Press, 1992), 30, 661.

18. Carl Bridenbaugh, ed., *Gentleman's Progress: The Itinerarium of Dr. Alexander Hamilton, 1744* (Chapel Hill: University of North Carolina Press, 1948), 108.

GLOSSARY

adelantados. Spanish for firstcomers into a region

atole. thin mixture of cornmeal eaten or drunk in the Spanish Southwest

azafrán. safflower; used in Spanish Southwest

bannock. English flat bread baked over or in front of a fire

chicos. boiled, dried sweet corn used in the Southwest

cocido. dish of boiled meat and vegetables eaten in the Southwest

cocina con fogón de campana. kitchen with bell-shaped fireplace, found in Southwest

cocina con fogón de pastor. kitchen with a shepherd's fireplace, found in Southwest

comal. flat earthenware pan for cooking corncakes, used in Southwest

dent corn. soft corn with a dimple at the top of the kernel

encomienda. system of tribute in Spanish colonies

estofado. meat stew of the Southwest

flint corn. hard, smooth-kerneled corn

frumenty. boiled wheat

gordos. cakes of wheat baked on a flat stone in the Southwest

head cheese. jellied loaf made from head, feet, and organs, especially of pigs

hoecake. See bannock

horno. freestanding adobe and clay beehive-shaped oven of the Spanish Southwest

hutspot. Dutch stewing pot; also a stew of meat or fish and vegetables

johnnycake. See bannock

mano. Spanish for mortar

masa harina. corn flour used especially in tortillas and tamales

meslin/maslin. mix of grains (usually rye and wheat) grown in the same field; also bread made from the mix of grains

metate. Spanish for pestle

nixtamal. kalai-soaked corn

olla. dish of boiled meat and vegetables eaten in the Southwest

panhaas. scrapple; a pudding made from pig's head and feet, and small pieces of meat

pearlash. potassium carbonate, a leaven

posole. corn treated with lye; used in the Southwest

potager. a "stew stove," a benchlike structure with a fire beneath and iron grates on top

pottage. thick soup

pulque. fermented juice of the agave plant; drunk in the Southwest

race. a lobe of ginger

ristra. a string, often braided, of chiles, onions, or garlic

samp. corn treated with lye, used in the East

suppawn/supaen. cornmeal mush

sweetmeat. candied or crystallized fruit

SELECTED BIBLIOGRAPHY

Acrelius, Israel. *A History of New Sweden.* Translated by William M. Reynolds. Philadelphia: Historical Society of Pennsylvania, 1874.

Anderson, Virginia DeJohn. "Animals into the Wilderness: The Development of Livestock Husbandry in the 17th Century Chesapeake." *William and Mary Quarterly,* 3rd ser., 59, no. 2 (2002): 377–408.

Ballard, Martha. *The Diary of Martha Ballard, 1785–1812.* Edited by Robert McCausland and Cynthia MacAlman McCausland. Camden, ME: Picton Press, 1992.

Barnes, Donna R., and Peter Rose. *Matters of Taste: Food and Drink in Seventeenth-Century Dutch Art and Life.* Syracuse, NY: Syracuse University Press, 2002.

Bernard, John. *Retrospections of America 1797–1811.* New York: Harper and Bros., 1887. Reprinted in *American Social History as Recorded by British Travellers,* edited by Allan Nevins. New York: Henry Holt, 1923.

Bidwell, Percy Wells, and John Falconer. *History of Agriculture in the Northern United States 1620–1860.* New York: Peter Smith, 1941.

Bradbury, John. *Travels in the Interior of America.* March of America Facsimile Series, no. 59. Ann Arbor, MI: University Microfilms, 1966.

Bradford, William. *A Journal of the Pilgrims at Plymouth: Mourt's Relation.* Edited by Dwight Heath. New York: Corinth Books, 1963.

Brickell, John. *The Natural History of North-Carolina.* Dublin: James Carson, 1737. Facsimile reprint with introduction by Carol Urness. New York: Johnson Reprint, 1969.

Bridenbaugh, Carl, ed. *Gentleman's Progress: The Itinerarium of Dr. Alexander Hamilton, 1744.* Chapel Hill: University of North Carolina Press, 1948.

Butterfield, L. H., Marc Friedlander, and Mary-Jo Klein, eds. *The Book of Abigail and John: Selected Letters of the Adams Family 1762–1784.* Cambridge, MA: Harvard University Press, 1975.

Byrd, William. *The Secret Diary of William Byrd of Westover 1709–1712.* Edited by Louis B. Wright and Marion Tinling. Richmond, VA: Dietz Press, 1941.

Candler, Allen D., ed. *The Colonial Records of the State of Georgia.* Atlanta: C. P. Byrd, 1904.

Carr, Lois Green, et al. *Colonial Chesapeake Society.* Chapel Hill: University of North Carolina Press, 1988.

Chastellux, François-Jean, Marquis de. *Travels in North America, in the Years 1780, 1781, and 1782.* Revised translation with introduction and notes by Howard C. Rice, Jr. 2 vols. Chapel Hill: University of North Carolina Press, 1963.

Child, Lydia Maria. *The American Frugal Housewife. Dedicated to Those Who Are Not Ashamed of Economy.* 12th ed. Boston: Carter and Hendee, 1833.

Cobbett, William. *A Year's Residence in the United States of America.* London, 1818.

Craven, Wesley Frank. *The Southern Colonies in the Seventeenth Century, 1607–1689.* Vol. 1, *A History of the South.* Edited by Wendell Holmes Stephenson and E. Merton Coulter. Baton Rouge: Louisiana State University Press, 1949.

Cronon, William. *Changes in the Land.* New York: Hill and Wang, 1983.

Danckaerts, Jasper. *Journal of Jasper Danckaerts.* Edited by Bartlett Burleigh James and J. Franklin Jameson. New York: Scribner's, 1913.

d'Artaguiette, Diron. "Journal of Diron d'Artaguiette 1722–1723." In *Travels in the American Colonies.* Edited by Newton D. Mereness. New York: Macmillan, 1916. Also American Memory Project, Library of Congress, http://memory.loc.gov/cgi-bin/query/r?am mem/lhbtn:@field(DOCID+@lit(lhbtn09410div19)).

Davis, Edwin Adams. *Louisiana: A Narrative History.* Baton Rouge, LA: Claitor's, 1961.

Diner, Hasia R., and Beryl Lieff Benderly. *Her Works Praise Her: A History of Jewish Women in America from Colonial Times to the Present.* New York: Basic Books, 2002.

Dwight, Timothy. *Travels in New England and New York.* Edited by Barbara Miller Solomon. 4 vols. Cambridge, MA: Belknap Press of Harvard University Press, 1969.

Emery, Sarah Anna. *Reminiscences of a Nonegenarian.* Newburyport, MA: William H. Huse, 1879.

Evans, Estwick. *A Pedestrious Tour of Four Thousand Miles—1818.* Concord, NH: Joseph Sears, 1819. Reprinted in vol. 8 of *Early Western Travels, 1748–1846.* Edited by Rueben Gold Thwaites. Cleveland, OH:

A. H. Clark, 1904. Also American Memory Project, Library of Congress, http://memory.loc.gov/cgi-bin/query/r?ammem/lhbtn:@field(DOCID+@lit(lhbtnth008_0091)).

Farish, Hunter D., ed. *The Journal and Letters of Philip Vickers Firthian, 1773–1774: A Plantation Tutor of the Old Dominion*. Williamsburg, VA: Colonial Williamsburg, 1943.

Glasse, Hannah. *Art of Cookery Made Plain and Easy, Which Far Exceeds Any Thing of the Kind Ever Yet Published . . . by a Lady*. 2nd ed. London, 1747. Reprinted as *Art of Cookery Made Plain and Easy*. Alexandria, VA: Cottom and Stewart, 1805. Also Facsimile with historical notes by Karen Hess. Bedford, MA: Applewood Books, 1998.

Goode, George Brown, ed. *The Fisheries and Fishery Industries of the United States*. 8 vols. Washington, DC: Government Printing Office, 1884–1887.

Gregg, Josiah. *Commerce of the Prairies*. Edited by Max L. Moorhead. Norman: University of Oklahoma Press, 1954.

Harbury, Kathryn. *Colonial Virginia's Cooking Dynasty*. Columbia: University of South Carolina Press, 2004.

Hazard, Thomas Robinson. *The Jonny-cake Papers of "Shepherd Tom," Together with Reminiscences of Narragansett Schools of Former Days*. Boston: for the Subscribers, 1915.

Higginson, Francis. *New England's Plantation, with Sea Journal and Other Writings*. Salem, MA: Essex Book and Print Club, 1908.

Hoffman, Kathleen. "Cultural Development of La Florida." *Historical Archaeology* 31, no. 1 (1997): 24–35.

Horry, Harriot Pinckney. *A Colonial Plantation Cookbook: The Receipt Book of Harriot Pinckney Horry, 1770*. Edited with introduction by Richard Hooker. Columbia: University of South Carolina Press, 1984.

Johnson, Edward. *Wonder-Working Providence of Sion's Saviour in New England*. Edited by J. F. Jameson. New York: Charles Scribner and Sons, 1910.

Josselyn, John. *New-England's Rarities Discovered*. Reprinted with a foreword by Henry Lee Shattuck. London: G. Widdoes, 1672. Boston: Massachusetts Historical Society, 1972.

Kalm, Peter. *Peter Kalm's Travels in North America: The America of 1750*. Reprint of English version of 1770 translated from the Swedish by John Forster. Edited by Adolph Bensen. 2 vols. New York: Dover, 1966.

Kiple, Kenneth F., and Kriemhild Coneè Ornelas, eds. *Cambridge World History of Food*. 2 vols. New York: Cambridge University Press, 2000.

Labaree, Benjamin W. *Colonial Massachusetts: A History*. Millwood, NY: KTO Press, 1979.

Lawson, John. *New Voyage to Carolina*. Edited with an introduction by Hugh Talmage Lefler. Chapel Hill: University of North Carolina Press, 1967.

Melish, John. *Travels in the United States of America, in the Years 1806 & 1807, and 1809, 1810 & 1811.* Philadelphia: Thomas and George Palmer, 1812.

Morton, Thomas. *The New English Canaan.* Boston: Prince Society, 1883.

Otto, John Solomon. *The Southern Frontiers, 1607–1860.* Westport, CT: Greenwood Press, 1989.

Peckham, Howard H., ed. *Narratives of Colonial America, 1704–1765.* Chicago: R. R. Donnelley, 1971.

Penn, Gulielma. *Penn Family Recipes.* Edited by Evelyn Abraham Benson. York, PA: G. Shumway, 1966.

Perkins, Edwin. *The Economy of Colonial America.* 2nd ed. New York: Columbia University Press, 1988.

Pike, Zebulon. *The Journals of Zebulon Montgomery Pike with Letters and Related Documents.* Edited by Donald Jackson. 2 vols. Norman: University of Oklahoma Press, 1966.

Randolph, Mary. *The Virginia House-wife.* Historical Notes and Commentaries by Karen Hess. Columbia: University of South Carolina Press, 1984.

Rhule, Donna. "Oranges and Wheat: Spanish Attempts at Agriculture in La Florida." *Historical Archaeology* 31 (1997): 555–580.

Rorabaugh, William J. *The Alcoholic Republic: An American Tradition.* New York: Oxford University Press, 1979.

Rose, Peter, ed. and trans. *The Sensible Cook: Dutch Foodways in the Old and the New World.* Syracuse, NY: Syracuse University Press, 1989.

Roth, Rodris. "Tea Drinking in 18th-Century America: Its Etiquette and Equipage." *Contributions from the Museum of History and Technology.* Paper 14, 61–91. U.S. National Museum Bulletin 225. Washington, DC: Smithsonian Institution.

Sewell, Samuel. *The Diary of Samuel Sewell, 1674–1729.* Edited by M. Halsey Thomas. 2 vols. New York: Farrar, Straus and Giroux, 1973.

Simmons, Amelia. *American Cookery; or, the Art of Dressing Viands, Fish, Poultry, and Vegetables.* Hartford, CT: Hudson & Godwin, 1796, Facsimile reprint with introduction by Mary Tolford Wilson. New York: Dover, 1984.

Simmons, Marc. *Coronado's Land: Essays on Daily Life in Colonial New Mexico.* Albuquerque: University of New Mexico Press, 1991

Smith, Andrew F. *Peanuts: The Illustrious History of the Goober Pea.* Urbana: University of Illinois Press, 2002.

———. *The Tomato in America: Early History, Culture, and Cookery.* Columbia: University of South Carolina Press, 1994.

———, ed. *The Oxford Encyclopedia of Food and Drink in America.* 2 vols. New York: Oxford University Press, 2004.

Taylor, Alan. *American Colonies: The Settling of North America.* New York: Viking, 2001.

Thomas, David Hurst, ed. *Columbian Consequences*. 2 vols. Washington, DC: Smithsonian Institution Press, 1990.

Trabue, Daniel. *Westward into Kentucky: The Narrative of Daniel Trabue*. Edited by Chester Raymond Young. Lexington: University Press of Kentucky, 1981.

Van der Donck, Adriaen. *A Description of the New Netherlands*. Edited with introduction by Thomas F. O'Donnell. Syracuse, NY: Syracuse University Press, 1968.

Wansey, Henry. *The Journal of an Excursion to the United States in North America, in the Summer of 1794*. Salisbury, UK: J. Easton, 1796.

Washington, Martha. *Martha Washington's Booke of Cookery*. Transcribed with historical notes and annotations by Karen Hess. New York: Columbia University Press, 1981.

Weaver, William Woys. *Heirloom Vegetable Gardening: A Master Gardener's Guide to Planting, Growing, Seed Saving, and Cultural History*. New York: Henry Holt, 1997.

———. *A Quaker Woman's Cookbook: The Domestic Cookery of Elizabeth Ellicott Lea*. Rev. ed. Mechanicsburg, PA: Stackpole Books, 2004.

Webb, James Josiah. *Adventures in the Santa Fe Trade 1844–1847*. Edited by Ralph P. Bieber. Lincoln: University of Nebraska Press, 1995.

Wilson, David Scofield, and Angus Kress Gillespie, eds. *Rooted in America: Foodlore of Popular Fruits and Vegetables*. Knoxville: University of Tennessee Press, 1999.

Wood, William. *New England's Prospect*. Edited by Alden T. Vaughan. Amherst: University of Massachusetts Press, 1977.

Woodmason, Charles. *The Carolina Backcountry on the Eve of the Revolution: The Journal and Other Writings of Charles Woodmason, Anglican Itinerant*. Edited with an introduction by Richard J. Hooker. Chapel Hill: University of North Carolina Press, 1953.

Woods, John. *Wood's Two Years' Residence in the Settlement on the English Prairie—June 25, 1820–July 3, 1821*. London: Longman, Hurst, 1822. Reprinted in *Early Western Travels, 1748–1846*. Edited by Rueben Gold Thwaites. Vol. 10. Cleveland, OH: A. H. Clark, 1904.

INDEX

Acadians, 42

Adams, John, 85, 199

African American diet, 57, 58, 71

African influences on American foodways, 134–135, 175–176, 181–184

Albany, New York, 103

"Albany beef," 53

Ale, 59, 80

Alewives, 52

Algonquians, 60

American Cookery, 1, 22, 52, 69, 155, 160, 163

American food habits, 2, 15, 16, 26–27, 28, African, influences, 134–135, 175–176, 181–184; archeological evidence of, 125–126, 183; Dutch influences, 133, 154, 158–163; English influences, 132–133, 164–171; fast eating, 26–27; French influences, 134, 179–181; German influences, 136, 171–172; Hispanic influences, 137–143; Native American influences, 8–10; other ethnic influences, 136; Scotch-Irish, 185; Spanish influences, 4, 173

American Frugal Housewife, The, 57

American Revolution, 28, 45

Anchovies, 77

Ancient New-England Standing Dish, recipe for, 61

Apples, 63; apple dumplings, recipe for, 63

Art of Cookery Made Plain and Easy, 1, 153, 154, 199

Asparagus, 56

Atole, 140

Backcountry, 184–188

Baked beans, 56–57; recipe for, 57

Baking powder, 27

Baking soda, 27

Ballard, Martha, 55, 72, 157, 210

Baltimore, Maryland, 28

Bannock, 22, 146, 151, 153, 186

Barley, 42–43

Barter, 14, 15

Bartram, John, 17

Beans, 56–57, 129

Bear, 48

Beef, 43–44

Beer, 59, 80, 113–114

Beets, 61

About the Author

SANDRA L. OLIVER has been a food historian for 30 years, is the author of *Saltwater Foodways: New Englanders and Their Food in the 19th Century* (1995), and is the Publisher/Editor of *Food History News*, a quarterly newsletter. She is also a food columnist for New England publications.